Group Counselling

PROFESSIONAL SKILLS FOR COUNSELLORS

The *Professional Skills for Counsellors* series, edited by Colin Feltham, covers the practical, technical and professional skills and knowledge which trainee and practising counsellors need to improve their competence in key areas of therapeutic practice.

Titles in the series include:

Counselling by Telephone
Maxine Rosenfield

Time-Limited Counselling
Colin Feltham

Long-Term Counselling
Geraldine Shipton and Eileen Smith

Client Assessment
Stephen Palmer and Gladeana McMahon (eds)

Counselling, Psychotherapy and the Law
Peter Jenkins

Contracts in Counselling
Charlotte Sills (ed.)

Counselling Difficult Clients
Kingsley Norton and Gill McGauley

Learning and Writing in Counselling
Mhairi MacMillan and Dot Clark

Counselling and Psychotherapy in Private Practice
Roger Thistle

Referral and Termination Issues for Counsellors
Anne Leigh

The Management of Counselling and Psychotherapy Agencies
Colin Lago and Duncan Kitchin

Group Counselling

Keith Tudor

SAGE Publications
London • Thousand Oaks • New Delhi

SAGE Publications Ltd
6 Bonhill Street
London EC2A 4PU

SAGE Publications Inc
2455 Teller Road
Thousand Oaks, California 91320

SAGE Publications India Pvt Ltd
32, M-Block Market
Greater Kailash – I
New Delhi 110 048

British Library Cataloguing in Publication data

A catalogue record for this book is available from
the British Library.

ISBN 0-8039-7619-4
    0-8039-7620-8 (pbk)

Library of Congress catalog record available

Typeset by Photoprint, Torquay, Devon
Printed in Great Britain by Biddles Ltd, Guildford, Surrey

Contents

No man is an island, entire of itself; every man is a piece of the continent, a part of the main.

John Donne (1624) *Devotions, XVII*

No individual is self-sufficient; the individual can exist only in an environmental field. The individual is inevitably, at every moment, a part of some field. His behavior is a function of the total field, which includes both him and his environment.

Fritz Perls (1973) *The Gestalt Approach and Eye Witness to Therapy*

I am because we are

African proverb

In memory of
Margaret Proctor, FBPsS
Principal Educational Psychologist, ILEA
generous Godmother and enlightening witness
(1914–1997)

Acknowledgements

Although writing is often a lone and isolated task, writing a book especially about groups is not possible without the experience, help and support of a number of people. My heartfelt thanks and acknowledgements go: to past and present clients, supervisees and trainees with whom I have been and continue to be privileged to work and who consistently remind me about the resilience, potential and aspiration of the individual and collective human condition; to Jenny Robinson, a valued colleague, who – and whose radical therapeutic work – deserves more recognition; to friends and colleagues for their help through discussion and research – Kevin Brown, Mike Fitter, Colin Lago, Adrienne Lee, Fiona Purdie, Val Smith and Ian Stewart – who, for me, formed a conceptual group matrix around this book; to Colin Feltham for his constructive editing; to Susan Worsey at Sage for her support and patience; to Jo and Simon Browes for their secretarial and design skills; and, finally and mostly, to Louise Embleton Tudor, my most valued colleague, best friend and life partner who, as ever, provides both support and constructive criticism and whose love and understanding contributes to my immediate facilitative environment and who, with Saul and Raiya, forms my most immediate family group.

Appendix 1, 'Best Practice Guidelines for Groupwork', © ACA. Reprinted with permission. No further reproduction authorized without written permission of the American Counseling Association.

Introduction

Group – An assemblage of objects standing near together, and forming a collective unity; a knot (of people), a cluster (of things) . . . a confused aggregation . . .
– A number of persons or things in a certain relation, or having a certain degree of similarity.

(Shorter Oxford English Dictionary,
3rd edn, 1973, p. 896)

– A social aggregation that has an external boundary and at least one internal boundary.

(Berne, 1963, p. 319)

Human beings are social animals. This is the sense of Aristotle's dictum that 'man is a political animal'. We live in a social world and live, love and work in social groupings. We are born into and raised in a family group (however we define 'family'); as children we often play in groups; we are educated in groups; we may dance and sing in groups; we work in groups – I spend the majority of my working life working in and with groups; we socialise mostly in groups; using computers we even network with others in groups; many people die surrounded by a group of family and friends. Despite this, Western psychology in its development and application to the field of counselling over the past hundred years has focused its attention predominantly on understanding the individual, individuality, *self*-actualisation, autonomy, the concept of the *self*, and the importance of *self*-development. More recently – in the past fifteen to twenty years – criticisms have been made of such an emphasis on the individual (e.g. Hillman and Ventura, 1992), self-actualisation (e.g. Rigney, 1981; Lukas, 1989), autonomy (e.g. Whitney, 1982; LeVine, 1990), self-development and individual *self*-concept – Nobles (1973), for instance, theorises that there is a 'we' self-concept, an awareness of an historical and cultural reference group. Donne's famous reflection on the human condition represents a view that we are inextricably linked each with each other. The social nature of the human condition and experience is as relevant a subject of enquiry as the individual psyche and, arguably, more so. This leads to a greater appreciation of the structure, dynamics, influence and value of both accidental groups (such as family) as well as intentional groups (such as counselling groups).

Since the first therapeutic groups were established in the late 1920s a wealth of experience has been garnered and libraries of papers and books have been written about the phenomena of 'the group'. The current list on group psychotherapy from the specialist bookshop Karnac Books comprises well over 100 titles and there are at least twelve journals on groups in the English language alone. This literature includes a number of books which serve as introductions to groups, the theory of groups and groupwork practice as well as those on 'how to create and run a group'. Yalom's *The Theory and Practice of Group Psychotherapy* (first published in 1970 and now in its fourth edition) (Yalom, 1995), is still the most comprehensive text available on group therapy. From a North American perspective, Shaffer and Galinsky (1974) give an overview of the major group approaches across psychiatry, social work and education which includes a useful section on the role of the leader within each model of group reviewed. More recently, Corey (1995), in his *Theory and Practice of Group Counseling* (also in its fourth edition), introduces basic elements of group process and, similarly, a number of theoretical approaches, although his basic elements appear separate from their theoretical foundations. Issues about pre-group information, confidentiality, psychological risks, ethics, use of techniques etc. all have a basis in (different) theoretical traditions: they are not atheoretical or neutral. Here in Britain, both Whitaker's (1985) guide to the principles of groupwork and Hinshelwood's (1987) introduction to groups are written from a psychodynamic perspective. Attention to the dynamics of groups is a feature of both analytic and humanistic counselling and does not feature so much in groups informed by cognitive-behavioural or rational emotive behaviour therapy. This present book aims to fill a gap in the literature in that it is written from within the humanistic/ existential tradition of psychology, psychotherapy and counselling. Within this tradition, I have inevitably been influenced by my own experience, study and training: first in gestalt therapy, then transactional analysis (TA) and the person-centred approach (PCA). TA and the PCA represent both similar and significantly different perspectives on human nature, personality, diagnosis/ assessment, change, interventions and on working with individuals and in groups (elaborated in Chapter 1). This book reflects a study of groups and group phenomena, influenced by humanistic/ existential and cultural psychology (see Shweder, 1990), which views culture and social issues as central to our knowledge and understanding of humans and our social psyches (see Singh and Tudor, 1997). Indeed, the experience and study of groups both reflects culture and represents the individual in the context of culture, community and society. In this sense, group counselling is – and must be – culturally located and culturally intentional.

This book is one of a series titled 'Professional Skills for Counsellors'. Skills, however, cannot – or should not – be divorced from theory and thus this book does draw on, refer to, summarise and introduce theories and concepts about groups. Significantly, the several dictionary definitions of skill (*Shorter Oxford English Dictionary*, 1973) identify reason, cause, knowledge and understanding as the (back)ground of practice. Furthermore, an undue emphasis on skills at the expense of the development of the counsellor's philosophy of practice and their therapeutic attitudes – of genuineness, respect and understanding – is positively dangerous as it perpetuates the myth that technique and interventions are 'tricks of the trade' which may be bought, sold and passed on, divorced from their roots in personal philosophy and a way of being. Theory is indeed the best practice. The ability to articulate a conceptual framework to guide group practice is considered good practise, as outlined by the Association for Specialists in Group Work (ASGW) division of the American Counselling Association (ASGW, 1998) (see Appendix 1). In being both practical and theoretical (and full of attitude!) this book reflects a position of praxis. It is thus less of an instructive 'How to . . .' book than one which encourages the practitioner in how to be and how to think about 'How to . . .'. None the less, readers from a variety of professional backgrounds (counselling, social work, medical and complementary health care, community work, organisation and industry) who are involved with or interested in setting up and facilitating groups will find help with the mechanics as well as the dynamics of groupwork. This is also a resource book. Whilst written from a broadly humanistic/ existential perspective, I acknowledge and draw on other traditions, especially the analytic, and references provide the reader with both source material and further reading on a wide range of relevant and related subjects.

Following a brief history of different approaches to groups and an introduction to group development (Chapter 1), the structure of the book in the next four chapters reflects a developmental approach to groups which is descriptive rather than prescriptive and which follows the concerns and considerations of the practitioner, by introducing and reflecting on concepts and theory that support practice. Thus, Chapter 2 discusses the concept of the group and stages of group development and considerations in setting up a group; Chapter 3 focuses on establishing the group and the first meeting of the group and reflects on issues of leadership and of contracting; Chapter 4 considers the developing group and ways of recording what happens in groups; and Chapter 5 presents issues in ending groups. Chapter 6, written by a colleague, Jenny Robinson, who is Project Manager of a therapeutic community, discusses issues raised by facilitating groups in residential settings. Chapter 7 explores the social (plural and collective) nature of the human condition and reflects on issues of the large group, inter-group relations, organisation and community. The implications of ethical issues raised in and by working with groups are considered throughout, whilst specific implications for education/training, personal development and supervision of the group counsellor are considered in Chapter 8.

A note on language

This book is one of a series on counselling and in this context I refer to group counselling and to group counsellors. Nevertheless, much of the content of the book draws on and is equally applicable to the theory and practice of group psychotherapy including the psychodynamic and group-analytic approaches. Much of the debate about the differences, particularly between counselling and psychotherapy, centres on superficial distinctions such as the notion that counselling is short-term, focusing on present problems, whilst psychotherapy is long-term, focusing on the influence of the past. In theory, practice and organisation and as regards the education and training of counsellors and psychotherapists, there are many overlapping areas between the two. The differences which exist and which are perceived are based on differences defined by different theoretical orientations. Thus, for example, the person-centred approach does not distinguish between counselling and psychotherapy, transactional analysis does (but not coherently in my view (see Tudor, 1997c), much of the psychoanalytic literature does, and so on. Difference is also promoted by the organisational context by which training institutes may or may not distinguish between the two in terms of entry requirements; or by the legislative context whereby some practitioners are registered as counsellors or psychotherapists and some titles, such as 'psychoanalyst' and 'child psychotherapist', are protected. In the context of the theory and practice of group counselling/psychotherapy, there is another term – *socio*therapy – which generally describes the exploration of *inter*personal, as distinct from *intra*personal activity (this is further discussed in Chapters 1 and 7).

Although I generally use the term 'counselling' in this book, I use the terms 'counselling' and 'psychotherapy' interchangeably and the generic 'therapy' to stand for both. When I use one or the other specifically I am reflecting their use either by the authors cited or in the context of the particular discussion and thus, for consistency, certain passages or sections refer to counsellor or to therapist. I generally use 'counsellor', 'group counsellor' or 'facilitator' to refer to the person facilitating or leading the group, except in Chapter 3 in which 'leader' is used in the context of a discussion of group leadership. Perceived differences between different terms such as groupwork, group counselling, group psychotherapy and group analysis are discussed in Chapter 1. I use the plural pronoun 'they' to refer to the singular she or he, and 'you' to refer to you the reader. Although a number of authors quoted are men of their time who, at least in their writing, did not account for women, I maintain the integrity and accuracy of quotations and leave you the reader to insert '[sic]' after 'he' and 'his' or to make your own translation. Excerpts from and references to clients' counselling work have been effectively disguised.

1

Groups: History and Development

In this chapter I offer a brief history of groups, and distinguish between counselling groups across the three traditions or 'forces' of psychology – the psychodynamic, the behavioural and the humanistic/existential. I introduce the conceptual distinctions between working *in*, *through* and *of* the group and the implications of such distinctions for practice. Finally, I discuss concepts of group development and illustrate their usefulness to the counsellor working in, through and with groups.

A brief history of groups

Although histories vary, it seems that Worcester, an associate of the psychologist James, and Pratt, an internist, were the first practitioners of group therapy. From 1905, they organised consumptive patients at the Massachusetts General Hospital Outpatient Clinic, Boston into groups or classes. In establishing a preventive programme of 'home sanatorium treatment', Pratt was initially concerned to monitor patients' progress and to educate them about their diet and environment. Later, he came to realise the importance of the mutual support created by patients having 'a common bond in a common disease' (Spotnitz, 1961, p. 29). He then became more interested in the psychological aspects of the groups and the interactions between group members. At around the same time as Worcester and Pratt were developing their outpatient groups, in 1909 Moreno was working with school children in Vienna, getting them to act out little plays, initially written for them, about various problems and issues of behaviour.

Soon the children were presenting their own plays and Moreno was applying this impromptu role playing – *psychodrama* – to working with adults. In 1922 Moreno established the Theatre of Spontaneity in Vienna. This therapeutic method had – and has – three aspects: *psychodrama*, the acting out of roles; *sociometry*, the method of investigation about attitudes and relationships; and *group psychotherapy*, a term first coined by Moreno in 1932, which describes the philosophy of treatment (see Moreno, 1946/1964, 1958). Later, during the Second World War, Moreno and his colleagues, now in the United States, developed *sociodrama*, in which the audience became the community, acting out and dealing with issues, for instance, of racial conflict.

Also in Vienna at this time, Freud was establishing a Psychological Society study group, comprising amongst others Adler, Ferenczi and Rank, which met weekly on Wednesday evenings and which may be regarded as the first training group, if not group training.

From these different beginnings, historically the next major development was that the group began to be viewed from within the conceptual framework of psychoanalysis. In 1921 Freud published a short book on *Group Psychology and the Analysis of the Ego* (Freud, 1921/1985a) in which he drew heavily on the work of the French psychologist Le Bon (1896/1920). Freud's views on group psychology (summarised in the next section) led to a number of distinct traditions of group therapy within psychoanalysis.

Three figures were influential in the early application of psychoanalytic concepts to groups: Burrow (1927), who referred to his procedures as *group analysis*, that is, analysis *in* groups; Schilder (1936, 1939), who applied the technique of free association by encouraging his group patients to discuss whatever came into their minds; and Wender (1936), who observed that transference phenomena developed in groups as much as in individual analysis. In 1938, Wolf, an American psychiatrist and psychoanalyst who had read the works of Burrow, Schilder and Wender, established his first psychotherapy group. Over the next ten years he developed his practice and by 1947 began to hold seminars in psychoanalytic group therapy at the New York Medical College. A year later, Wolf began a training workshop at the Postgraduate Center for Psychotherapy in New York and by 1954 the Center introduced a certification programme in group therapy. Wolf and his colleagues applied psychoanalytic concepts – resistance, transference, interpretation etc. – to the patients in the group, with very little modification of them, other than developing the notion of *multiple transference* which acknowledges that the patient's transference manifests itself in and onto the multiple relationships in the group and not just with/onto the therapist. The advantage of such group therapy is that the patient shows more evidence of their neurosis and pathology and thus there is more data available to be analysed and interpreted.

Also in the 1940s, Lewin (1952) was developing field theory, whereby psychological relationships were viewed in terms of their surrounding field – in this case the group, which was understood as an entity in itself. Lewin established the training group (T-group), comprising volunteers (not clients) in order to study the qualities of the group – what he referred to as 'group dynamics'. Following Lewin's death in 1947, some of his associates founded the National Training Laboratory (NTL) in Bethel, Maine, in which the T-group formed the basic education instrument (see Gottschalk, 1966).

Around the same time as Wolf was establishing his first psychotherapy groups in New York, in Britain Bion (who did not publish his work until 1961) and Foulkes (1948/1983, 1964) (who was also heavily influenced by Lewin) were developing a group dynamics approach to group psychotherapy which emphasised the importance of viewing the group itself as a coherent entity. This took place at a military rehabilitation hospital in Northfield in what became referred to as the Northfield experiments, and at the Tavistock Clinic in London. This focus on the dynamics of the group also led Bion, Foulkes and others to develop theoretical concepts relevant to the *group-as-a-whole* as distinct from applying concepts to the group borrowed from individual psychoanalysis. In 1952 Foulkes and other colleagues formed the Group Analytic Society; formal training developed with the founding in 1971 of the Institute of Group Analysis. This tradition has influenced the theory of systems (systems theory) in many groups such as families and organisations.

In the 1950s and 1960s, various psychologists and therapists, working within what has come to be known as the 'third force' of humanistic/existential psychology and psychotherapy (see pp. 14–20), began experimenting with and promoting more experiential approaches to psychotherapy, including working with groups in which the members' – and therapists' – experiencing of themselves and of each other became the focus of the group and interpersonal process and often dynamic encounter (see, for example, Whitaker and Malone, 1953; Gendlin and Beebe, 1968; Rogers, 1970/1973). Around the same time, gestalt therapists, influenced by Lewin's field theory, were recognising the impor-tance of both field and ground: 'only the interplay of organism and environment...constitutes the psychological situation, not the organism and environment taken separately' (Perls et al., 1951/1973, p. 19). Also, Berne, the founder of transactional analysis (TA), was developing his ideas on the principles, structure and dynamics of groups and of organisations (Berne, 1963, 1966). In 1970 Yalom first published his seminal work on *The Theory and Practice of Group Psychotherapy*, based on his research into the curative or therapeutic factors of groups (Yalom, 1970) (see Chapter 2). Although Yalom is an existential psychotherapist, his research and influence spreads across all schools of psychology.

Over the past thirty years, group analysis, group psychotherapy and group counselling have developed, been applied to more and a greater variety of settings, and have become more integrated into professional practice, with many individual counsellors/psychotherapists and other professionals such as social and health care workers, psychologists, management and organisational con-sultants leading or facilitating groups. Groupwork theory, in turn, has been influenced by other fields such as social work (which generally uses the term 'groupwork') (see Douglas, 1979, 1993; Glassman and Kates, 1990; Brown, 1992), family therapy (e.g. Satir, 1982) and by recent developments in social theory such as cybernetics and postmodernism (see Becvar et al., 1997). During the past twenty years, exponential development in electronic technology in the field of human communication has also had a significant impact on counselling – through the increasing provi-sion and use of telephone counselling and communication through electronic e-mail and the world wide web of the internet. Whilst there appear obvious disadvantages about counselling via such media, the advantages of greater mutuality, that is relation-ships often with a team or group equalised through language (plain text) and the timing of the communication (stimulus and response, sending and receiving), and of relationships less medi-ated by social conventions and therefore perhaps more honest, should not be underestimated. In taking up the challenges of 'computer therapeutics', Lago (1996) argues for a theory of e-mail counselling and, from a person-centred perspective, considers its application to the early, pre-therapy phase of contact with the client. Rosenfield and Smillie (1998) discuss group counselling by telephone.

The three traditions

Broadly, there are three different traditions or 'forces' within psychotherapy: the psychoanalytic or psychodynamic, the behavioural and the humanistic (also referred to as the humanistic/existential). Theoreticians and practitioners within these different forces have different ideas about human nature, personality development, pathology or maladjustment, even differences between the terms used to describe the same phenomena, society, the process of change, groups, group dynamics and the role of the analyst/conductor/psychotherapist/counsellor. These are briefly reviewed as regards their contribution to our understanding of group counselling.

The psychoanalytic tradition
Psychoanalysis is, strictly, an individual therapy. The rules of treatment, requiring as near total privacy and confidentiality, and the format it takes, requiring regular attendance of anything from three to six times a week, make it almost exclusively an individual form of treatment. It is thus more accurate to discuss group therapy within this tradition as *informed by* psychoanalysis. None the less, Freud (1921/1985a) did write about group psychology and this informs psychoanalytic approaches to groups. His views of group psychology can be summarised thus:

- The individual in a group is less repressed and therefore displays 'the manifestations of this unconscious [his instinctual impulses], in which all that is evil in the human mind is contained as a predisposition' (p. 101).
- The individual 'readily sacrifices his personal interest to the collective interest' (p. 101).
- The condition of the individual in a group is one of being hypnotic.
- By virtue of being in a group, the individual becomes a barbarian, a creature acting by instinct, with a lowered intellectual ability, an ass.

- 'A group is impulsive, changeable and irritable . . . led almost exclusively by the unconscious . . . incapable of perseverance . . . it has a sense of omnipotence . . . is extraordinarily credulous and open to influence, it has no critical faculty . . . the feelings of a group are always very simple and very exaggerated' (pp. 104–5).
- A group requires excessive stimulus to produce an effect on it; it is nevertheless open to the influence of suggestion or suggestibility.

That Freud's statements about group psychology appear somewhat undeveloped, is due to the fact that, for a number of reasons, he did not further elaborate his theory and analysis of groups. Other psychoanalytic influences also inform group theory and practice: from Adler, the value of social equality; from Jungian analytic psychology, the collective unconscious (see Boyd, 1991); whilst Kleinian theory influenced Bion (1961). Convergences between Jung and Foulkes are described in a special issue of *Group Analysis* (Fiumara, 1989). From these different historical influences, as well as developments in social and political theory, four distinct traditions may be discerned within psychoanalytic approaches to groups.

In one strand of psychoanalytic thinking, Freud's approach to group psychology, together with psychoanalytic principles, are applied to individuals *in* the group and, to a limited extent, to the group itself. A Freudian psychoanalysis of the processes in the group between the group members relies on:

1. A theory of the unconscious.
2. An analysis of defence mechanisms of individual members – Freud (1921/1985a) describes identification as the principal neurotic defence operating between members of a group – and of any resistance to interpretation.
3. An analysis of transference and counter-transference phenomena.
4. Interpretation of group processes.

This is represented by the 'Tavistock model' of group analysis in which themes develop from free-flowing discussion (the group equivalent of free association) and all material is understood in terms of the transference with the group therapist. In response, the therapist makes a specific tripartite interpretation: firstly, of the group; secondly, of individual members, relating the group interpretation to how the individuals in the group are behaving; and, thirdly, viewing the group as analagous to and evocative of a family, pointing out how this (current) behaviour is a repetition of responses from early life experiences. In his chapter on the psychoanalytic approach to groups, Corey (1995) reflects this classical approach to group psychotherapy.

It was the work of Bion (1961) and Foulkes (1948/1983, 1964) which moved the focus from (individual) psychoanalysis to group analysis, that is, analysis *of* the group itself. Bion developed the interpretation *of* the *group-as-a-whole*. Based on the notion that any group has 'work' to do and that this provokes anxieties, especially in relation to the group leader, Bion identified three 'basic assumptions' of groups:

■ Dependency – when the group looks to the leader to lead and to do the work for them.
■ Fight/flight – when the group resists any attempt on the part of the leader or group members to structure the group by rebelling against them (fight) or ignoring them (flight).
■ Pairing – when members pair off psychologically, hoping that the pairs will provide the structure they need to do the work and produce a solution to the work task.

For Bion all interpretations were group interpretations made towards the goal of helping group members to function effectively in work groups and helping groups-as-wholes to function effectively as work groups.

Foulkes, who was influenced not only by Lewin's field theory but also by the critical theory of the Frankfurt School of philosophy and social theory, generally referred to his work through the group as group-analytic psychotherapy, and had a different focus to that of Bion. Foulkes' philosophy, principles and practice may be summarised thus:

■ The primary focus of treatment is on 'the individual as a whole in a total situation' (Foulkes, 1948/1983, p. 1).
■ The group situation is the best forum in which to study both the group and the individual.
■ Neurotic symptoms disguise what is not expressed within relationships.

■ Communication in groups takes place on four levels, in terms of: current relationships, individual transference relationships, shared and projected feelings and fantasies, and archetypal images.

■ The focus of group-analytic psychotherapy is on the group matrix, 'the hypothetical web of communication and relationship in a given group . . . the common shared ground' (Foulkes, 1964, p. 292).

■ The aims of group-analytic psychotherapy are: activation (active participation, communication and self-observation), adjustment or adaptation, and insight (Foulkes, 1948/1983).

For an introduction to Foulkes' work and developments based on it see Pines (1983).

A fourth tradition within analytic group psychotherapy is represented by the 'group focal conflict model' (Whitman and Stock, 1958), which conceptualises group dynamics in terms of nuclear conflict, utilising concepts of 'disturbing motive', 'reactive motive' and 'solution' (see Whitaker, 1985). Hyde (1988) sees this model as having a number of similarities to the Tavistock model and as compatible with group analysis.

The behavioural tradition
This tradition has its roots in the work of the Russian physiologist Pavlov, his discovery of the conditioned response and reflex in animals and his application of classical conditioning and the conditioned stimulus and response to the neurotic behaviour of humans (see Pavlov, 1941 [a posthumous publication]). In America, the work of the behaviourist and experimental psychologist Watson on maladaptive behaviour (Watson and Rayner, 1920) and Skinner (1938) on operant or instrumental learning, was influential on the development of behaviour modification. In Britain, two approaches have developed: one behavioural and the other cognitive-behavioural, which focuses in therapy on cognitions first and then on behaviour (O'Sullivan, 1996). Behaviour therapy (a term coined by Skinner in the early 1950s) is predominantly an individual therapy and does not have a specific approach to or model of groups. Apart from the economic advantage of working in groups by providing services to more people, there is a therapeutic gain of conducting behaviour therapy in groups in dealing with certain social behaviours such as assertiveness, anger

and shyness. Shaffer and Galinsky (1974) identify and describe three distinct categories of group approaches within the framework of behaviour therapy: systematic desensitisation groups, which use various techniques and steps to control forms of anxiety (see Wolpe and Lazarus, 1966); behavioural practice or behaviour rehearsal groups, for example, in assertiveness (see Lazarus, 1968); and specific behaviour control therapies over, for example, smoking (see Marrone et al., 1970). Although cognitive-behavioural group therapy is, strictly speaking, not itself a group therapy (see Alladin, 1988), the behavioural tradition has influenced practitioners across the other two traditions and the use of its techniques (for example, coaching, confrontation of behaviour, beliefs, constructs and thinking; feedback; goal-setting; homework; modelling, paradox; rehearsal; and suggestion) is equally widespread in both individual and group counselling/ psychotherapy and other approaches to working with groups.

The humanistic/existential tradition
This tradition represents a broad church of psychological, psychotherapeutic and counselling theory and practice. Maslow (1962) first identified this as the 'third force' in psychology, defining it as a developing science (some would say an art) concerned less with pathology and disturbance (psychoanalysis) and that which is simply explained in terms of mechanistic theory (behaviourism), and more with human motivation, self-development and aesthetics. Humanistic psychology, as Maslow describes it, is 'epi-Freudian' and 'epi-behavioural' ('epi'=building upon) and thus includes previous traditions. In any case, it includes, amongst others, psychodrama, neo-Reichian therapies, gestalt therapy, personal construct psychology, transactional analysis, the person-centred approach, psychosynthesis etc. Whilst each school or approach has its own contribution to group counselling, one form of group which draws on many models and which, in representing the accumulated thinking and practice of a variety of people, reflects this 'epi' tradition is encounter.

Encounter   Encounter literally describes a 'meeting', sometimes defined as 'face to face' or 'in conflict', is a form of group and is – or was – for some even a social movement. Encounter is essentially holistic, based as it is on a belief in the unity of mind, body and spirit. A central concept is that of *identity*, which has an inner aspect including the rules we have which govern us as well as an outer expression of this – which we express in groups. Although the first mention of encounter goes back to a series of poetic writings published by Moreno in 1914, the two major influences on encounter were Schutz (1973), who came from a psychoanalytic tradition, and, from within the humanistic tradition, Rogers (1970/1973). Schutz, who joined the staff of the Esalen Institute in California in 1967, developed what became referred to as an 'open encounter model' of group. Drawing on the work of Reich and neo-Reichians, Schutz prioritised the somatic in his analysis that body tensions are and represent blocks against feelings. In open encounter the group leader brings the client's awareness to bear on their body and encourages them to express their feelings in the form of some physical activity such as pushing against or falling back on others. Although Rogers was running groups training counsellors as early as 1946, and included a chapter on groups (Hobbs, 1951) in *Client-Centered Therapy* (Rogers, 1951), it was not until the 1960s that Rogers himself became more involved in groups. Applying his research and ideas about the facilitative conditions for change, and favouring a more participative approach on the part of the facilitator, Rogers (1970/1973) describes the following patterns in the process of encounter groups, 'roughly in sequential order' (p. 22):

1. Milling around
2. Resistance to personal expression or exploration
3. Description of past feelings
4. Expression of negative feelings
5. Expression and exploration of personally meaningful material
6. The expression of immediate interpersonal feelings in the group
7. The development of a healing capacity in the group
8. Self-acceptance and the beginning of change
9. The cracking of facades
10. The individual receives feedback
11. Confrontation
12. The helping relationship outside the group sessions
13. The basic encounter
14. The expression of positive feelings and closeness
15. Behaviour changes in the group.

Barrett-Lennard (1979) suggests that this formulation may be summarised in three phases:

- Engagement
- Trust and process development
- Encounter and change.

At around the same time as Schutz and Rogers were running or facilitating encounter groups, Bach (1966) and Stoller (1972) were extending the format of conventional group therapy in terms of its time frame to the point of running groups of 24 to 48 hours' duration, referring to these as marathons and later as marathon group encounter.

Wibberley (1988) traces four influences on encounter: one from the 1940s from Lewin and the NTL training groups which, over time, became more concerned with personal growth than organisational development; a second from the more aggressive confrontational style of groups run originally in a residential therapeutic community for drug addicts called Synanon, founded in 1958 (Yablonsky, 1965); the third from Schutz; and the fourth from Rogers. The influence of these roots is seen in encounter and, more commonly, groups influenced by encounter today.

1   Encounter groups are generally directed towards and comprise 'healthy' people rather than existing counselling and/or disturbed clients. Whilst often therapeutic, with their focus on the here-and-now, they are not generally regarded as therapy. Rogers and Sanford (1980) view the purpose of encounter as the enrichment and enhancement of personal development and distinct from group therapy in its response to serious problems – although they state that the process is much the same. They are – or were – part of the self-development and growth movement, especially from the late 1960s to mid 1970s. Wood (1995b) reflects:

> with less stable communities and the decline of organized religion, the small group also could offer a congenial communal setting for the creation of a stabilizing mythology and inspirational ritual. Perhaps the encounter group served as a microcosm of American idealism where the defeat of loneliness, finding a sense of meaning, anti-intellectualism, and religiosity were all possible (p. 5).

2   One strand and influence in encounter is the intensive, confrontational approach which, in its extreme form at Synanon, involved 'attack' therapy whereby a person is cross-examined about their behaviour or attitudes, criticised and even ridiculed.

This found a cultural resonance at the time amongst people who supported the Chinese cultural revolution, which employed similar tactics, especially against intellectuals and those perceived to be intellectual. The Erhard Seminar Training ('est') marathon groups developed some similar techniques in their promotion of personal growth and transformation in a short period of time – for a review of Erhard's subsequent and more recent initiative, The Landmark Forum, see Wruck and Eastley (1997).

3   The open encounter of Schutz was highly structured with movement, group exercises and suggestions and directions from the leader. Experimentation was encouraged – the nude marathon was one example (Bindrim, 1968) – and in many ways reflected the times.

4   The fourth branch of encounter, which developed from Rogers, is less structured, with more emphasis on communication between members of the group and on congruence or genuineness. In the later years of his life Rogers became more involved in the resolution of conflict, intercultural tension and in peace initiatives through facilitating groups in several of the world's 'hot spots'. This reflects the strong counter-cultural influence of encounter which led it at the time to be an influential social experience – Rogers (1970/1973) even claimed that the encounter group was one of the most successful modern inventions:

> those who may have thought of the encounter group as a fad or phenomenon affecting only a few people temporarily would do well to reconsider. In the troubled future that lies ahead of us, the trend towards the intensive group experience is related to deep and significant issues having to do with change . . . in persons, in institutions, in our urban and cultural alienation, in racial tensions, in our international frictions, in our philosophies, our values, our image of man himself. It is a profoundly significant movement. (Rogers, 1970/1973, p. 169)

In present times, the legacy of encounter finds expression in social applications such as consciousness-raising groups, and, more recently, in community-building initiatives (see Chapter 7).

For further reading on encounter see Merry (1995) and Yalom (1995).

Transactional analysis and the person-centred approach   As far as approaches to groups and to working with groups are concerned, each school within the humanistic/existential tradition has its own emphasis: psychodrama – and sociodrama – offers a rich literature on groups (e.g. Røine, 1997); gestalt approaches to group have been collected in a unique volume by Feder and Ronall (1994). From my training and experience, given that I draw particularly on transactional analysis (TA) and the person-centred approach (PCA), I summarise their respective approaches to groups (Table 1.1). Developments in and applications of both TA and the PCA are referred to throughout the book.

Integrating the traditions

Over the past fifteen years there has been an increasing interest in the concept of integrative counselling/psychotherapy and, indeed, many counsellors and psychotherapists refer to themselves as 'integrative'. This term, however, which is broadly used to describe some combining of parts of the whole field of counselling, covers a multiplicity of meanings and is open to (mis)interpretation and confusion. I discern three strands or strategies in this combining of parts: 'the first is the development of different models for integration; the second argues that integrative psychotherapy constitutes a separate school or 'fourth force'; the third that a particular approach to psychotherapy *is in itself* integrative' (Tudor, 1996c, p. 330). The relevance of these debates for the group counsellor is that these strands may also be seen in the field of group counselling:

- *Different models for integration* – represented, for example, by the application of Gelso and Carter's (1985, 1994) framework of components of counselling relationships to group counselling (see Chapter 4). Aveline and Dryden (1988) apply a literary thematic structure – romantic, ironic, tragic and comic visions – to their brief comparative review of small group therapies across a range of therapeutic orientations. Corey (1995) presents his 'integrated eclectic model' of group counselling which addresses the three factors of thinking, feeling and doing.
- *Integration as a fourth force* – represented by the interest, again over the past fifteen years, in a systems approach to group counselling/psychotherapy which relates the parts (the group members) to the whole (the group). Manor (1994) identifies a number of authors from different orientations who

Table 1.1 *Comparison between transactional analysis and person-centred approaches to group counselling*

	TA	PCA
Philosophical roots	Humanistic/existential, phenomenological and empirical: 'insofar as living in the world is concerned, transactional analysis shares with existential analysis a high esteem for, and keen interest in, the personal qualities of honesty, integrity, autonomy, and authenticity, and their most poignant social manifestation in encounter and intimacy' (Berne, 1966, p. 305)	
Goal/s	Classically, to cure clients: to achieve social control over behaviour, symptomatic relief, transference cure, and script cure (see Berne, 1961/1975a, 1972/1975b)	None set by therapist
Focus	Classically, on the analysis of transactions between group members	On the facilitation of communication between group members and on learning; on group functioning and cohesion (Lietaer and Dierick, 1996)
Method	Contractual	No specific method (see attitude of group facilitator)
Structure	Negotiated through contractual method	Little formal structure (see Coghlan and McIlduff, 1990): this is based on a belief in the organismic actualising tendency of individuals and of the group.
Rules and contract	Rules prescribed by the counsellor, contract defined and agreed bilaterally (see Chapter 3)	Generally none, any decided and agreed by group
Responsibility	Shared, based on the contract	Shared between members and facilitator/participant
Process	Defined by transactions both within the group (internal group process) and those impacting on the group (external group process)	No formal process – this is based on trust in the group as an organism (see Wood, 1982) and 'the wisdom of the organism'

Table 1.1   *Continued*

	TA	PCA
Techniques	Many, including the use of diagnosis; analysis of ego states, scripts and games etc.; eight therapeutic operations (Berne, 1966) including confrontation	None (see attitude of group facilitator)
Attitude of group counsellor/ therapist/facilitator	Classically, didactic, teaching clients, for instance, to recognise ego states, transactions and psychological games	Facilitative, drawing particularly on Rogers' (1957, 1959) six conditions for therapeutic change. The facilitator is also a participant
Group development	Viewed in sequential terms of group imago (see Berne, 1963, 1966) and see below	From 'milling around' to the basic encounter and (behavioural) change (see above and Hobbs, 1951; Rogers, 1970/1973)

have moved to a systems approach to group psychotherapy, and suggests that 'quite a number of group analysts . . . would privately express the view that very little would be lost if group analytic ideas were couched in systems terms' (Manor, 1994, p. 257).

■ *Particular approaches as integrative* – represented by theoreticians and practitioners who argue that their particular approach to counselling/psychotherapy is itself integrative. Rogers, for instance, presented his 'necessary and sufficient conditions' initially as an integrative framework for all helping relationships (Rogers, 1957).

There are a number of other traditions which are more difficult to place. Feminist and transcultural counselling/psychotherapy, for instance, are both influenced by all three traditions, especially the analytic and, to a lesser extent, the humanistic and their practitioners identify themselves variously. Some view the transpersonal tradition in therapy as an alternative fourth (or fifth) force. Very little has been written from these perspectives specifically as regards group therapy (see Butler and Wintram, 1991; Thomas, 1997).

Working in, through and of the group

The different traditions of psychotherapy/counselling, as well as the counsellor's own experience and training, influence the way an individual thinks and works. These differences explicitly – or, more often, implicitly – inform the way a group counsellor leads, conducts or facilitates a group. Roberts (1982) conceptualises these differences as that between psychotherapy *in* the group, *through* the group and *of* the group. Therapy *in* the group, developed by the early practitioners in both the psychoanalytic and humanistic traditions, focuses on the individual client often 'working' or doing 'pieces of work' in the group, sometimes literally with the counsellor and client sitting in the middle of the group, following which the individual client may invite and/or get feedback about themselves and their 'work'. Perls' invitation to people to take the 'hot seat' in his gestalt therapy is an example of such psychotherapy *in* the group. Therapy *through* the group focuses on the relationships between group members themselves and between them and the counsellor/psychotherapist. The group counsellor may also work *through* the relationships established in the group; the group transactional analyst, for example, analyses and intervenes in transactions between group members. Therapy *of* the group, developed by Bion (1961), treats the group-as-a-whole with interventions directed at the whole group. These are developed in relation to organisations in Chapter 7.

Several approaches and many practitioners combine different elements, based on the notion that every input, contribution or transaction may be viewed as both an individual and a group contribution; thus, *in* and *of* the group (e.g. Tavistock model and TA), *through* and *of* the group (e.g. group-analytic psychotherapy, many humanistic approaches), *in* and *through* the group (e.g. gestalt). Table 1.2 summarises these different foci of group counselling/psychotherapy with examples of possible opening and closing statements.

Conceptualising the group

As we reflect on groups in which we have grown up, lived, worked, participated etc., we inevitably conceptualise our experience. Craib (1987) refers to this as the unavoidability of theory: 'we never have a direct access to the world outside ourselves; it is

Table 1.2 *A comparison of counselling/psychotherapy in, through and of the group*

	In the group	*Through* the group	*Of* the group
Focus of afftention	The individual/s	The individual member/s	The group-as-a-whole
Example of opening statement	How are you, Adam? (addressing an individual)	What do people want to work on this evening?	____(silence)
Example of closing statement/s	Take care. See you on Wednesday … (addressing different individuals)	We'll finish there.	____(silence)

always mediated by our language, which contains implicit and explicit theories of what the world is like and how it works' (p. 33). Two conceptualisations of groups are especially useful in thinking about, planning and working with groups: the image of groups and stages in the development of groups.

The image of groups

We all have images of groups: groups we have grown up in, worked in, played in, groups we have enjoyed and groups we have hated, groups we have experienced and those we have imagined. Berne (1963) referred to this subjective image of the group as the *group imago*: 'any mental picture, conscious, pre-conscious or unconscious, of what a group is or should be like' (p. 321). Later, Berne (1966) defined it as 'a mental image of the dynamic relationships between the people in the group, including the therapist; idiosyncratic for each individual patient' (p. 364). This concept is thus especially useful in understanding how group members, *subjectively* and *individually*, as well as the group counsellor, experience the group over time – from before they join it to after they leave it; indeed Berne suggests that this 'private structure' of the group 'is the most decisive structural aspect for the outcome of the individual's therapy' (Berne, 1966, p. 153). Berne identifies four phases in the development of the individual's group imago in the course of the group:

■ *The provisional group imago* – an individual's image of the group before they enter the group or before the group becomes active.

- *The adapted group imago* – the image as 'superficially modified in accordance with the member's estimate of confronting reality' (Berne, 1963, p. 321).
- *The operative group imago* – the further modification of the image 'in accordance with the member's perception of how he fits into the leader's imago' (Berne, 1963, p. 321).
- *The secondarily adjusted group imago* – 'in which the member relinquishes some of his own proclivities in favour of the group cohesion'. (Berne, 1963, p. 321)

Citing Berne (1963), Clarkson (1991) suggests a further stage or phase of the development of an individual's group imago, that of:

- *The clarified group imago*:
  insofar as the group imago is a facsimile of an infantile group imago or a reproduction of a childhood group imago, its clarification and differentiation is part of facilitating individuals and groups to live more in terms of their current needs. (p. 46)

In addition, I suggest that there are a further two phases of an individual's subjective experience of groups:

- *The secondarily operative group imago*, a fifth phase before Clarkson's clarified group imago, in which the individual member is concerned with clarifying and developing interdependent relationships in the context of the group which are free from any adaptation (rather than being concerned primarily with group cohesion).
- *The historical group imago*, a seventh and final phase, which represents images of the group which the individual carries beyond the end of the group or their ending with the group.

An individual's changing experience of the group may thus be represented as in Figure 1.1. Alpha, a new group member, knows the group therapist but has not met or differentiated 'those others' whom she knows to be in the group. A prospective new member may only know that the group comprises a particular number of members; equally, existing group members may only know that

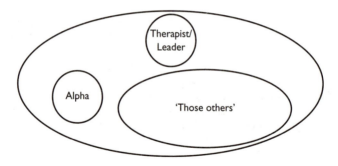

Figure 1.1 *Alpha's provisional group imago (based on Berne, 1966)*

someone is joining the group. Figure 1.1 thus reflects the provisional group imago held by all members joining a newly established group. Berne suggests that differentiation is based on early experiences of groups, family history as well as present attitudes towards groups.

In Figure 1.2, by this beginning stage of group therapy Alpha has differentiated two group members from 'those others', in this case by seeing them – and herself – in a hierarchical relation to each other and to the group therapist ostensibly on the basis of her perception of their emotional maturity. Her concern about the hierarchy in the group reflects and represents her experience in her family of origin.

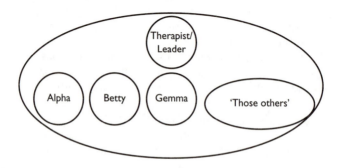

Figure 1.2 *Alpha's adapted group imago (based on Berne, 1966 and Clarkson, 1991)*

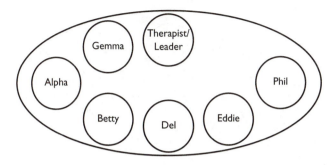

Figure 1.3 *Alpha's operative group imago*

In Figure 1.3 Alpha has now differentiated all the members of the group, although she is still focusing on how she fits into the leader's imago at this stage, also seeing Gemma as closer to the group therapist and as in between herself and the therapist.

In Figure 1.4 Alpha's experience of herself in the group is now one of a number of differentiated individuals in an increasingly cohesive group.

In the phase of the group shown in Figure 1.5 Alpha's experience is of herself and other individuals in the group moving, experimenting and changing (represented by the double circles). Each member is increasingly differentiated both (with)in themselves, that is, from previous images of themselves, and in relation to others, that is, from previous images and models of relationships.

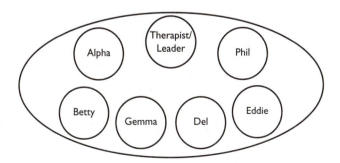

Figure 1.4 *Alpha's secondarily adjusted group imago*

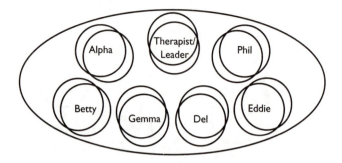

Figure 1.5 *Alpha's secondarily operative group imago*

In Figure 1.6 Alpha and Gemma are leaving the group. Alpha's imago of the group is clear (clarified), based on her experience in the present with no interference from the past.

After Alpha has left the group, she none the less still carries an image – many images – of it. Figure 1.7 shows Alpha's view of 'her group' as it was at one particular moment or phase, together with her image of 'those others', that is new members, who have subsequently joined the group (see Chapter 5 for a further historical group imago in the context of discussion about what happens after a group ends).

The concept of the group imago is clearly based on the individual's subjective (phenomenological) experience of groups. Thus the group counsellor only knows subjectively their own group imago and may only *infer* the group imagoes of individual

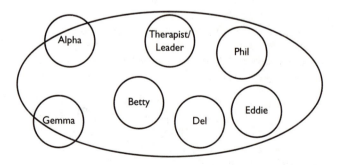

Figure 1.6 *Alpha's clarified group imago*

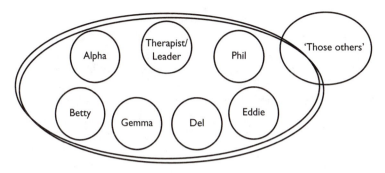

Figure 1.7 *Alpha's historical group imago*

group members – although such inferences are crucial in understanding individuals' differing experience of the group as well as the origins of such experiences. In reviewing and applying different concepts of groups and in representing a range of approaches to science, it is therefore also useful to consider an objective (empirical) view of group development.

Stages of group development

There are a number of theories and conceptualisations about group process and development – see, for instance, Rowan (1976), who includes a series of poems to describe his experience of a particular group process in a Tavistock group, Mackewn (1997), who reviews and compares different gestalt approaches to group development . . . and even Mearns (1997) who, whilst acknowledging the contradiction between predictive developmental stages in either human or social development and the person-centred approach, nevertheless offers a heuristic sequence of stages within the development of the larger group in a learning context:

I   Polite tolerance
II   Confusion and disorientation
III   Glimpsing the potential
IV   Valuing and working in the open process.

In a seminal article on the 'Developmental sequence in small groups' (Tuckman, 1965), which, in turn, reviewed and analysed fifty articles on stages of group development, Tuckman proposed four general stages of group development: forming, storming, norming and performing – although he acknowledged that some authors reviewed also identified a Pre-stage 1 (e.g. Shellow et al., 1958). Later, Tuckman and Jenson (1977) amended the model to include a fifth stage, adjourning. This is similar to Lacoursiere's (1980) termination stage, although this four stage model – orientation, dissatisfaction, production and termination – is different in some respects from that of Tuckman. It is important to note that in his review of groups in their various settings and in developing his developmental sequence Tuckman was focusing on the task of the group and task-activities. It is also postulated that these phases may be identified within the lifetime of a particular group meeting. Table 1.3 summarises Tuckman's phases (with these additions), together with his sequential view of the group structure and key task-activity in these phases. It also compares Tuckman's phases of group development with Berne's developing group imago as well as my own additions and completion to the table (in italicised type). In comparing these schemas of group development I am bringing together different approaches to theories of knowledge – the subjectivist (e.g. Berne, 1963) and the objectivist (e.g. Tuckman, 1965). On a conceptual level this offers a comprehensive view of group development; on a practical level, it connects the image of the group with the notional task associated with that image: with a provisional image, the task is orientation, etc. Whilst these are two major theories on group development, they are not the only ones. In many respects group counsellors draw on the developmental model consistent with their theoretical orientation; Corey (1995), for instance, applies Freudian and Eriksonian developmental stages to groupwork; MacKenzie and Livesley (1983) apply a six-stage model also based on epigenetic processes to brief group therapy; and a further developmental approach to *inter*-group relations is explored in Chapter 7. Yalom (1995) challenges what he views as confusion about group development: 'each group is, at the same time, like *all groups, some groups, and no other group!*' (p. 306, original emphasis). This said, Yalom accepts that there are modest advantages to group

Table 1.3 *Comparative phases of group development*

Group imago (Berne, 1963)	Stages of group development (Tuckman, 1965)	Group structure (Tuckman, 1965)	Task-activity (Tuckman, 1965)
Provisional group imago	Pre-Stage I (Shellow et al., 1958) *Pre-forming*[1]	(For the individual) Resistance and hostility	*Orientation to the idea of the group*
Adapted group imago	Forming	Testing and dependence	Orientation to the task and testing
Operative group imago	Storming	Intragroup conflict	Emotional response to task demands
Secondarily adjusted group imago	Norming	Development of group cohesion	Open exchange of relevant interpretation/ discussion
Secondarily operative group imago	Performing	Functional role-relatedness	Emergence of insight and solutions
Clarified group imago (Clarkson, 1991)	Adjourning (Tuckman and Jenson 1977) Termination (Lacoursiere, 1980)	*Differentiation*	*Appreciation of importance of group and individuals*
Historical group imago	(For the individual) Mourning	*Separation and distance*	*Disinvestment from group and reinvestment in new relationships*

[1]Clarkson (1991) attributes this to Sue Fish.

therapists having some broad schema of a group's development and it is in this questioning spirit that these two conceptualisations of group development are offered and used as a broad organising framework in this book.

The following vignettes, taken from work with individuals (vignettes 1 and 7) and with groups, illustrate the practical usefulness of such developmental conceptualisations of the group. In these examples the counsellor draws on these concepts in responding both to individual members and to the group as a whole.

Vignette 1
Adam: I'm worried about joining the group. What happens? What sort of people are they? Will they accept me? What are the rules?
Counsellor: You sound worried and anxious. The group is a good place to talk about such feelings.

Comment
This client (in individual counselling) is, in terms of the group, in the *preforming* stage. Depending on the counsellor's style and theoretical orientation, they will say less or more in response to such questions, bearing in mind that the client is expressing a need for some orientation to the group. At the same time the counsellor should not be overly reassuring. Here the counsellor acknowledges the client's feelings and encourages him to take them to the group, thereby giving him some information, without detracting from his anxiety.

Vignette 2
Bea: [*seeing a notice about 'No shoes in the group room'*] Do we have to take our shoes off?
[*Pause*]
Celine: Yes.
Bea: Oh.
[*Pause*]
Derek [addressing the counsellor]: Are you going to say something?
Counsellor: What do you want me to say?

Comment
This is the beginning of a new group who are *forming*. Bea is testing the counsellor's boundaries whilst Derek is expressing some dependence on the counsellor to get the group started – to which the counsellor responds by challenging Derek to be clear about what he wants.

Vignette 3
Evelyn: [to *Ferdinand*] I'm vexed with you.
Ferdinand: Well, you're always vexed with someone. I'm really pissed off with you for always finding fault with someone and [*to counsellor*] I'm cross with you for not controlling her [Evelyn] more.
Counsellor: It seems like you are cross with each other and you [Ferdinand] at least are cross with me. I don't want to control anyone's emotions. Now the group's been meeting for a while, it seems to me that you are really getting to know and trust each other with your feelings.

Comment
This interchange reflects the *storming* phase of the group in which there is conflict between group members and between group members and the group counsellor. Here the counsellor responds directly to Ferdinand and indirectly to the whole group about the role of emotions in relation to the task of this group at this stage, i.e. getting to know and trust each other.

Vignette 4
Gil: You know, I'd like it if everybody said something at the beginning of the group. I'd sort of know where everyone was at then.
Harika: I'm not sure about that: it would seem too formal, especially if I didn't have anything to say.
Iain: I agree. I was in a group once where everyone had to say what they wanted and how much time they wanted. I didn't like that.
Jasmine: I wouldn't want things to get too formal. On the other hand having a 'go round' or some sort of 'check in' might actually help us feel

Comment
Here the group is discussing the pros and cons of having some introductory 'check in' time – an example of *norming*. The group counsellor chooses not to intervene in the discussion, rather encouraging the group members to discuss this possible group norm (see Chapter 4). The group cohesion, indicative of this stage is reflected by the fact that each person acknowledges in some way what the other/s have said.

like a group.
Kay: Yes, I want to know how people are before I start talking.

. . .

Vignette 5

Len: You seem distracted Mal. You haven't been with us all evening. What's the matter?
Malik: I'm thinking about a colleague at work who is really not pulling his weight and it's upsetting me. He's taking a lot of time off and when he's there he's not there, if you know what I mean.
Counsellor: . . . a bit like you this evening.
Malik: Yes, I guess . . .
Noni: So what are you going to do?
Malik: I'm not sure. I can't think straight.
Noni: Yes you can. Your thinking is excellent.
Malik: I suppose . . .
Counsellor: You don't seem yourself this evening Mal and, unusually, you're not responding to what others are saying. It seems like you're feeling – and being – like your colleague.

Comment
This extract reflects a group whose members know each other well and, whilst not yet achieving or helping Malik achieve a solution, certainly provides some insight into a parallel process between him and his colleague. This familiarity, care and process is indicative of the *performing* stage of the group.

Vignette 6

Oliver: . . . so I'm going to be leaving the group.
[*Pause*]
Peter: Well that's a bit of a shock . . . I don't want you to leave the group.
Quinn: I'm going to miss you.
Roger: Yeah, me too . . . Hey, that leaves four of us. [*To counsellor*] Are we going to be able to continue as a group?
[*Pause*]
Stan: Wait a minute, the guy's not left yet. I want to talk more about this, like 'what's happening?' and then 'what about us?'
Peter: Yeah, but someone leaving – Oliver leaving – affects us as well as him . . . both are important.

Comment
Oliver's announcement that he's leaving provokes a variety of reactions, common to endings (see Chapter 5). The appreciation of the importance of both the group and the individuals, especially reflected in Stan's and Peter's responses, reflects this *adjourning* phase of the group. The counsellor was about to say something in the second pause when Stan came in and, due to what he and then Peter said, chose not to say anything at this point.

Vignette 7

Oliver: Yes, I'm getting on with my life but I really miss the support of the group. Maybe it was a mistake to leave when I did . . . maybe it was too soon . . .
Counsellor: You sound regretful. You're 'getting on' and you're wanting more support. You seem to be saying that you can't get or don't have support outside the group . . .

Comment
Here the client (in individual counselling) is talking about the group which he has recently left, the loss of which he is *mourning*. The counsellor reflects the client's thoughts, having in mind the client's task of disinvesting from relationships in the group and looking outside the group for new, supportive relationships.

This chapter has summarised a brief history of groups as well as the influence of different theoretical orientations and has discussed two conceptualisations of group development. The next four chapters develop this framework by considering practical issues in counselling groups, beginning in Chapter 2 with discussion of the practical preparatory work necessary for the counsellor in preparing for a counselling group.

2

Preparing for the Group

In this chapter I consider the practical issues involved in preparing to establish a counselling group which has, or which is expected to have, a certain continuity of existence. I begin with a brief review of therapeutic factors of groups – on the basis that these will vary according to the counsellor, the client group and any therapeutic goals, and that these variables will influence the establishment of the group. This also raises the issue of the importance of research and evaluation. Following this, I expand on ideas about the nature, composition and function of the group through discussions on:

- Defining the group
- Advertising and pre-group information
- Assessment
- Fees

Therapeutic factors

A therapeutic factor is defined as 'an element of group therapy that contributes to the improvement in the patient's condition and is a function of the actions of the group therapist, the other group members, and the patient himself' (Bloch and Crouch, 1985, p. 4). Although Bloch (1988) makes a distinction between this element and a condition for change (such as a shared sense of motivation or commitment), which allows therapeutic factors to operate, Rogers' (1957, 1959) six necessary and sufficient conditions for growth and therapeutic personality change may be taken as both, that is, psychological contact between counsellor and client/s, client incongruence, counsellor congruence, unconditional positive regard (UPR) and empathic understanding and the client's receiving of the counsellor's UPR and empathy. Despite widespread misunderstanding and misrepresentation of the necessity and sufficiency of these *six* conditions (*as distinct from* the 'core conditions'), it is clear that Rogers viewed them as necessarily and suffficently applied to groups and specifically to resolving group tension and conflict (Rogers, 1959). The universality and integrative nature of these conditions are confirmed even when tested against more widely accepted factors such as Yalom's.

The first systematic study of therapeutic factors in groups dates from a review article by Corsini and Rosenberg (1955), who identified nine such factors applying to group therapy as a whole across orientations. Bloch and Crouch (1985) identify ten therapeutic factors and, in his seminal work on *The Theory and Practice of Group Psychotherapy*, Yalom (1995) identifies eleven therapeutic factors in group therapy (or twelve as he subdivides interpersonal factors into input and ouput):

- *The instillation and maintenance of hope* – group members observing the improvement of others.
- *Universality* – the notion that we are not unique, alone or isolated in our 'wretchedness'.
- *Imparting of information* – which may be didactic instruction in various aspects of interactional group therapy or may be direct advice.
- *Altruism* – the notion that people receive through giving support, reassurance, suggestions, insight etc.
- *The corrective recapitulation of the primary family group* – for which the group provides a greater range of possibilities (than does individual therapy).
- *Development of socialising techniques* – and social learning.
- *Imitative behaviour* – in groups the imitative process is more diffuse and varied (than in individual therapy in which this factor is entirely dependent on the therapist).
- *Interpersonal learning* – gained, according to Yalom, primarily through transference and insight.
  Interpersonal learning – input concerns the client's learning about themselves as regards how they come across.

Interpersonal learning – output focuses on the person's contribution to others in the group.

■ *Group cohesiveness* – which '*must encompass the patient's relationship not only to the group therapist but to the other group members and to the group as a whole*' (Yalom, 1995, p. 48, original emphasis).

■ *Catharsis* – the expression of 'suppressed, choked affect' (Yalom, 1995, p. 80) together with a sense of liberation; catharsis *in itself* is not necessarily therapeutic.

■ *Existential factors* – defined as representing 'responsibility, basic isolation, contingency, the capriciousness of existence, the recognition of our mortality and the ensuing consequences for the conduct of our life' (Yalom, 1995, p. 88).

Yalom's research was based on a Q-sort of sixty therapeutic factor items (reproduced in Appendix 2) which was constructed a priori by Yalom and other experienced practitioners; and indeed the language of the statements/items describing the sixty therapeutic factors reflects these practitioners, their orientations and their underlying assumptions about therapy. When I used these same items as the basis for my own research, one piece of feedback I received was that the statements 'weren't *you*' – which bears out Dierick and Lietaer's (1990) criticism of research based on pre-constructed categorisations (see below). The only alteration I made to the statements used by Yalom was to change some of the verbs in the items to the present tense as I was conducting research into ongoing groups. The sixty items reflect the therapeutic factors thus (although this is unknown to the subjects of the research):

Items 1–5   Altruism
Items 6–10   Group cohesiveness
Items 11–15   Universality
Items 16–20   Interpersonal learning – input
Items 21–25   Interpersonal learning – output
Items 26–30   Guidance
Items 31–35   Catharsis
Items 36–40   Identification
Items 41–45   Family re-enactment
Items 46–50   Self-understanding
Items 51–55   Instillation of hope
Items 56–60   Existential factors

In a study of twenty long-term (mean duration 16 months) group therapy patients, who each made a simple rank ordering of the sixty items, Yalom and his colleagues (Yalom et al., 1968) discovered that seven out of the first eight items represented some form of catharsis or of insight. Yalom (1995) relates that two other studies using the sixty item Q-sort report remarkably similar findings, although he acknowledges

> these research findings pertain to a specific kind of therapy group: an interactionally based group with the ambitious goals of symptom relief and behavioral and characterological change. Other groups with differ-ent goals may capitalize on a different cluster of therapeutic factors. (p. 80)

This is borne out by my own research into one ongoing therapy group comprising eight members, each of whom completed a similar exercise, rank ordering the sixty items. The ten items deemed to be most helpful, were, in order of importance:

1	Item 10: Belonging to a group of people who understand and accept me.
2	Item 6: Belonging to and being accepted by a group.
3	Item 43: Being in the group is, in a sense, like being in a family, only this time a more accepting family.
= 4	Item 17: Learning how I come across to others.
= 4	Item 22: Feeling more trustful of groups and of other people.
6	Item 18: Other members honestly telling me what they think of me.
7	Item 47: Learning why I think and feel the way I do (that is, learning some of the causes and sources of my problems).
= 8	Item 26: The therapist's suggesting or advising something for me to do.
= 8	Item 60: Learning that I must take ultimate responsibility for the way I live my life no matter how much guidance and support I get from others.
= 10	Item 8: Revealing embarrassing things about myself and still being accepted by the group.
= 10	Item 21: Improving my skills in getting along with people.
= 10	Item 58: Recognising that no matter how close I get to other people, I must still face life alone.

These represent a different ranking of factors than in Yalom's research: five out of the first six items represent group cohesion (nos. 10 and 6) and interpersonal learning (nos. 17, 22 and 18). These factors can also be understood in terms of the 'core conditions' of the person-centred approach (PCA): item 10 reflecting the importance of the empathic understanding of others and items 17, 47, 60 and 58 of empathic self-understanding; items 10, 6, 43 and 8 of acceptance or unconditional positive regard; and item 18 of the valuing of genuineness or congruence. The first (item 10) bears out Giesekus and Mente's (1986) observation that *clients'* empathic understanding of each other is the most important therapeutic factor in therapy groups – and is, therefore, one of the therapist's primary tasks – and is the basis for group cohesion.

From Corsini and Rosenberg's (1955) review, it follows that 'the relative importance of these factors in a particular form of group therapy is a function of, *inter alia*, the group's purpose, the members' clinical needs, the duration of treatment, and the stage in the group's development' (Bloch, 1988, p. 287). Yalom (1995) suggests that the importance of the therapeutic factors varies not only according to these considerations but also according to the clinical population, therapeutic goals and, of course, the individuals in the group. This kind of research is thus useful both in terms of defining your practice and what you are aiming to offer in facilitating a therapy group and in evaluating how individuals in a particular group are experiencing and understanding the therapeutic effect of what you are offering. Notwithstanding the interest and value of such research, research studies that analyse data according to previously established categories of factors are limited. From a person-centred perspective, one which values the subjective experience as an approach to evaluation and indeed the structure of research, Dierick and Lietaer (1990) describe their study, in which more than 100 group members were asked open questions, the answers to which were then used to construct a category system describing 'helpful events'. From the responses Dierick and Lietaer (1990) derive three broad categories: relational climate and structural aspects of the group, specific interventions by group members or therapist, and process aspects in the group member – by which they organise the more detailed responses. They then compare these with therapeutic factors found in the literature and argue that many of these are enhanced by the findings of their research. Thus group cohesion includes 'an array of Group relational climate dimensions. Within these Rogers' basic relationship attitudes are easily recognizable' (p. 765). The field of research into group therapy is extensive, covering issues such as leadership, group development and group process, and is well reviewed by Bloch (1988). As with theory, research forms the background to and informs both good practice and the practical consideration in preparing for a group.

Defining the group

In practical terms, the group counsellor also needs to define the group in terms of purpose, type, constituency, size, regularity and lifetime, and duration, and to consider the setting of the group.

Purpose

The purpose of a group is the objective the therapist or facilitator has in view when planning and establishing it. General purposes of groups may be: 'to better understand ourselves', 'to become more aware', 'to learn to relate to each other in ways which would be helpful' – these are taken from Rogers' (1970/1973) report on the establishment of the early (that is, post-Second World War) encounter groups. Berne (1966) defines the purpose of 'group treatment' specifically as 'the alleviation of psychiatric disabilities' (p. 3), thus distinguishing 'treatment' groups from other therapy groups (whose central purpose or aim is not to 'cure' patients), discussion groups, support groups, growth groups, community groups etc., all of which have different purposes which are generally clear from their titles. Berne cautions against the loose use of terms such as 'sharing', 'integration', 'maturity' and 'growth' as goals for groups and argues for further, more precise definition in the context of a well-planned therapeutic programme. Groups, however, do not have to have a therapeutic purpose in order to be useful. Consciousness-raising, support and focus groups all have their specific purposes, as do a variety of work-based groups (see Chapter 7).

Although the initial purpose of the group is the therapist's, once established, the purpose of the group and that of the therapist may be different. Stewart's (1996) concept of an outcome matrix is useful in understanding the potential for difference and conflict. The outcome matrix encourages the counsellor to identify *their* outcome for the client (as distinct from the client's outcome for themselves) at both a social level (that is, within awareness) and a psychological level (initially, at least, outside awareness). Thus, in the context of a men's group:

■ Counsellor for client/s (social level): That they have an opportunity to discuss gender issues.
■ Counsellor for client/s (psychological level): That they change their use of oppressive language.

If the counsellor operates out of awareness then they may well take a punitive stance about the use of language in the group and indeed the direction of the client/s therapy. In my view, this is the problem underlying a lot of anti-discrimination/anti-oppressive practice training and psycho-educational work with men who have been violent, work which operates at an implicit, psychological level rather than an explicit, social level of contracting and purpose.

Type
There are many types of group – treatment, therapy, support, community, discussion, consciousness-raising, encounter – whose purpose, constituency and perhaps orientation is usually indicated by their title, for example, psychiatric in-patient treatment group, gestalt therapy group, gay men's support group, therapeutic community group, Marx reading and discussion group, men's consciousness-raising group, open weekend encounter group. Clearly it is important that the therapist is clear about what type of group they are offering.

Another aspect of 'type' is whether the group is open, that is, open to new members, or closed, that is, a fixed membership for the lifetime of the group. Decisions about this usually relate to the purpose and planned lifetime of the group. Closed groups tend to run for a fixed term with a clear ending. A therapist may then run another, new group incorporating some members from the previous group. In terms of open groups, which tend to run until the therapist gives notice, Henry (1988) develops a classification or typology: the drop-in (drop-out), the replacement and the re-formed group (see Figure 2.1), although I regard the re-formed group as, in effect, a new closed group.

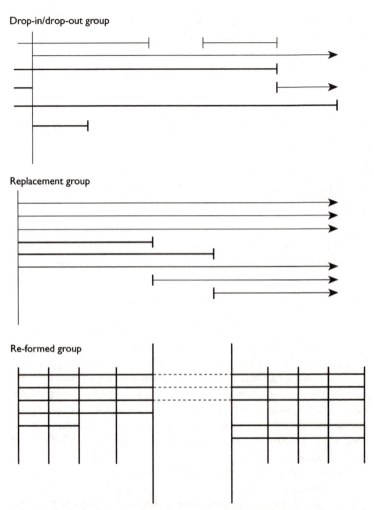

Drop-in/drop-out group

Replacement group

Re-formed group

Each single horizontal line represents the attendance of individual members, the vertical lines represent time boundaries, i.e. sessions.

Figure 2.1   *Types of open group (Henry, 1988)*

Constituency
This refers to the eligible membership. Le Bon (1896/1920) first distinguished between heterogeneous crowds (anonymous

crowds, juries, parliamentary assemblies) and homogeneous crowds (sects, castes, classes). From this, a distinction may be drawn between heterogeneous groups, whose members are not selected, and homogeneous groups, whose members are defined and therefore selected in some way by specific criteria:

- by diagnosis or symptom, for example, a group of people diagnosed as having schizophrenia or people with eating disorders
- by experience, for example, adult survivors of childhood sexual abuse
- by common interest or purpose, for example, a fell walking group
- by common task, for example, a work-based group/team/ project
- by gender, for example, a women's group
- by sexuality, for example, a group of gay men and/or lesbians
- by a combination of classifications, for example, a gay men's group.

The arguments for heterogeneous groups date back to Freud (1921/1985a) who, paraphrasing Le Bon, suggests that 'the particular acquirements of individuals become obliterated in a group, and that in this way their distinctiveness vanishes. The racial unconscious emerges; what is heterogeneous is submerged in what is homogeneous' (Freud, 1921/1985a, p. 100). From a more positive viewpoint, we know that our social world is also a plural world: there are many worldviews of how to understand people as individuals and in groups and as we live in a plural world we need to deal with plurality and difference. Berne (1966) argues strongly against homogeneity (unless on the basis of a particular psychiatric condition), suggesting that

> it is usually based on personal prejudices, supported by rationalizations which may become untenable in the face of systematic criticism . . . The real issue . . . is not the one commonly debated, 'What are the criteria for the selection of patients?', but the underlying, usually unstated assumption 'Criteria for selection are good.' (p. 5)

On the basis that selection criteria are no good, Berne makes several radical suggestions about selection and allocation: that clients should be assigned to groups by someone unconnected with the group, or by random allocation, or, indeed, that every client should be put into a group. Berne also argues that siblings, parents, spouses, lovers – and rivals – of clients could be included in the same group. As a result, within Transactional Analysis (TA) there is a strong emphasis on non-selected groups.

Within an essentially heterogeneous group there are some arguments for selection, precisely (if somewhat ironically) in order to maintain the heterogeneity, especially in a group comprising a particular cultural majority. Thus, a counsellor wanting to facilitate a genuinely mixed group – mixed by culture, age, gender, sexuality etc. – may have to select, through targeted advertising and recruitment say in a minority community. When members leave a mixed group, for instance, they inevitably change the balance; the therapist then has to decide whether to take the next client, whoever that is, or to wait until a new client 'matches' the group member who has left. In the case of a mixed gender group, I used to keep the numbers even (four men, four women); thus, at any one time if the group comprises seven, there may be a space for, say, one man – and, therefore, not a woman – and vice versa. I have recently rethought this and, in the spirit of non-selection and in consultation with the then current group, have changed this so that I allow a certain imbalance and uneven numbers – down to a minimum of, say, two of either gender – and working through any individual and/ or group process which arises from this.

Another issue that requires balance or at least consideration arises when the group comprises clients who are themselves counsellors or psychotherapists or in training as such. In my experience, beyond a certain number (that is, three in a group of eight), the group may feel imbalanced. This may be expressed by suspicion (usually amongst those who are not therapists) that the client/therapist is better than or less 'ill' than them; or that they are only observing or are in some way an assistant therapist and thus not fully participating in the group process; or by frustration – by both the 'lay' people and the trainee therapists. One solution to this issue is to have a selected group comprising therapists. (This issue is compounded by the requirement for training counsellors themselves to have experience of therapy, a requirement which further complicates the dynamics of any therapy and any therapy group in which such counsellors are members. This situation requires special care and experience on the part of the group therapist, see Chapter 8.)

Arguments for homogeneous or specifically selected groups are generally related to the group's purpose and the therapist's goals.

If the purpose of a group is to increase the self-esteem of gay men then the constituency of the group is most likely to be gay men only. Equally, if the purpose of a group is to confront homophobia in heterosexuals then such a group will generally comprise hetero-sexual people only – which is the argument underlying the organisation of much anti-discrimination or anti-oppression train-ing work, in heterosexual, white, middle-class, able-bodied (etc.) groups. If the goal of a group is 'the abandonment of stereotyped relationship patterns' (Berne, 1966, p. 8) then, it could be argued that this is best achieved in a single gender group (that is, a men's group or a women's group) as a mixed group tends to reflect stereotyped relationship patterns (for a feminist contribution to groupwork see Butler and Wintram, 1991). On the other hand, given that we live in a plural, mixed world, ultimately there is also a purpose to resolve such issues in a mixed environment – both inside and outside the therapeutic environment.

Finally, in terms of homogeneity, sometimes the context in which the group is being offered makes it homogeneous, that is, a group for 'problem drinkers' in an alcohol recovery centre, or the constituency of the group, for example a children's group (see Ginott, 1961), a couples group (see Coche and Coche, 1990) or a particular family group. Counsellors working with such groups need to take account of particular issues of size, setting, contact and contracting – and, in the case of minors obtain appropriate consent (see Appendix 1). Ultimately, the question of homoge-neous or heterogeneous groups is a consequence of the group therapist's values.

Size

Whilst there are no hard and fast rules about the size of counsel-ling group, discussions about the optimal size of such a group tend to conclude that eight is a standard number for a small counselling/therapy group. Bion (1961) suggests that the mini-mum size of the group is three: 'two members have personal relationships; with three or more there is a change of quality (interpersonal relationships)' (p. 26). A minimum number also allows for any occasional absences or fall in the numbers regularly attending the group: you may have eight places in your group but be prepared to work with six or four for a while. Hopper and Weyman (1975) provide a sociological view of the psychology of groups and the relation of size to participation, citing the *pan-chayat* or council of an Indian village which has five members and the 'ideal' dinner party which apparently consists of five to seven people! Many parish councils, which some now view as the smallest and most local unit of participatory 'political' decision-making, often operate with similar numbers. Foulkes (1975) suggests that from eight or nine upwards (excluding the conductor) the character of the group changes. De Maré (1972) develops the principles of group analysis to larger, 'median' groups of between fifteen and thirty people, a tradition and practice which is active within the Institute of Group Analysis (see Appendix 4). As its name suggests, the median group fills the numerical gap between the small therapy group and the large group, which Foulkes (1975) identifies as requiring a minimum membership of thirty and preferably fifty or one hundred. At this end of the spectrum and across different therapeutic traditions are the large psychoanalytic groups of the Leicester Conference sponsored by the Tavistock Institute for Human Relations (see Rice, 1965; Wasdell, 1997) and the community meetings at conferences and intercultural workshops of the person-centred approach at which numbers may reach 300. Size also needs to be linked to purpose: an ongoing therapy group would tend to be smaller than, say, either a median group or a community-building weekend workshop (with numbers anywhere between twelve and 200). In terms of dealing with interactions in a group and group dynamics it is worth noting that as a group's size increases arithmetically, the number of relationships between group members and within the group increases geometrically (see Chapter 4).

Regularity and lifetime

Again, this varies and needs to reflect the aims of the group. Some therapists run open-ended groups for many years; others time-limited groups which may be short-term (see Scott and Stradling, 1998). The most important issue as regards regularity, especially in planning and establishing a therapeutic group, is that of consistency: it is better to offer a regular group which you can realistically maintain over the planned lifetime of the group (for example, once a week for a year, once a fortnight for an open-ended group) than enthusiastically to offer a twice-weekly group which both you as the group counsellor and the clients may subsequently find it difficult to sustain.

Duration

Again, the standard, depending on the frequency of the group, seems to be between 1.5 and 2.5 hours for a weekly group. Foulkes (1948/1983) suggests that more than 1.5 hours does not serve much purpose and, interestingly, states that the termination of the group should not be too rigid or abrupt, letting it find a natural halt (somewhere between 75 minutes and 90 minutes). Some therapists run, as a supplement to their weekly group, occasional day or weekend groups or marathons (see Chapter 1). Berne (1966) makes a number of practical suggestions about such 'continuous group therapy', including: that food and (soft) drinks should be available, buffet style, but that there is no need to break for meals; that a tentative time should be set for sleeping but that this could and should be extended when necessary; that the therapist should absent themselves for rest and reflection (thereby leaving the group to themselves); and that the therapist needs to protect 'fragile' clients. Berne's final comment distinguishes his group treatment with its aim 'to get patients well' from 'doing group therapy' or the open encounter group marathon experience undertaken for its own sake or for general growth. As with other defining considerations, duration needs to reflect the purpose of the group.

Setting

The setting for a group is crucial. It provides and represents the safe space, container or *temenos*, 'a space set aside' for the group: a facilitating environment. The physical boundaries of the meeting area should be clear. It should be somewhere in which members experience privacy so that confidentiality is not only agreed but felt – a basic lack of soundproofing often undermines clients' confidence in confidentiality. It needs to be a space in which people may be heard easily, even when talking in a low voice. Again, as with the issue of size, the setting needs to be appropriate to the group's size and to facilitate its purpose with no or few distractions (noise, provocative decor etc.). Generally, it needs to be comfortable and utilitarian with, for instance, a larger space if you encourage or use expressive therapies or a washable floor if you are using art or a variety of play materials (sand, water etc.).

The broader setting of the context of the group is also important. The setting (or context) of a GP's surgery will have a different impact on the group than one meeting in the setting of a counsellor's private practice. The different physical (external) characteristics of the different settings (plastic chairs or soft cushions), as well as issues of constituency and fees or payment also affect the group's internal dynamics. Some groups meet or some group meetings are held in members' own homes – such is the case of the 'alternate' group, whereby the group meets alternately without the counsellor (for a discussion of which see Chapter 3).

Advertising, pre-group information and initial contracting

In its *Code of Ethics and Practice for Counsellors*, the British Association for Counselling (BAC) (1997) states that 'any publicity material and all written and oral information should reflect accurately the nature of the service on offer, and the relevant counselling training, qualifications and experience of the counsellor' (Section B.4.2.1). In its ethical guidelines, the United Kingdom Council for Psychotherapy (UKCP) also refers to accuracy as regards qualifications and advertising (UKCP, 1996, p. xv, 2.1 and 3). Thus a group advertised as 'a short-term, closed counselling group for up to twelve young men attending ante natal classes in order to help them adjust to becoming and being fathers' defines the group offered in terms of duration (short-term), type (closed counselling group), size (up to twelve), constituency (young men) and purpose (to help them adjust . . .). Such clarity promotes potential group members choosing and participating on the basis of *informed* consent. In practice, many therapists advertise their groups rather less specifically, for example:

Places available in Therapy Group
Contact F. Bloggs, CQSW, Counsellor
Telephone number

It is doubtful whether such an advert fulfils the BAC's requirements in terms of reflecting accurately the nature of the service, and whilst it cites the qualification of the counsellor, a CQSW is a social work qualification rather than a counselling one and there is no reference to *relevant* training, qualifications or experience.

Places available in an ongoing, weekly Person-Centred Therapy Group

This established mixed group aims to provide an environment in which its members may explore and resolve issues and difficulties in relating to others in relationships, at home and/or at work. For further details, information and a free initial mutual assessment interview, contact

F. Bloggs, Counsellor in Training

As a social worker I have many years' experience of working with families and in groups. I have completed two years' training as a person-centred counsellor and am running this group under professional supervision.

Telephone number

The second advert may cost a little more, but it is accurate and, in terms of the BAC's (1997) Code, also ethical and professional. The logic of this approach to advertising and pre-counselling information raises the issue of what training, qualification and experience is regarded as relevant to *group* counselling – which is discussed in Chapter 8.

As regards (initial) contracting with clients, the BAC's (1997) Code also states that 'counsellors are responsible for reaching agreement with their clients about the terms on which counselling is being offered . . . [and that] the communication of essential terms and any negotiations should be concluded by having reached a clear agreement before the client incurs any commitment or liability of any kind' (B.4.3.1). Although this is a slightly reworded version of the same section in the previous Code (BAC, 1992), given that it is highly unlikely that such communication *and negotiations* can be satisfactorily completed or even should be attempted by letter or by telephone conversation, I view this as a clear statement of the counsellor's obligation to offer a free initial assessment meeting (– 'before . . . incurs any . . . liability'). Personally, I regard such meetings as a *mutual* assessment in that the client is assessing me as much as I am assessing them.

Assessment

At an initial meeting, in addition to wanting to know more about what brings them to this meeting with me at this point in their lives, I am interested to cover the following options:

- Group therapy or individual therapy.
- Therapy group or other group.
- Mixed therapy group or homogeneous therapy group.

Having discussed these areas, the client and I reach some conclusion and usually agree the outcome.

Group therapy or individual therapy

Clients come to an initial meeting with certain assumptions as well as more or less knowledge about the form (or modality) of therapy they are seeking. One common assumption – amongst both clients and counsellors – is that individual therapy is the therapy of (first) choice and that therefore there have to be good reasons to join a therapy group. The implication of Berne's challenges to this status quo concerning selection and allocation is for the therapist in any initial assessment interview to view group therapy *at least* as an equal option to working individually or, indeed and perhaps more radically, *to regard group therapy as the therapy of choice* and, therefore, that there have to be good reasons for working with clients only in individual therapy. Schmid (1996) refers to this as the 'therapeutic primacy' of the group. Perls (1967) hypothesises that 'trust in the group seems to be greater than trust in the therapist' (p. 311). This has implications for the training of both individual and group therapists (discussed in Chapter 8) and for educating the general public about forms of therapy. Wolf and Swartz (1975b) argue that the fact of the *therapist's* choice to do individual or group therapy is an expression of their values. The discussion about the form or modality of therapy thus reflects both the client's concern and the therapist's values. On this basis, however a client presents themselves, all assessment may be viewed as a systemic assessment: an assessment of the client-in-context, represented in Figure 2.2. Someone may come to see you as an individual, with their partner or as a member of a family, they may be referred to you as a part of a sub-system such as a workplace or a community. In any/every case a comprehensive, systemic assessment takes account of not only the presenting or presented client but also other identified people in their life, not only the presenting problem or issue but also other relevant issues, not only the form in which they present themselves (for example, as an individual) but also other appropriate forms of working with them-in-context.

People presenting with particular issues may be more amenable to group than individual therapy. Survivors of childhood physical and/or sexual abuse may prefer to work in the context of a group for reasons of safety and protection: the group may act as 'enlightened, *conscious* witnesses' (Miller, 1988/1990). It is also arguable whether full resolution of issues that entail secrecy,

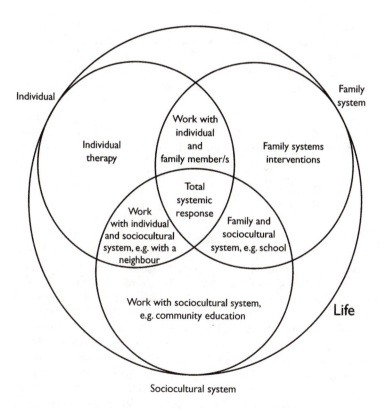

Figure 2.2 *The client-in-context (based on Clarkson and Fish, 1988)*

shame and stigma can be achieved only in individual therapy (Herman and Schatzow, 1984).

Table 2.1 lists some common statements in initial interviews, together with the therapeutic factors and values which may inform the therapist's thinking, together with the possible modality of therapy. Obviously, such assessment is not made on the basis of one sentence; nevertheless, these examples from practice give a general indication of a therapist's thinking, values and options.

Based on the information I perceive (and subceive), I discuss these options at initial assessment interviews - and, indeed, throughout an individual or group therapeutic relationship - so that potential clients and I distinguish between their rationale for group or individual or other form of therapy.

A note on 'combined' therapy   So far I have discussed various options as 'either–or' choices, for instance, *either* individual *or* group therapy. A further series of options arises from a 'both–and' perspective in assessment and therapy, for example, *both* individual *and* group therapy, that is, combined or concurrent therapy.

Practitioners across different orientations take different views about the efficacy of combined therapy. Whilst it is common practice amongst many psychoanalytic practitioners, there is also a strong group analytic tradition of working only with groups; Wolf and Swartz (1962) do not recommend combining therapy, arguing that group treatment is valid in its own right. In the behavioural tradition practitioners tend to work with individuals, and may combine this with group work to deal with specific social behaviours (see Chapter 1). Combining modalities of therapy is perhaps most common in the humanistic/existential tradition, although there is little discussion of this. In research comparing individual client-centred psychotherapy and group therapy (Dierick and Lietaer, 1990), all the helpful processes (therapeutic factors) experienced in individual therapy were also found in group therapy, although intrapsychic exploration of personal problems and subsequent self-insight was mentioned twice as often by those who experienced individual therapy. One way in which individual and group therapy are combined by some therapists is 'individual therapy first then group therapy'. Yalom (1995) warns against this method of therapy weaning: 'group therapy is not a modality to be used to facilitate the termination phase of individual therapy' (p. 234). Table 2.2 summarises the

Table 2.1 *The implications of common statements in initial assessment interviews*

Presentation	Statement	Therapeutic factor/s (Yalom, 1995)	Values (Wolf and Swartz, 1975b)	Modality of choice
Individual	'I'm shy in groups'	Interpersonal learning – Input Development of socialising techniques	Relating is good	Group therapy
Individual	'I'm frightened of groups'	Interpersonal learning – Input and/or Output	Awareness of others	Group therapy Individual therapy
Individual	'I'm frightened of groups'	Family re-enactment	Out of conflict comes gain	Group therapy
Individual	'My partner and I are just not communicating'	Interpersonal learning – Input and Output	Relating is good	Couples therapy Group therapy
Couple	(One partner to the other) 'Now I know that I'm angry with my father (and not you)'	Corrective recapitulation		Individual therapy
Couple	'We wouldn't want to be in a group with so-and-so'	Interpersonal learning – Input	Rejection of absolutism, totalism and exclusivism Awareness of others	Group therapy (couples group)
Group	'We don't get on as a Team'	Imparting information Development of socialising techniques	Rejection of absolutism, totalism and exclusivism	Group consultation (inter-group experience) Individual consultation
Group	'We don't get on as a Team'	Group cohesiveness	Differences of opinion are OK	Group consultation

advantages, disadvantages and questions raised by combining individual and group therapy.

Table 2.2   *Advantages, disadvantages and questions raised by combined individual and group therapy*

Advantages	Disadvantages	Questions
Individual therapy provides a preparation for group therapy, combined therapy continues this process		Re. confidentiality – Is there open confidentiality between individual and group meetings? Does this extend to situations in which different therapists are doing the individual and group work?
Combined therapy provides a forum (i.e. in the individual session) in which the client may work through problems with the group, e.g. feeling threatened, or with the group therapist, e.g. an intense transference reaction to the therapist	The client may avoid working through difficulties with the group in the group, e.g. about authority	Re. therapist – Is there a preference as to who does the therapy? Yalom (1995) states his preference: (1) all or some members in concurrent individual therapy with other therapists – 'conjoint therapy'; (2) all group members in concurrent individual
Group therapy provides a rich supplement to individual therapy	Group therapy may be viewed as supplementary to the 'primary', individual therapy and therapeutic relationship Combined therapy may exacerbate sibling rivalry in the group, particularly if only some group clients are in individual therapy with the group therapist	therapy with the group therapists – 'combined therapy'; (3) some members in concurrent individual therapy with group therapist (p. 414)

Some of the practical implications of combining therapy, for instance, issues of confidentiality, are discussed in Chapter 3.

Therapy group or group
Another issue I explore with potential group therapy clients is whether they are specifically seeking group *therapy* or whether they are wanting to join *a* group. There are many kinds of groups. We may belong to, or feel we belong to, 'identity' groups by virtue

of our identity, for example, as parents, as workers, as black, as gay, as survivors, etc. 'Associations' are groups such as a variety of social, political or psychological groups or organisations, based on an association of ideas or aims, which people join voluntarily. 'Issue' or 'campaign' groups are formed around a particular issue or campaign, from local matters such as road safety to national campaigns such as the Snowdrop Petition (campaigning against private ownership of handguns) and international concerns such as Amnesty International. There are also 'casual' groups which form usually and perhaps spontaneously for a one-off event or happening such as a concert or festival. In asking potential clients 'Why group *therapy*?' the therapist is ascertaining their interest not only in participating in a group but also in their commitment to the explicit purpose of the group as defined, including to personal change in the context of group therapy. As a result of discussing this issue, I have known some clients realise that they are more interested in joining a social group with a view to meeting friends and perhaps a potential partner or in joining a choir; others have clarified what sort of group they are looking for and join a men's (consciousness-raising or support) group or a campaigning group (for example, of men against male violence).

One step further on from assessment is selection. Following our mutual assessment, a client and I may agree that they will join a therapy group – or not. Selection implies that the power to decide, to select and allocate clients rests solely in the hands of the therapist. Selection implies that the therapist has a set of (usually hidden) criteria by which they decide whether someone is suitable for group therapy, whether any contraindications to group therapy are present, and whether the individual is suitable to be 'matched' to the group. A therapist may match an individual to a group (whether new or existing) in terms of diagnosis, for example having only one or two people with a diagnosis of narcissistic borderline personality disorder in any one group; by contrast, that is, by personality 'type'; and/or to achieve a balance, for example of gender, culture, sexuality, age, backgrounds, interests etc., with the needs of the group in mind – Foulkes (1948/1983) refers to this as 'group-centred' selection. Such matching is based on the belief and value that balance is desirable and that the therapist is in the best position to weigh that balance. Ultimately, the therapist may use matching to homogenise the group or to achieve greater heterogeneity.

Mixed therapy group or homogeneous therapy group
Finally, having ascertained that the client does want to be in group therapy and that both client and therapist are agreed, there is the matter of whether a mixed (heterogeneous) group or a 'special' (homogeneous) group would be more therapeutic. Again, this partly relates to the purpose of the group and the client's purpose and aims in joining a group. For further discussion of issues raised by working with a heterogeneous group, see Price (1988) on single sex (i.e. women's) groups, Thomas (1997) on a black men's psychotherapy group, and Tudor (1998a) on issues of relationship and leadership in a mixed men's therapy group – mixed, that is, in terms of culture and sexuality.

A reflection on assessment
It is interesting to reflect on the fact that assessment for group therapy is conducted predominantly in the context of an *individual* interview with the group therapist/leader, although Foulkes (1948/1983) views the group situation as 'the vantage point for Diagnosis and Prognosis' (p. 31) and selection as well as the primary locus for treatment. However, generally as regards assessment in groups, it is considered more feasible to run a number of small assessment groups for a new therapy group (see, for instance, Knowles, 1995) than for places in an ongoing group. Assessing potential group clients in the therapy group has advantages and disadvantages and raises some questions (see Table 2.3).

Fees

Group counsellors working in the public sector (within the NHS) or in the voluntary/independent sector perhaps do not need to consider the issue of fees as much as do their colleagues in the private sector, although in some voluntary agencies offering counselling there are issues regarding the contribution clients are expected to pay, the collection of these 'donations' and how this affects the therapeutic relationship and dynamics in individual, couples or group counselling. In any case, having regard to setting fees is good practice (see Appendix 1).

Krueger (1986) describes the issue of money in counselling and psychotherapy as *The Last Taboo*; elsewhere (Tudor, 1998b), I discuss the received and perceived wisdom about the role of

Table 2.3 *Disadvantages, advantages and questions raised by group assessment*

Disadvantages	Advantages	Questions
It may breach both parties' confidentiality, especially if the potential client is not accepted as a group member	It is democratic, a value identified by Wolf and Swartz (1975b)	Re. responsibility – Is it the task of the group to assess potential new members? Foulkes (1948/1983) advocates using the group situation itself as a test for selection, commenting that 'it was rather a question of ruling unsuitable patients out, than of selecting particularly suitable ones for Group treatment' (p. 59)
	It promotes mutual assessment	
Such assessment is likely to provoke anxiety	Such assessment is likely to provoke anxiety	

money as a form of exchange (value) for counselling services (including being valued). Here, I briefly review the issues involved in setting the fee and the payment of the fee specifically as regards group therapy.

In terms of setting the fee, most group counsellors appear to charge individual members of a group about half of what they charge for an individual session: thus a counsellor charging £30 per hour (or 50 minutes) may charge £15 per client per group. A two-hour group comprising eight people gives the counsellor an income of £120, i.e. £60 per hour. This is by no means rare and, indeed, particularly in London, may be a conservative example of 1998 prices. Such fees reflect the additional costs in running groups in terms of preparation, thinking, supervision and administrative time regarding a number of people, let alone the fact that a group may not be 'full' and that, over time, a counsellor is unlikely to earn (literally) the 'full rate' from a group. Given that money is such a basic and emotive issue, counsellors need to be particularly clear about the basis on which they set their fees and their motivation for so doing, for instance, whether the money they earn from groupwork subsidises their other work with, for example, individuals on low incomes, children, trainees, or voluntary work. In the context of running a group, counsellors who offer free or low-cost counselling or who operate a sliding scale also need to decide whether you charge everyone in the group the same fee. Whether you do or not – and Foulkes (1972) suggests that you do – and especially if you do not, you need to be prepared for the subject of money to be discussed openly in the group.

As regards payment of the fee, I ask group members as they gather before the group to put their money in a box and to tick their name on a card (see Figure 2.3); thus everyone sees who has paid, who (if anyone) has not, who pays ahead and who is behind – Freud (1913/1958) cautions against allowing 'large sums of money to accumulate' and suggests asking for payment 'at fairly short intervals – monthly, perhaps' (p. 131). From this payment card is clear that, at 6.8, Alpha has not paid, Effie (who left the group on 9.7) did not pay for her last group and Theo has also not paid for that group, despite the fact that he has paid for the sessions since. Clearly some group issues are being reflected and expressed through non payment.

Some group counsellors insist on being paid in cash on the basis that this heightens the client's awareness of the exchange and the value of the counselling. Whilst this may be therapeutic for some clients, it is clearly not true for those clients in the public sector who value their therapy, and for others any insistence on this point may create fantasies about their counsellor not declaring all their income for tax purposes. In any case, money and issues of value, worth, poverty, welfare, scarcity, relative wealth and difference all need to be brought into the therapeutic space. If some group members pay their fee in the form of barter (an

Date of group	2.7	9.7	23.7	30.7	6.8
Alpha	√	√	√	√	
Beattie	√	√	√	√	√
Gemma	√	√	√	√	√
Effie	√				
Theo	√		√	√	√

Figure 2.3   *Counselling group payment card -I[1]*

1. This does not note attendance, only payment received. Other versions might reflect both, for instance, by incorporating an A for absent.

arrangement strongly discouraged by the American Counseling Association, 1995) or through a Local Economic Trading Scheme (LETS), this also needs to be acknowledged. The indirect nature of a LETS, whereby the barter arrangement is separate, outside of and not linked to the counselling, appears more straightforward but may miss the psychological aspect of the struggle of exchange and value. Again, if all this is explicit in respect of the group, the counsellor needs to be prepared for the issues of difference this raises, for example, knowing that one client does barter work for the counsellor, another, who pays the fee, may decide that she would prefer to do barter work too. If their barter work involves a particular client with more contact with the counsellor, others may express their jealousy or envy about this. The counsellor's rules (non-negotiable) and contracts (negotiable) about fees with individual clients are equally applicable to groups, except that any negotiations take longer! The argument for charging for missing sessions (Freud, 1913/1958; Syme, 1994) is probably stronger in the context of group counselling, as you cannot replace that client in that group meeting. Similarly, the issue of giving notice of missing group meetings is more one of courtesy to the counsellor and other group members as, again, it is not possible to replace that client (and therefore their fee). Once a client agrees to join a counselling group, it is usual that they are committed to attending and paying even for missed sessions. I also insist on clients giving at least three weeks' (or three groups') notice to the group of their leaving. This gives them and the group a minimum period of time in which to end and say goodbye (see Tudor, 1995 and Chapter 5). In my experience only one client refused to attend these last sessions (although he did pay for them) and, perhaps predictably, the group felt bereft, cheated and angry.

In this chapter I have reviewed the main issues in preparing for a group. Other issues that the group counsellor needs to take into consideration are those equally involved in organising any counselling practice. Two further considerations which have implications for practice and establishing the group – the issue of leadership (including co-leadership) and the concept of the alternate group – are discussed in the next chapter, which focuses, heuristically and developmentally, on establishing the group.

3

Establishing the Group

McDougall (1920), one of the earliest writers on groups and one cited by Freud, identifies five conditions for groups – conditions, that is, for raising collective mental life to a higher level:

1. That there should be some degree of continuity of existence in the group.
2. That the individual (participant) should have some definite idea of the nature, composition, function and capacities of the group.
3. That the group should be brought into interaction with other groups.
4. That the group should possess traditions, customs and habits, including those which determine group relations.
5. That the group should have a definite structure.

In Chapter 2 I discussed the nature, composition and function of the group in terms of preparing for group counselling. In this chapter, which considers the initial phases of the group's development, from before its first meeting to its first and initial meetings, I discuss issues of leadership, the initial meetings, contracts and the concept of the alternate group meeting – which cover McDougall's other conditions for collective mental life. The interaction between groups – *inter*group relations as distinct from *intra*group relations – is discussed in Chapter 7. These discussions are preceded by consideration of pre-group time, the time immediately before a group when the group members are gathering.

The provisional group – pre-forming

Prelude – pre-group time

This pre-group time is important in practical terms: it gives clients time to have a drink and to go to the lavatory, and it ensures that the formal group time starts on time. It is also significant psychologically: it allows for what Rogers (1970/1973) refers to as 'milling around'; as a way of structuring time (Berne, 1966, 1970/1973), it provides for ritual and pastiming. For some clients this is both the most difficult aspect of the group experience ('the loathsome small talk'), and eventually the most therapeutic. Issues that arise during this time – clients feeling nervous, ignored by others, etc. – may be and are brought into the group. This time may also be thought of as an 'alternate' group meeting (see below). Conceptually, this time reflects the pre-forming phase of the group's development which, to a greater or lesser extent, is experienced on each occasion the group meets.

As far as I am aware, no research has been conducted into this aspect and phase of a counselling/therapy group and, by definition, it is not directly accessible to the group counsellor (as they do not participate in this pre-group time). From my research (see Appendix 2), the following observations were made by clients in two separate psychotherapy groups about the purpose and value of this time (15 minutes before the beginning of their respective groups) as well as how their perceptions about this time changed over time. When establishing a group I make the point that the group meets at 7.15pm or 15 minutes before the formal group. In the research, some clients reported being very precise about the time they would aim to arrive, as the majority of these stated that they did not want to be the first to arrive – one client said that they felt more withdrawn if they were there for the whole time. Arrival time, members' actions, reactions and interactions during this time may become as much the subject for discussion, confrontation etc. in the group as any other issue.

Purpose Three themes emerge from clients' views of the purpose of pre-group time: sociality, attachment and transition. The time was seen as informal, social time which provides an opportunity for them to 'catch up' with each other, and to exchange 'normal' ideas. A number of clients also saw the time as an opportunity to practise social intercourse and for the whole process of making initial contact with each other. Following on from this, there is the theme – and purpose – of attachment, of connecting and re-familiarising themselves with each other. This (re-)attaching and connecting with each other, on an everyday but nevertheless meaningful level, was acknowledged by some as particularly difficult: one client feared that this intimacy (that is, any intimacy during this time) was only skin deep. Answering the ritual question 'How are you?' has a different significance in the waiting/social area in a counselling practice: the answer to that question is what many clients seek through the process of coun-selling. The third theme which emerges is that of transition, 'a passage into deeper things': the transition between the clients' outside worlds and counselling, 'a time for transition and quiet-ening', and the transition between the waiting/social area and the counselling group itself, as one client put it: 'it eases me into the group time'.

Value   The reported value of this pre-group varied enormously: from some clients finding it easy to others finding it difficult and challenging; from those valuing it as being time for 'non-therapy issues' to those valuing this time in which they interact with others and which thereby provides them with material on which to reflect and from which to learn in the group. One client reported the uneasiness they felt as a result of the conflict between various purposes, needs and values they attributed to this time: wanting attention, being socially appropriate, being well behaved and having a genuine interest in others – which relate to various identified therapeutic factors (Yalom, 1995) (in this example, family re-enactment and altruism). Others found this time difficult if they were feeling annoyed or resentful and a time of trepidation – emotions which, although they did not find easy, they did value.

Changing perceptions   Generally, clients reported that, over time, the pre-group time had become easier for them: from a time to be survived (endured to tolerated) to being an opportunity from which to learn. At the time of the research, the use of this time as 'catching up' was experienced at a more intimate level, and the difference between the time and the content of the time being social and 'business' (counselling) was not so pronounced:

life becomes the subject and business of therapy and therapy a part of life and not apart from life.

Whilst it generally appears that pre-group time has a useful purpose and is experienced as valuable, there is an argument for going from the outside world straight into the inside world of therapy, carrying all the joys, fears, issues and 'baggage' directly into the group. Wolf and Swartz (1962), for instance, see no need for 'warm up' periods, arguing that most groups move easily into interaction. Indeed, having a pre-group time creates another transition – that between the waiting room and the consulting/ group room – which can detract from immediate interactions. The silence at the beginning of some groups may reflect the difficulties of unseen and unheard interactions in the pre-group time and of such transitions (see Chapter 4).

Leadership

In planning and running a group the counsellor needs to consider the issue of leadership: 'without leadership, we believe, there can be no insight, no reorganization, no integration' (Wolf and Swartz, 1975a, p. 66). Here, at least for the present, I use 'leadership' and 'leader' as generic terms to cover discussions about the group counsellor/psychotherapist/analyst/conductor/facilitator/etc. Depending on their theoretical orientation, training, their own experience of group leaders, temperament and style, as well as particular issues with which they are working, counsellors will have different perspectives on leadership. In this section I discusss leadership as a relationship, as a task which connotes a role, leadership and power and issues involved in co-leadership.

Berne (1963) identifies three types of leadership, which correspond to the three aspects of the group's structure:

- The responsible leader, that is, the leader in the organisational structure.
- The effective leader, that is, the leader who makes the actual decisions.
- The psychological leader, that is, the most powerful in the private structures (imagoes) of the individuals in the group.

Such leadership may be combined in one person such as the group counsellor or may be distributed between a number of people in the group. Ultimately, for Berne, 'a practical test of leadership is the power to make decisions that are not subject to revision or veto by anyone else present; most convincingly, decisions concerning group structure' (Berne, 1963, p. 146). This has a practical application when we consider the issue of group rules and their enforcement. Rogers (1970/1973), on the other hand, was more concerned about whether and how he could be a facilitative person in a group, describing his hope to become as much a participant in as a facilitator of the group.

In a unique volume (in remembrance of Swartz), Liff (1975) introduces various views on *The Leader in the Group*, including:

- The absent leader, the psychological leader of the alternate group (see below).
- The creative leader who models flexibility.
- The responsible leader (not in the Bernian sense), who participates in the client's real life decisions, for instance, in response to a client's self-harming behaviours.
- The charismatic leader, who tends to create a group dependent on her/him.
- The affiliative leader, who can 'bring about a feeling of being understood, strengthened and an equal to the leader' (Christ, 1975, p. 105).
- The leader as a model, for instance in examining themselves and others (Wolf and Swartz, 1975b).
- The existential leader.

Leadership and relationship These nominal descriptions of leaders may be viewed as descriptions of the *relationship* between the group 'leader' and the group members. This also enables us to locate clients' conflict and competition with the group leader in terms of the therapeutic relationship rather than simply in diagnostic terms which tend to pathologise and individualise the client. This is not to deny or minimise the impact of anti-leadership behaviour; it is to understand it as a goal-directed (or mis-directed) expression of need. From a TA perspective, Novellino (1985) describes two types of anti-leadership competition from the client against the therapist: social and psychological, involving, respectively, direct and indirect transactions with the group leader, fuelled by jealousy and envy and with the aim of becoming the actual or the psychological leader.

Drawing on Gelso and Carter's (1985, 1994) three components to therapeutic relationships – the working alliance, the transferential and the real relationship – and Clarkson's (1990, 1995b) sub-division of the transferential relationship into the developmentally needed or reparative relationship, I consider elements of such relationships as regards various types of leader and illustrate them with the leader's responses to specific group issues (Table 3.1). Of course, the responses depend on the group leader's training, theoretical orientation and experience, for instance, in working through or confronting the transference. (I view what Clarkson refers to as the transpersonal relationship as transpersonal *moment/s* in therapeutic encounters.)

Leadership – task, role, attitude and intervention In terms of the stages and phases of group development discussed in Chapter 1, the group leader may facilitate the identified task and respond to common issues discussed in the group (for further details about the destructive and constructive behaviours at each stage of the group see Clarkson, 1991). Table 3.2 (which relates to the group structure and task-activity identified in Chapter 1, Table 1.2) summarises these issues as well as the leader's focus and tasks in relation to the pre-forming and forming stage. In the pre-forming phase, prior to the group, the leader's focus is on preparation and their tasks are to prepare the individual prospective members by explaining to them about groups and *the* (this) group and informing them about practicalities such as venue, time, numbers etc. (see Chapter 2). The counsellor also needs to discuss and decide about the necessity or desirability of preparatory individual therapeutic work at this stage (see Chapter 2). Possible problems for the leader include: being under- or, more commonly, over-prepared, being anxious or unclear, as well as having to deal with practical difficulties such as potential members 'dropping out'. In the forming phase, the leader's focus is on facilitating contact, contracts and communication, as well as attending to any difficulties and misunderstandings. Their tasks include being prepared (in themselves, preparing the room and facilities), being clear about structure, boundaries, task and leadership – which tasks are not necessarily work that has to be done but are equally facilitative attitudes on the part of the group counsellor. Problems or difficulties at this stage for the leader, indicative of the pre-forming stage, are anxiety and confusion, which may lead to rigidity and an authoritarian attitude about rules or a lack of consistency and to a focus on the individual rather than the group. As with discussion

Table 3.1 *Group leadership and therapeutic relationship: issues and responses*

Therapeutic relationship (Gelso and Carter, 1985, 1994; Clarkson, 1990, 1995b)	Kinship metaphor (Clarkson, 1990, 1995b)	Types of leader/ship (Liff, 1975)	Group issues in relation to leader/s	Group leader's response
Working alliance	Cousins	The responsible leader	The goals and tasks of the group	To discuss desirability and appropriateness of goals and tasks
		The affiliative leader	Bonding, emotional alignment	To demonstrate genuine concern and compassion, consistency and constancy
Transferential/counter-transferential relationship	Godparent/godchild or step-parent/step-child	The absent leader	Absence, disappointment	To be present both psychologically and – with the exception of the 'alternate' group – physically (see Wolf and Swartz, 1962 on projective presence)
		The charismatic leader	Worship, reification	To analyse and/or confront the transferential – and counter-transferential – need for dependency
		The leader as model	Impetus for role modelling	To distinguish between productive and counter-productive modelling, or to eschew the use of modelling (see Wood, 1995a)
Developmentally needed or reparative relationship	Parent/child	The creative leader	Attachment, dependence, parenting, separation, independence	To identify developmental deficit and/or reparative need, to contract for parenting and to fulfil contract
		The leader as model		
Real/person-to-person/I–You relationship	Siblings	The responsible leader	Engagement	To be genuine
		The affiliative leader	Mutuality	To be understanding
		The existential leader	Life and death	To be open, to be a whole person

Table 3.2 *The group leaders' focus and tasks/attitude in relation to phases of group development and common issues – Part I*

Group imago (Berne, 1963)	Stages of group (Tuckman, 1965)	Common issues	Leader's focus	Leader's tasks/ attitude
Provisional group imago	Pre-stage 1 (Shellow et al., 1958) *Pre-forming*	(For individuals) Joining, commitment	On preparation	To inform, explain and prepare
Adapted group imago	Forming	Attachment, dependence, structure, boundaries, leadership	On facilitating and encouraging contact and communication, on attending to descrepancies and incongruence	To be prepared, to be clear about structure, boundaries and task

of the group, Table 3.2 is developed in Chapter 4 (storming, norming and performing stages) and completed in Chapter 5 (adjourning and mourning stages).

In performing tasks a person takes on, however temporarily, a role associated with that task. In this sense leadership may be viewed as a *role* and one of a number of roles people take on in groups as they do in the rest of their lives. As a strand of social psychology, role theory, which describes the formal and predictable attributes associated with a particular position such as (cleaner, father, leader), has been highly influential on groupwork theory and practice and especially ideas about leadership (see, for instance, Rowan, 1976; Houston, 1982). Another way of viewing task, and one which moves away from task-centredness and role-relatedness, is as an attitude, a way of being: that is, having a sense of focus at any stage or point in the group and, for instance, before the group having an *attitude* of preparation, of being informed and of being able to inform and explain, without this becoming an absolute necessity, checklist or task to be performed.

Group leaders' input into groups are often seen as interventions. Berne (1966), for instance, defines eight 'therapeutic operations' which he divides between interventions and interpositions. In articulating a dialogue between client-centred group psychotherapy and other orientations, Lietaer and Dierick (1996) develop, from a cluster and factor analysis which yielded nine scales, a group therapist intervention style which they divide into four umbrella sections:

A. Facilitating the experiential process
Scale 1: Deepening individual exploration
Scale 2: Stimulating interpersonal communication
B. Personal presence
Scale 3: Personal commitment and support
Scale 4: Give personal here-and-now feedback
C. Meaning attribution
Scale 5: Providing individual insight
Scale 6: Clarification of interactions and group process
Scale 7: Psychodynamic interpretation
D. Executive function
Scale 8: Direction, advice and procedures
Scale 9: Process rules and evaluation.

This is useful in a number of respects. It accords with factors found by Lieberman, Yalom and Miles (1973): emotional stimulation, caring, meaning attribution and executive function. It elaborates and develops our understanding of group therapists' style of interventions across different orientations in which we may discern some similarities and commonalities between the person-centred approach (PCA) and other more analytic approaches, for instance, in meaning attribution. Finally, this research is especially important in offering the person-centred group therapist something beyond the mantra of 'trust the process' and a view that intervention and structure do not necessarily equate with direction (see also Coghlan and McIlduff, 1990).

Leadership and power   The terms 'leader' and 'leadership' evoke the concept and issue of power: the power the leader has in the group by virtue of their responsibility, authority, knowledge, experience, etc. – and of the fact that others give them or let them take that responsibility, authority etc. Jacobs (1987) examines the dyadic, symbiotic relationship between leaders (or masters), who foster dependency, and followers, without whom leaders have no power. Given the dynamics of power inherent in the counsellor–client relationship and the power dynamics which can be fostered and/or adopted in groups, it is essential that group counsellors understand and address issues of power, influence and authority (see Embleton Tudor and Tudor, 1994). Such working through their own history and relationship to power is not only good practice (see ASEW, 1998), but also provides protection for themselves as well as their clients. One practical exercise is to be able to distinguish the characteristics of a counselling group from those of a religious or psychological cult.

In discussion both outside and within the counselling and psychotherapeutic literature, power is often seen as negative and *in itself* abusive. Steiner (1987) objects to the concept of power being universally linked to the control of and over others and concludes that 'the greatest antidote to the authoritarian use of power . . . is for people to develop individual power in its multidimensional forms and to dedicate themselves to passing on power to as many others as can be found in a lifetime' (p. 104). This positive individual power in the counsellor may be referred to as therapeutic potency or authority. This authority is conscious, whole, integrated and often quiet and engenders 'power in the patient'. It reflects affiliative rather than charismatic leadership. A group leader with authority is one who encourages group members to express their own power – at all levels of *content*, *process* and *structure* of the group, thus:

Content – Helping two group members to assert themselves in relation to each other.

Process – Encouraging other group members to respond to a client (rather than always responding her/himself).

Structure – Opening up the effective leadership of the group, for instance, about the decision-making process, to the group itself, for example about the length of meetings, the ending of the group etc.

In a discussion about men in counselling and psychotherapy, Stein (1982) proposes that the male group therapist needs 'to establish a balance between leadership, which can provide some consistent direction and facilitation for group exchange, and *non-adherence to traditional patterns of leadership*, which are often directive, prescriptive, or authoritarian' (p. 287, emphasis added, see also Tudor, 1998a). Ultimately, of the leader with authority (genuine, positive power),

> When actions are performed
> Without unnecessary speech,
> People say, 'We did it!'
> (Lao Tzu, 1973, *Seventeen*).

Rogers (1978) cites this as a definition of an effective group facilitator and as consistent with his perspective on power: that of not taking away people's power. The specific qualities of effective group counsellors are described and discussed in Chapter 8.

Co-leadership   From this discussion about power, it follows that all members of a group have – and/or may take – the leadership role. It also follows that formal (effective) leadership does not have to reside in one leader; and that having two leaders may well affect the philosophy and process of passing on power or not taking it away. The first example of co-working was probably Adler's employment of two counsellors to work with children and their parents in his Child Guidance Clinic in Vienna in the late 1920s.

Advantages of co-leadership for the group include:

- *Complementarity* – a mutual completing of experience in some way, for instance, by co-leaders being male and female, black and white, gay and heterosexual etc.
- *Supplementarity* – literally adding something to supply a deficiency, for instance in experience or skills, 'two counsellors are better than one'.
- *Observation* – ten senses are better than five, whilst one facilitator is working with one group member, the other may be 'holding' the rest of the group.
- *Safety* – a co-therapist may be perceived as providing a safety in terms of being a separate witness to therapeutic work undertaken by the other therapist with a group client. This may be especially important in working with adult survivors of childhood sexual abuse and/or in terms of male and female group counsellor or with counsellors from dominant and minority cultures working together.
- *Modelling* – of the working alliance, of real relationships, of healthy conflict and the resolution of differences.

In a unique book on co-therapy, Roller and Nelson (1991) emphasise the relationship aspect of co-therapy, arguing that working with a co-therapist is not only selecting a special practice but is also choosing a relationship. Specific advantages of co-therapy for the two leaders are:

- Greater opportunity for learning – through working with, observing, and receiving feedback from each other.

- Widened perspectives – including possibly different theoretical understanding.
- Monitoring – the opportunity for counsellors to check and balance their complementary (and supplementary) behaviour and to adjust any emotional or perceptual bias.

The disadvantages of co-leadership for both the group and the counsellors focus on the possible breakdown in the relationship between the co-leaders and the potential for confusion and conflict within the group. Roller and Nelson (1991) identify five dilemmas for co-therapists:

1. Competition
2. Counter-transference
3. Confusion and lack of communication
4. Lack of congruence between co-therapists
5. Co-dependency between co-therapists

and a further four dilemmas for couples who also work as co-therapists:

6. Jealousy
7. Falling in love (with a client)
8. Exposure of inequality in relationship
9. Spillover into and from personal lives and relationship.

Any facilitative co-working (and for that matter living and loving) relationship needs to be based on honesty, integrity, regard, respect and mutual understanding, especially when working with and across difference/s – of class, culture, gender, sexual and theoretical orientation. In terms of planning a group, the choice of the person with whom to facilitate a group is crucial. Values, preferences, temperaments, differences and similarities – all need addressing, and thorough preparation, including good supervision, is essential. Whilst, in general, difference/s are to be welcomed and celebrated, some differences may be too much for the group to deal with: counsellors working from within different theoretical orientations, for instance, may work in different directions towards different goals. Roller and Nelson (1991) provide a number of practical tools to help work through these issues, including a co-therapy issues questionnaire and guidelines for co-therapy couples.

Most co-leader arrangements are just that: leading together as equals, whether experienced counsellors or counsellors in training (co-learners). Some group leaders work with an apprentice or assistant – Roller and Nelson (1991) refer to this relationship as '*nequipos*' meaning an unequal team. Whilst this may be a good opportunity for the apprentice to learn from a more experienced practitioner, the difference in the relative status between apprentice and leader inevitably impacts on the group. Interventions made by the apprentice may be seen as having to be 'checked out' with the 'real' group counsellor; group members may resent having to work with someone who is 'only' an apprentice; others may rescue the situation by trying to please the leaders. Gender dynamics between the two leaders (the experienced male leader and the female apprentice and vice versa) and others around class, culture, disability, race and sexual orientation may further exacerbate already complex dynamics. Whilst there is an argument that such issues are 'all grist for the mill', such arrangements may constitute an unnecessary burden on a group. Again, Roller and Nelson (1991) provide practical help in the form of example contracts between *nequipos* and between a supervisor and co-learners.

Some groups, for research purposes and usually for a specific and limited time, may have an observer present. Again, there are difficulties with such arrangements, whether the person is a participant–observer or a separate, non-participative observer; either way, they affect the phenomenological field and dynamics of the group. In either case, of the apprentice or the observer, careful consideration needs to be given to their purpose and effect. The primary purpose of a counselling group is therapeutic and not educative – of counsellors or the public. At the same time, such arrangements may be workable, especially if arranged and agreed in advance. It is one thing to establish and recruit members to a group with such arrangements made explicit; it is another to introduce such arrangements during the lifetime of a group. If this is the case, it is important to give the group a genuine choice, especially to say 'No' – and in such cases one 'No' should stand for the whole group, and without prejudice.

In conclusion, successful co-therapy relies on:

■ Openness in communication – both with each other and with the group

- Liking each other as people
- Respect and equality of partnership and acknowledgement of any inequalities
- Compatibility of counsellors' values and theoretical viewpoints and clarity about any differences and their implications
- Complementary balance of counsellors' experience, knowledge and skills.

The adapted group – forming

The initial meeting/s

The first decision the group counsellor has to make is how to begin. This applies to each group, but particularly so to the first group. The counsellor may say nothing, something, or a lot.

Counsellor: [*Looks around at each member of the group. Smiles. Silence.*]

A: Aren't you going to say anything?

B: I want you to say something and start the group.

C: Why are you smiling?

D: I feel really uncomfortable.

E: [*After some minutes' silence*] Well, my name's Emily and I'd like to know other people's names.

Counsellor: [*Looks around at each member of the group.*] Welcome [*pause*]. We have two hours together and we can make of it what we wish.

F: Well, I'd like to know a bit about everyone.

G: What do you mean by 'what we wish'? Does that mean anything goes?

H: I really appreciate being welcomed. I joined a group before and nobody said anything for ages and I didn't know what was going on.

Counsellor: Hello. My name's Theo. As this is the first group I'd like each of you to say your name, something you're feeling and what you want from being in this group.

I: Well, my name's Ilsa and I'm feeling nervous. What I want from being in this group is to overcome my anxiety.

J: I'm Jim and I'm glad you [Theo] asked everyone to say something 'cos I can't stand long silences when everybody stares at everybody else and nobody says anything. I'm here to work on my anger and deal with people's reaction to me being angry.

K: My name's Kay and I'm here because Theo suggested that I come into a group.

L: My name's Len and I've been feeling increasingly wobbly as it's got to my turn to say something. I'm not sure what I want from the group. I'm not even sure if I want to be here.

These are just three examples of what the group counsellor might say and of various responses to them. The choice of what and how you say it depends on your intention, your theoretical orientation, your inclination and, probably most importantly, your culture. All counsellors reflect different cultural norms – welcoming people individually/collectively, shaking hands/not shaking hands, talking/being silent – the point is to be intentional rather than unintentional or unaware of your culture. Decisions about whether and, if so, how you start have implications for subsequent meetings and the norms and culture of the group. In the third example, the counsellor invites members to 'check in' which, if repeated, may well lead to this becoming a group norm by which, as a matter of course, members check in at the beginning of each group. The advantage of the check in (and particularly one structured as in the example), is that everyone gets to speak at the beginning of the group; everyone knows, at least to some extent, how each other is feeling; and everyone gets an idea of what people want from the group and, therefore, roughly how much time everyone will have. Psychologically, it enhances a sense of belonging and attachment. The disadvantage of the check in is that it structures the proceedings, leaving little room for spontaneity; it may feel artificial, particularly if neither the counsellor nor group members respond to each other ('because it's the check in'), waiting until everyone has spoken before interacting with each other; and it fosters a segmented view of the group in which everyone has 'their time' (usually the total meeting time divided by the number of people in the group) which may lead to the group becoming individual counselling *in* the group rather than *group counselling*.

Where the counsellor does not direct proceedings this leaves the group more open-ended – or 'open-beginninged' (as in the first two examples). It is the subsequent interactions or transactions and the processing of these which makes 'group time' or, indeed, the whole of the group, distinct from check in time. Whilst the focus of the check in is on the individual, the focus of group time is on the individual-in-the-group and on the group itself. Whilst check in is individual-centred, group time is group-centred.

Contracts

There appears to be an increasing interest in the subject of contracts and the process of contracting in counselling. Due to the centrality of the contractual method in transactional analysis, TA is an especially rich source of literature on this subject and informs many of the contributions to *Contracts in Counselling* (Sills, 1997b) (a companion volume in this series). Appendix 3 outlines a contract for use in group counselling.

In the context of group counselling, the initial contract is between the counsellor and the individual potential client and thus the initial contract (written or unwritten) is agreed between them. However, in this context, other group members are involved in the contract in terms of competency, responsibility and delivery. Thus, a group member who wants feedback about how he comes across is requesting some interaction from other group members and, effectively, involving them in his therapeutic contract. As the group counsellor is generally viewed as 'holding' the contract with each client individually, then working in the context of a group involves the counsellor sub-contracting this responsibility to other group members from time to time and/or as regards specific issues such as giving feedback. This theoretical distinction becomes significant in practice when a client asks the group to support them in something which runs counter to their therapeutic growth, for example, to confirm 'how stupid I've been'. The group counsellor thus holds a number of individual contracts as well as the group contract, one aspect of which may be sub-contracted elements of the individual contract. Thus:

Individual contracts

A: 'To express my feelings and to ask for feedback about how I come across to others especially when I feel angry.'

B: 'To learn to trust people by sitting next to people and asking to be held.'

C: 'To clarify my thinking about what was abusive about my parents' parenting of me and what may be abusive about my own parenting.'

Group contracts

All: 'To attend; to participate; to respond to others; to take responsibility for my own actions, comfort, etc. which includes not being violent to myself or others in the group.'

A: 'To ask you all for feedback about how I come across to you, especially when I feel angry.'

Counsellor's contract with A: 'I will help you to express your feelings and I will give you feedback about how you come across, especially when you're angry.'

Group's sub-contract with A: 'We will give you feedback . . .'

The group's contract with A is essentially a *sub-contract* as it is the counsellor who 'holds' their part of the contract with A and who therefore has the main responsibility, in this case, to respond to A. This does not detract from the fact that the group counsellor may well confront the group about not responding to A. Nevertheless, if the group does not respond or the group members change and do not agree to respond or the group ends, it is the counsellor who still retains their responsible part for the therapeutic contract.

There are a number of terms in this area of counselling and of work with groups which are often confused, notably: contracts, rules and working agreements. Table 3.3 defines the differences between these terms with reference to common elements by which they are initiated and agreed, their mutuality, negotiability and timescale and, with reference to TA, the ego state in which they are made.

Berne (1966) suggests three contractual necessities or rules in establishing groups: clarity about time, and fees, and that the client can say anything without exceptions. However, a further consideration is the dictum 'Never make a rule you can't enforce' (M. Turpin, personal communication, October 1988). As enforcement usually involves some sanction, when considering what you want to state as group rules it is also worth considering what sanctions you are prepared to make and, indeed, have the power to make if someone then breaks a rule. In terms of the distinctions drawn above, I consider the first two of Berne's necessities as rules whilst the third is not a rule as it is not enforceable; as it

Table 3.3 *Comparison of contracts, rules and working agreements in group counselling*

	Contracts	Rules	Working agreements
Definition	'An explicit bilateral commitment to a well-defined course of action' (Berne, 1966, p. 362)	A non-negotiable requirement set by the counsellor prior to and as a pre-requisite for working with the client/s	'Stated intention of behaviors … to provide short-term protection' (Woollams and Brown, 1978, p. 255)
Initiated by	Counsellor or client/s	Counsellor	Counsellor or client/s
Agreed by	Counsellor: client/s Client/s: counsellor Client/s: client/s	Counsellor to client/s	Counsellor: client/s Client/s: counsellor Client/s: client/s
Laterality	Bilateral	Unilateral (multilateral acceptance)	Bilateral or multilateral
Ego state	Made in Integrated Adult	Made from counsellor's Integrated Adult	Made from any ego state
Negotiability	Renegotiable	Not negotiable	Negotiable in the session
Timescale	Made at any time	Made at the beginning of counselling	Made at any time Performed between meetings

stands, it is more a suggestion to which group members may or may not respond. If, after discussion, group members agreed, say:

> to communicate directly with each other both in and outside the group (that is, no gossiping) and that anything said outside the group between any group members may be brought into the group

then this would constitute a *group* contract.

In Chapter 2 I discussed fees and notice and distinguished between rules (non-negotiable) and contracts (negotiable). Thus, the amount of the fee may be an administrative rule, how the payment is made may be a part of my contract with a client; my requirement that clients give three weeks' (or groups') notice is also a rule. Issues about holidays also illustrate the usefulness of this distinction. As far as holidays are concerned, I set my core holidays around Winter, Spring and Summer breaks and half-terms (non-negotiable) and negotiate with the group over any additional weeks holiday. Thus, outside my given core holiday, the group decides how long or short a break they want and thus has control over the financial implications of their decisions: if the (majority of the) group decides not to meet and therefore there is no group I do not charge a fee, if the majority decides to meet I do charge anyone who subsequently does not attend. Thus fees, missing sessions and notice are group rules, whilst decisions about additional holidays are group contracts.

Being clear about the difference between rules and contracts both enables and requires you to be clear about the extent of and limits to those rules and contracts and, in general, to have a minimum number of rules: the counsellor's use of social control contracts may lead to becoming 'the agent of cultural transmission of injunctions' (Holloway, 1974, p. 16). This is particularly pertinent as regards the relationship between what happens in the group and what happens outside the group between group members. Different group counsellors draw different lines about such social intercourse. Some make it a group rule that group members do not have social contact outside the group, other than perhaps the minimum contact of walking to the bus stop together. In this context if it subsequently emerges that group members do have contact which breaches the group rule, then the group counsellor needs to be prepared to enforce that rule, with the ultimate sanction of expulsion from the group. Other group counsellors encourage social contact between group members. Wolf and Swartz (1962) make the point that:

> we do not regard all social relationships as necessarily resistive. We would attempt to analyze only those alliances which are neurotic pacts. For us, a social relationship often reveals resistances and often, as well, positive facets of character not otherwise seen as part of the therapeutic experience. (p. 110)

One group occasionally met socially as a group. Issues arose in these social times which were brought back to the group meetings (as the group had a contract to do so). This is a particularly important contract when groups or members of groups are meeting socially outside the group as it protects both the individual and the primacy and integrity of the therapeutic group. Later, the same group discussed the possibility of visiting a sex shop together. This led to important discussions about pornography, sex and sexuality, morality, politics, relationships between men and women, the possible therapeutic value of such a visit in confronting issues of shame. In such circumstances, and especially with such emotive material, it is easy for the group counsellor to allow themselves to be drawn in to the *content* of such discussions as distinct from staying with the *process* of such discussions and what it means for the group. Again, I find the distinction between contracts, rules and working agreements useful in being clear about the parameters and the processes of the group (see Box 3.1).

As far as the group counsellor is concerned, anything which happens between group members outside the group is, in strict contractual terms, ex-contractual and outside the direct and immediate therapeutic relationship. However, there is a very real sense in which the therapeutic relationship extends beyond the time the client is in contact with the counsellor (see Figure 3.1 and Tudor, 1999b).

As many counselling groups take place in agency or organisational settings, such as student counselling services, women's therapy centres etc., the concept of the three-handed contract between the client, the counsellor *and the agency* or 'the powers

---

Box 3.1   Differences between group rules, contracts and working agreements as regards social contact outside the group

Group rule/s	Contract/s	Working agreement/s
The counsellor forbids or determines the nature of the contact outside the group and that this must be reprted back in the group.	The counsellor and group define the relationship between the group and any outside contacts in relation to the individual group members' overall therapeutic contracts. The counsellor may be neutral, supportive or encouraging of such contact/s.	The counsellor and group member/s make specific agreements as regards contact outside the group between group meetings (for example, that someone will telephone another group member).

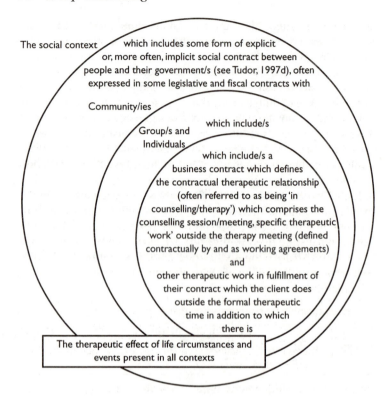

The social context   which includes some form of explicit
or, more often, implicit social contract between
people and their government/s (see Tudor, 1997d), often
expressed in some legislative and fiscal contracts with

Community/ies

Group/s and   which include/s
Individuals

which include/s a
business contract which defines
the contractual therapeutic relationship
(often referred to as being 'in
counselling/therapy') which comprises the
counselling session/meeting, specific therapeutic
'work' outside the therapy meeting (defined
contractually by and as working agreements)
and

other therapeutic work in fulfillment of
their contract which the client does
outside the formal therapeutic
time in addition to which
there is

The therapeutic effect of life circumstances and
events present in all contexts

Figure 3.1   *The contractual therapeutic relationship in context*

that be' is useful (see Chapter 6 and Tudor, 1997a). Finally, whilst this section has focused on the contract, which describes the content of the contract or bilateral or multilateral agreement, *contracting* describes the *process* of arriving at a contract (for more on which see James, 1971; Sills, 1997b).

Confidentiality   Perhaps the most common group contract is that of confidentiality. I consider this as a contract rather than a rule as its definition, negotiation, application and maintenance are most effective when initiated by either clients or counsellor, agreed by both/all parties, bilateral and renegotiable (see Table 3.3). Some counsellors – in my view, inaccurately – state confidentiality as a ground rule without defining it; and many clients assume it as such. Whilst many counsellors (and trainers and supervisors) raise the issue at or near the beginning of a group, it is often insufficiently defined because of certain assumptions ('We don't need to discuss confidentiality because we all know what we mean by it, don't we?') and may subsequently lead to misunderstandings ('But I thought it was OK to talk to my partner about the group') with serious consequences (people feeling betrayed). If you do raise the issue, it is useful to ask group members what they mean by confidentiality as this facilitates understanding, communication and, ultimately, agreement. It also enables people to discuss their previous experiences of confidential situations – which inform their current views. Another way of introducing the issue of confidentiality is, following some discussion about what people want or what they are doing here, to ask what they need in order to get what they want or to fulfil their aim. Usually people talk in terms of respect, understanding, self-responsibility (for example, making 'I' statements) – and confidentiality, typically:

> I agree to abide by confidentiality, that is, to talk to others outside the group only about what I have said or done myself and not to refer to others in the group by name or deed or in any way which could identify them. This extends to discussing my experience of the group with my partner/close friends.

In this way, confidentiality is properly viewed as supporting the group process rather than an end in itself. Having agreed such a statement, group members either say 'Yes' or nod their head to show their assent. It is worth paying attention to this detail as, again, misunderstandings can arise ('But I never agreed to that: I didn't say "Yes".'). Generally, rather than introducing the subject myself and thereby imposing this as an issue or concern for the group (which it may not be), I leave it to group members to raise it. This encourages people to think about what they need and to be active in getting it or raising the subject; it also encourages more group interaction in discussing *whether* confidentiality is important and, if so, *how*, rather than assuming *that* it is important. In his review of the issue Bond (1993) argues that 'the priority of the principle of autonomy suggests that confidentiality should not be imposed on the client . . . but should be the subject of negotiation' (p. 122). In my experience, such discussions and negotiations, although they generally take longer, have led to more thorough understanding of what confidentiality means both for individuals and the group. It is also worth appreciating – and reminding people – that in counselling there are *always* limits to confidentiality and that breaking confidentiality is both defensible and, in some circumstances, mandatory (see Bond, 1993; Jenkins, 1997). One such discussion centres on the issue of group members meeting other group members outside the group casually, which is particularly pertinent in small communities both geographically and culturally. Some people do not mind others knowing they are in a therapy group, others do. If two people who are part of a group meet each other in the street and say hello to each other there is no problem, but if either party is with someone else, who may well subsequently ask how their friend knows that other person, then this could be a breach of confidentiality and can create problems. There are no hard and fast rules about such issues, but clear contracts and contracting helps. In my experience, most group members agree to greet each other if they meet socially, although some prefer and ask to be ignored or unacknowledged. This can be both respected and worked with and may form part of 'the psychological aspects of the contract which become part of the therapeutic struggle' (Berne, 1966, p. 20). A similar situation is one in which, usually at the end of someone's membership of a group or at the end of the lifetime of the group, some people take group photographs – in which case they need to check whether group members mind them being seen by others. This is perhaps more relevant to a training group; nevertheless, if there is a group confidentiality contract, such consideration applies. Having agreed a group confidentiality contract, when a new member joins the group, there are two choices: either they agree to accept the existing contract or, preferably, this is restated and renegotiated. In my experience, some of the most dynamic discussions in a group take place as a result of this situation, with group members remembering and disagreeing about existing contracts and even the existence of contracts and new members raising issues and 'rules' which the group may not have considered, for instance, about no violence in the group or no sex between group members.

In many ways confidentiality defines and represents a boundary around the group which, in an ongoing group, includes existing and previous members and new members as they join. When someone leaves the group, I draw a line on the card (see Chapter 2,

Figure 3.2 *Counselling group payment card-II.*

	2.7	9.7	23.7	30.7	6.8	3.9	10.9	17.9	24.9	1.10	8.10	15.10	22.10
Alpha	√	√	√	√	√	√	√	√	√	√	√	√	√
Beattie	√	√	√	√	√								
Gemma	√	√	√	√	√	√	√	√	√	√	√	√	√
Effie	√												
Theo	√	√	√	√	√	√	√	√	√	√	√	√	√
Del						√	√	√	√	√	√	√	√
Zeta						√	√	√	√	√	√		
Eddie										√	√	√	√

Figure 2.3) after their name (Figure 3.2). At a practical, administrative level and at a psychological level it makes it clear that they have left. When a new person joins the group, they see their name, the names of the others in the group as well as names of those who have left, thus assimilating a sense of the group's history.

As far as the group confidentiality contract and boundary is concerned, this includes previous members of the group: thus, a new person knows the name/s of previous group members and present members may refer to previous group members. This draws a clear boundary around current and previous membership of the group. This raises the interesting issue of whether the group should know the names and any details about prospective members prior to their joining and whether prospective group members should know who is in the group before joining. For the group counsellor to share this information would usually break confidentiality (depending on the group contract) and that of their individual/prospective group client. On the other hand, if you do not share or exchange this information it is difficult to check any dual or conflicting relationships – which then have to be dealt with when a new person joins the group. One group agreed that the counsellor could disclose their names to prospective clients and, in turn, wanted to know the names of such clients.

The group contract that everything said or done outside the group, including any social contact, may be reported and worked through in the group also has implications for confidentiality.

When a group member wants a word with the counsellor outside the group, when the counsellor wants to raise an issue with a group member or when she/he reminds them about something they did in individual therapy, these are situations in which the confidentiality contract defines – or should define – the therapeutic primacy of the group.

One issue which is not much discussed is that of the counsellor's confidentiality. This is especially important for those counsellors who share more of themselves in the group – in studied self-involvement rather than promiscuous self-disclosure or 'indiscriminate frankness' as Kopp (1974) puts it. In terms of openness (to criticism) and the wider issue of public accountability, and in order to avoid the dangers of the preciousness of therapy (where it is viewed as removed and remote from the world), incestuousness (by which therapy becomes a closed clique) and discipleship (whereby the counsellor/therapist/guru is revered, followed and not challenged), I believe that counselling/therapy and the counsellor/therapist should be subject to the outside informal scrutiny of clients' partners and friends as well as more formal accountability of professional organisations and networks. At the same time, counsellors also have a right to be protected against misrepresentation and abuse; in response to this, some counsellors negotiate a group confidentiality contract which includes that what they say about themselves and what they say to a client, *if* reported, should be discussed *in context*.

Finally, although confidentiality is important and such details (as discussed above) are crucial to consider, there is a danger that we may become over-cautious and over-careful. In the context of increasing rules, regulations, registration and litigation this is an understandable if defensive fear. For some time now, in counselling and in training, I have left the issue of confidentiality to be taken up by the group, trusting that if it is an issue someone will raise it. My experience has proved this to be the case: some groups raise it at the beginning, others do not and some have reflected positively on the fact that they have undertaken a training day or a course without discussing it. In a similar vein, Shohet (1997), taking up the issue of the unenforceable nature of confidentiality contracts (such as the above example of what the counsellor says), suggests a 'goodwill contract' which encourages respect and mindfulness. This is actually supported by the legal position on confidentiality in groups. In an interesting article discussing this subject, Applebaum and Greer (1993) observe that 'although therapists who breach patients' confidentiality can be sued for malpractice or sanctioned in licensure or ethics proceedings, lay persons have no a priori obligation to protect others' communications' (p. 312). In the United States of America only two jurisdictions prohibit group members from disclosing outside the group information obtained in the group and only one explicitly refers to the context of group therapy (see Appendix 1). Thus, whilst the group counsellor may subscribe and legally be held to clients' confidentiality, group members' adherence to any agreements about confidentiality is ultimately only a matter of goodwill.

The alternate group meeting

This concept, of the group meeting without the therapist, was first introduced by Wolf in 1938 (see Wolf, 1949) and derives its name from the practice of the group meeting on its own alternately to its meeting with the therapist: 'a regularly scheduled, planned session as an integral part of the therapeutic experience' (Wolf and Swartz, 1962, p. 107). The alternate group is not a social gathering, its purpose is clearly therapeutic. Wolf and Swartz (1962) identify a number of purposes for this meeting:

- It facilitates interaction in the absence of the group counsellor/s, for example, a client who is quiet in the therapy group talks in the alternate meeting.
- It provides an opportunity for clients:
  - to be helped by and to help their peers, for example, in developing strategies for coping with anxiety;
  - to compare their behaviour in the respective alternate and therapy meetings; thus, a client who was perceived to be aggressive and threatening in the therapy group was experienced as helpful in the alternate meeting;
  - to function on their own – which enhances and reinforces clients' and the group's sense of health, well-being and functioning;
  - to experience each other more concretely than verbally, for instance, by meeting in each other's houses, in the way they live.

Although Wolf and Swartz (1962) note that termination is facilitated by the alternate session in terms of increasing client autonomy and independence, they argue strongly that the alternate meeting can be introduced at the beginning of the life of the group. They also discuss the pros and cons of the meeting taking place in the usual therapeutic setting and conclude that it best takes place in group members' homes as this encourages independence from the counsellor and the artificiality or separateness of the therapeutic setting. Wolf and Swartz (1962) comment on the impact that this has on the partner of the member hosting the group, perhaps becoming interested in therapy through contact with the group during any social time before or after the alternate meeting.

Much of Wolf and Swartz's (1962) original chapter on the alternate session is aimed at countering the resistance on the part of the traditional psychoanalytic establishment to the idea of 'patients' meeting on their own: 'not to permit the alternate meeting circumscribes the examination of actual and illusory attitudes among patients in both peer and authority directions' (p. 105), 'the therapist who fears what patients will say to one another and who must restrict them to a sterile environment reflects an overprotective and controlling attitude' (p. 111) and, in a passage that might equally have been written by humanistic practitioners:

> for the therapist concerned with the possibility that there is no reparative pressure at the alternate session, it should be said that the urge toward health persists in the therapist's absence, partly out of inherently constructive strivings resident in all patients, partly because the leader is projectively present at the alternate meeting. (p. 111)

My own relatively recent experience of establishing an alternate group meeting, which meets for an hour before a therapy group which I and a co-therapist facilitate, indicates initial support for Wolf and Swartz's theory and observations about the purpose and usefulness of this meeting as supplementing and complementing the therapy group. It also forms a bridge between group therapy and the wider social context in which group members live (see Chapter 7), and between therapeutic relationships which are dependent or which at least focus on the group counsellor/s and the wider and more sustaining value of therapeutic *relating* to others (friends, neighbours) and in community (see Tudor, 1999b).

Having now established the group, in the next two chapters I turn my attention to maintaining the group during the middle, working phase of its life (Chapter 4) and, in Chapter 5, to ending the group.

4

The Working Group

The operational or working stage/phase of the group refers to the middle phase of the group's life, characterised by the development of trust and group process. In terms of Berne's (1963) phenomenological approach (see Chapter 1), this is when the members' group imagoes are operative, secondarily adjusted and secondarily operative (my addition), which correspond to Tuckman's (1965) storming, norming and performing stages (see Table 4.1). In this chapter, using the developmental view of groups as a way of organising the material, I consider issues which are particularly pertinent to the operational/working group in these phases – 'difficult' clients and 'hostile' groups, silence in groups, new members and leaders, and contact in and outside the group. Following this I discuss a number of methods of recording what happens in groups.

The operative group – storming

Following the initial phase in which members 'mill around', engage and (at least to some extent) modify their image of and preconceptions about the group in terms of their own experience of it, there is a further modification of the image of the group 'in accordance with the member's perception of how he fits into the leader's imago' (Berne, 1963, p. 321). In Tuckman's (1965) meta model, this is the storming stage in which group members express conflict with and hostility to the therapist *and with each other* 'as a means of expressing their individuality and resisting the formation of group structure' (p. 386). For some, storming is viewed

Table 4.1 *The group leader's focus and tasks/attitude in relation to phases of group development and common issues – Part II*

Group imago (Berne, 1963)	Stages of group (Tuckman, 1965)	Common issues	Leader's focus	Leader's tasks/ attitude
Operative group imago	Storming	Intragroup conflict and challenge to leader, active and passive expressions of anger	On members owning their feelings, on discrepancies and incongruence	To validate and clarify members' feelings, to accept criticism and to be able to negotiate appropriately
Secondarily adjusted group imago	Norming	Ambivalence, enthusiasm and reluctance	On inclusion and exclusion of members	To facilitate discussion, to challenge rigid constructs
Secondarily operative group imago	Performing	Change, reliance and resolution, premature withdrawal	On task (where appropriate) On individuals and group	To encourage group autonomy and interpersonal support

specifically as challenging the leader and their authority. I prefer the term operative, as this gives more the sense that this is a necessary and positive part of the group's development, operation and life. In any case, in this phase, the group is concerned with conflict, challenge and expression, whilst the leader's task is to take such issues seriously – and to survive! The leader needs to clarify and validate such feelings – and the right to have feelings – of *all* group members, to empathise and hold all sides of any conflict and to facilitate improving relationships in the group (see Rogers, 1959/1970, 1973). Finally, the leader needs to be able to be flexible and to negotiate appropriately by 'discriminating between compromises/negotiations which would facilitate or handicap group task [or process]' (Clarkson, 1991, p. 43). Dangers for the leader (and for the group) at this stage include getting defensive, discounting or deflecting conflict, giving up or being emotionally absent, being persecutory (of individuals or of the group), rescuing (being too 'nice'), or standing by (letting things happen).

The brief example in Box 4.1 illustrates the storming phase of a group and the leader's task in clarifying and validating feeling and the expression of feeling, without getting defensive.

Box 4.1   Example of group storming

Group counsellor's commentary, reflecting a process recall

Sam: I'd like to go next. I've got something important to say to the group . . .

Sam looks and sounds angry. He is addressing the group and yet looking directly at Rose.

Rose: [*interrupting*]: You're looking straight at me and you sound angry.

Yes.

Sam: No I'm not.

Keith (Group Counsellor): Not what?

Sam: . . . angry. OK, I was looking at Rose but I'm not angry. It's just that she always starts the group and no one else gets a look in and I do have something really important to talk about.

I want to clarify whether he is saying he is not angry or (possibly) that he thinks he hasn't looked at Rose. Now he sounds angry/ defensive – with me? He's upping the stakes ('really important') and now sounds a little desperate.

Tonia: I agree with you, Sam. I've noticed that too, Keith. You always let Rose start the group. In the other group I was in we always had a 'check in' so everybody could say something before people launched in with what they wanted.

Now Tonia's (typically) piling in. She sounds angry with me. Also, I notice that she's the second person who's interrupted Sam. In extolling the virtue of her previous group, she is in some way putting all of us down. I'm beginning to feel irritated.

Una: I feel out of this. To me you all sound angry.

Una appears isolated (a usual position) but also is acting as the group barometer.

Keith: [*to Una*] . . . everyone except you.

I nearly summarised what was happening in the group and at the last minute changed my mind to focus on Una. In the light of what she said and where she got to, I think this was useful. Now I address the whole group. I decide to pick up the theme and name the connections, leaving the dynamic of people interrupting Sam until later.

Una: Yes . . . well, No. I guess I'm a bit pissed off with everyone saying what they're not . . . and, yes, that includes me.

Keith: It seems – and sounds – like most of you are angry in different ways – with each other, with me and maybe with the group as a whole.

Two issues which often emerge at this stage are those associated with 'storming': the view, based on analytic perceptions of defences, resistance and hostility, that people and groups are difficult and problematic; and the phenomenon of silence in the group.

'Resistance', 'disruption', 'difficult' and 'problem' people

In the literature on groups and especially about this developmental stage, these terms are often used. Some approaches and many practitioners, for example, translate the action of resisting (verb) (as above) into the label of 'resistant' (adjective) client/group. If you take the view – as I do – that defences in general are there for protection, then they become understood as part of a whole (holistic) picture of the person rather than only reflecting their pathology. Such defences may constitute a 'psychological maladjustment' of the organism (Rogers, 1951); it is nevertheless the best we can do, given our circumstances and the information we have at the time: being paranoid, that is, having heightened awareness ('*para noia*') about people, may be a defence against or a maladjustment to an abusive early environment. Thus the classic psychoanalytic defences (as identified by S. Freud, M. Klein, A. Freud and R.S. Lazarus) – may be viewed as 'creative adjustment coping mechanisms' (Tudor, 1996b). From this point of view or frame of reference, 'resistance' becomes rather 'an error of empathy on the therapist's side' (Speierer, 1990, p. 343). The same goes for the so-called 'disruptive group'; my concern and interest is in what needs to be disrupted, broken, burst asunder or shattered: viewing the nominal noun (disruption) rather as an active verb, to be understood and worked through. Moreover, disruptions in the form of asides between group members, disturbances in the field of the group, such as someone being late, or at the external boundary of the group, such as someone leaving the door open, and disharmony, as in a disagreement between group members: all these reflect and represent some meaning for the individual group member and the group itself and provide 'grist for the mill' of the process of the group.

Claiming that 'each patient *must* be a problem' (p. 375, original emphasis), and in doing so drawing no distinction between the person and their problem, Yalom (1985) devotes a whole chapter to 'problem patients' – the monopolist, the schizoid, the silent, the boring, the help-rejecting complainer, the self-righteous moralist, the psychotic, the narcissistic and the borderline patient, a curious cocktail of recognised diagnostic categories and informal labelling. (In the fourth [1995] edition of his book, Yalom drops the reference to the self-righteous moralist and, in reponse to diagnostic changes and self-psychology theory, clusters the schizoid and the narcissistic under the rubric of 'the characterologically difficult patient'.) This focus on the presenting problem and the symptom often misses the cause; in response to the so-called 'manipulative' client, I am interested to know how come they learned to be so dextrous (and where and why the therapist learned such terms!). In my experience, this empathic attitude both gives a more accurate and whole picture of the person and is more likely to lead to the development of a therapeutic working alliance, understanding and healing. (It is interesting to note that, despite enduring hostility in some psychoanalytic quarters, empathy, along with genuineness and respect, is more and more seen as essential to psychotherapy – by, amongst others, Kohut, Jaspers and self-psychologists such as Stern.) A further problem with any categorisation is that it may confirm the client in a particular role in the group: *the* harmoniser, *the* wallflower, *the* keeper of the rules etc. Again, I am more interested in either negotiated roles (for a useful exercise on which see Houston, 1990) or, more usefully, in making the noun into an action and in understanding the need underlying the behaviour: what is the client's need to keep or make things harmonious; what is useful to them and, indeed, the group, in being a wallflower; what are other people doing whilst one person keeps the rules?

The 'hostile' group

From a psychoanalytic perspective, hostility derives from pre-Oedipal rage and is particularly expressed in relationships in groups, more so than in the dyadic relationship of individual counselling and psychotherapy. Gans (1989) identifies a number of sources of hostility, linked to phases of human and group development:

- *Early phase* – anxiety, vulnerability to attack, prejudice and fear of exclusion, loss of control and narcissistic injury.
- *Reactive phase* – self-confrontation through another (parallel to Yalom's [1995] therapeutic factor of interpersonal learning – input), sibling rivalry, transference and premature termination.

■ *Mature phase* – disappointment.

Depending on the philosophy of human nature underlying the counsellor's theoretical orientation, these concepts will be more or less useful. For most practitioners there is a middle ground between the extreme pessimism and determinism of the traditional psychoanalytic position and the naïve optimism and extreme voluntarism of some humanistic practitioners. The reality is that groups are powerful entities and may be constructive and destructive. As I finished writing this book, I was reminded of both perspectives in reading newspaper reports of a gang of young women who had chased a man and beaten him to death and, the same day, another similar group of friends who had come together and raised money for charity by undertaking a long-distance walk.

One further example of negative forces or dynamics in groups is scapegoating. Significantly, the word comes from the ancient Mosaic ritual of symbolically heaping sins onto a goat who was then sent alive into the wilderness; this, together with the ritual sacrifice of a second goat, was considered an atonement ('at one ment') for the sins of the tribe, community or group. The brunt of criticism and exclusion which scapegoating involves may be understood as an 'anti-group' process, that is, one of 'the destructive processes that threaten the functioning of a group . . . [by which] the group as object becomes impregnated with the hostile projections of the membership' (Nitsun, 1996, pp. 1–2). In his seminal work on the anti-group Nitsun fills a gap in the literature by paying attention to the destructive processes in the group, especially those directed at the group itself. In doing so, he views the concept as an intermediary concept between the ideas of Foulkes and Bion. As far as scapegoating is concerned, Gans (1989) suggests that the task (role/attitude) of the leader is to support the person being scapegoated in order to acknowledge their feelings, to reassure the other group members that, in a similar circumstance, they will be protected and, most importantly (in my view), 'to assist members in acknowledging as their own feelings they wish to disown' (p. 510). Given that the victim of such processes is also participating in such responses, in my experience such individual and group processes are most effectively worked with by co-therapists. Recently, there has been an interesting debate conducted among an internet discussion group about scapegoating in groups and the necessity and sufficiency of Rogers' (1959) conditions as applied to groups (see Chapter 2). To date (January 1999), the discussion has not acknowledged the significance of all *six* of Rogers' conditions in dealing with hostile and destructive processes: for instance, that the facilitator is *in contact* with *all* members of the group and that on this basis, she/he can offer the 'core conditions' of genuineness, regard and empathy and that *all* members experience her/his regard and empathy. As a result, the differentiated perceptions of group members increase as does their *extensionality*, that is, extending their frame of reference and empathic understanding of the other – which Giesekus and Mente (1986) observe is the most important therapeutic factor in groups.

Reflections on silence
There are many reasons for silences in groups, some undoubtedly derive from family experiences, some are influenced by culture and by gender, typically women are more silent (and silenced) than men. There appears to be general agreement in the therapeutic literature that the greater the verbal participation and involvement in the group, the more the client is valued by others, the more she/he values themself, and the greater the therapeutic value of the group. Conversely, with rare exceptions, clients who are consistently silent do not appear to gain from the experience and often evoke frustration and exasperation in other group members. Yalom (1995) makes the point that silence is a behaviour and as such (and as with all behaviour) 'has meaning both in the framework of the here-and-now and as a representative sample of the patient's typical way of relating to his or her interpersonal world' (p. 376). However, many, including Yalom, go further and construe silence in groups as having only negative connotations. Here, both views are considered and negative, passive silent behaviour is distinguished from positive, active, therapeutic silence in groups.

The concept of passivity from transactional analysis (TA) is a useful one in understanding and confronting silent behaviour – and in distinguishing such behaviour from therapeutic silence. Schiff et al. (1975) identify four passive behaviours, which people use to establish and maintain unhealthy, symbiotic behaviours.

- *Doing nothing* – a non-response; energy is channelled into inhibiting responses; generally people who are doing nothing do not think about what is happening.
  Example
     Adam: [*to Ben*] What do you think about what I just said?
     Ben: [*looks scared and does not respond. Silence*]
     Adam: [*looks uncomfortable*]
     Counsellor: [*to Ben*] You look really scared, Ben, as if you can't think straight. *Or*
     You look scared, Ben. You can feel and think at the same time.

- *Over-adaptation* – usually by being helpful, adaptable or accommodating to people and in situations by complying to what the person *believes* other people want her/him to do.
  Example
     [*Cath is crying*]
     Dot: [*gets up, walks across the room, fetches box of tissues and gives them to Cath*]
     Counsellor: [*to Dot*] Dot, I know that you do a lot of looking after people. I also know that I feel irritated when you look after people when they haven't asked for it. Or
     Cath didn't ask for any tissues and she could take that as a message to stop crying. Besides tears are good for the skin.

In transactional analysis (TA) terms, this last intervention is designed to get Dot to utilise her Adult to define what is appropriate and what is not appropriate.

- *Agitation* – 'involves people engaging in repetitive, non goal-directed activity (Schiff et al., 1975, p. 12).
  Examples: coughing (when the person does not have a cough), leaving the room, shifting around in one's seat a lot, waggling or kicking one's feet.
  The counsellor may confront any of these passive behaviours simply by drawing the client's attention to them, inviting the client to think about what they are doing and suggesting that they can function *and* experience whatever sensations they are feeling.

- *Incapacitation or violence* – 'the discharge of energy built up while people are being passive' (Schiff et al., 1975, p. 13) – either of which often follow a period of agitation. As people generally do not accept responsibility for their incapacitation (for instance, some forms of psychosomatic disorders such as 'hysterical conversion') or violence ('She made me do it', 'I couldn't help myself: I just lost control') etc., the counsellor needs either to confront this belief or to contain the escalation until the energy is discharged (for example, by the client hitting a cushion), after which the client can cathect (put energy into) their Adult.

Identifying such passive behaviours may help the counsellor to distinguish between a passive silence and active, therapeutic silence.

Silence forms a significant part of human communication. Silence in groups is *potentially* a particularly potent and profound experience – as traditional councils, Quaker meetings and group meditation attest. It occurs, with rare exceptions, at some point in every group and, indeed, in time may form a large part of a particular group. It carries different meanings – for each person and for the group at different times and in different phases. Silence may be golden – 'speech is silver, silence is golden' (proverb) – it may also be simmering, awkward, friendly or frosty. It may be more meaningful than speech: 'silence is deep as Eternity; speech is shallow as Time' (Thomas Carlyle, *Critical and Miscellaneous Essays*); 'speech is the small change of silence' (George Meredith, *The Ordeal of Richard Feverel*). Some groups may incorporate a ritual of silence at the beginning and/or the end of the group which may develop spontaneously or be agreed or be guided by the leader. Discussing *The Way of Council*, Zimmermann and Coyle (1996) recount the powerful impact on decision-making of silence and stories: 'in council one listens in the silences between the words with the ears of a rabbit' (p. 3). Silent meditation is a way of focusing on the subject, for instance in a theme-based group (see Cohn, 1972). It may have a still, quiet quality – ''tis visible silence, still as the hour-glass' (Dante Gabriel Rossetti, *The House of Life*) – and be facilitative:

At the midnight in the silence of the sleep-time
When you set your fancies free.
(Browning, *Epilogue to Asolando*)

For some individuals, and at some times, silence is the most genuine expression: 'Silent? Ah, he is silent. He can keep silence well. That man's silence is wonderful to listen to' (Thomas Hardy,

Under the Greenwood Tree). For others it is an unhelpful, isolating and anti-therapeutic retreat from human interaction and the world: 'Silence is become his mother tongue' (Oliver Goldsmith, *The Good-Natured Man*).

The literature quoted generally reflects the importance and value of silence; it also hints at the limitations of speech. Drawing on Wittgenstein's linguistic philosophy, Lynch (1997) suggests that the limitations of language necessarily imply limitations of 'talking therapy' and recognises two different kinds of silence: the silence of oppression (or repression) and a silence of the limits:

> which represents the recognition of the limits of language in describing our existence. This is the silence of prayer and meditation, the silence of awe in the midst of beauty. It is also the silence that may be experienced in the face of tragedy, where words cannot adequately express our response . . . [it is] an affirmation of our existence in all its depth and mystery. (Lynch, 1997, p. 127)

Thus, one of the necessary qualities of the group counsellor is to be able to distinguish between passive, silent behaviour and active therapeutic silence, between the silence of oppression and of the oppressed, especially if reproduced in the group environment and process, and a collective silence of limits which acknowledges and expresses the human condition. In a rare article on the positive power of silence in groups, Harris (1996) considers the phenomenology of silence and distinguishes between *individual* silence, silence *between* group members and group *silence* – a useful framework for discerning the positive or problematic meaning of silence in groups.

The secondarily adjusted group – norming

Berne (1963) refers to the fourth phase of group development as the secondarily adjusted group imago, as one in which 'the member relinquishes some of his own proclivities in favour of the group cohesion' (p. 321) – which I place parallel to the norming stage (see Chapter 1, Table 1.3, and Table 4.1 above). The group structure (Tuckman, 1965) is concerned with the development of group cohesion through negotiating, establishing, maintaining and re-negotiating group norms. Examples of group norms are:

- *Participation* – for instance, that everyone checks in or says something during the group.

- *Responsiveness* – that group members respond to each other (rather than leaving it to the group counsellor).
- *Self-responsibility* – that individuals talk for themselves, using 'I' rather than 'you' or 'one' (also see Corey, 1995).
- *Group responsibility* – that group members take some responsibility for each other, for example, asking 'How are you this week?' or observing 'You seem quiet'. I refer to this as 'interfering with play', a phrase inspired by the words of the late (and great) Bill Shankley, manager of Liverpool Football Club who, when questioned about the then off-side law whereby a player who was not interfering with play could be deemed not to be offside, replied 'If a player isn't interfering with play then he shouldn't be on the pitch'. The point of being in a group is precisely 'to get in each other's way' and to be able to deal with and learn from such interference (meaning, literally, 'doing with').

Note that these are neither group rules nor contracts (see Chapter 3), although they may be developed as contracts; rather they may be seen by the group as desirable qualities, attitudes and behaviours in that particular group. Common issues at this stage centre on ambivalence to such adjustment and to establishing norms, which task is seen as expressing a commitment to the group: members often show (both) reluctance and enthusiasm for the task. The leader's focus and tasks/attitude are summarised in Table 4.1. Difficulties for the leader at this stage centre on her/his response to the establishment of norms: being defensive, rigid or too flexible. One issue that highlights the significance of group norms, both conceptually and most practically, is that of new members joining an open, ongoing group – and indeed is a major argument for having open groups which are more representative of life, in which people join and leave group situations.

New members
When new members join an ongoing counselling group they often act as a catalyst for the group to change, to review and, sometimes, to regress – the group often recycles earlier phases/stages of development. Introducing new members is certainly interfering with play and may be likened to dropping a stone in a pond: it creates ripples. He, she or they immediately change the group dynamics even before they arrive – even whether they are a

she, he or they! In view of the prospect of a new member joining, the group may consolidate around its identity. Kaplan and Roman (1961) refer to this as 'a hypercathexis of group membership and of the symbolic representation of the group, which [is] seen as a psychological entity' (p. 380). When there is a space in a group, that is whenever the numbers fall below the maximum (for example, eight), I remind the group that another person may join at any time. Once I accept a client into the group, I give the group one week's (or group's) notice of this, at which point the group often expresses curiosity about the new member – which I tend not to satisfy. At this point groups often reminisce about their shared history which is about to change and in this respect joining always evokes mourning (see Chapter 5). The group may also depersonalise or categorise '*the* new member' as such, both in advance of and during their early membership of the group.

When the new member arrives they come straight into the pre-group time where their name is already on the group payment record card (see Chapter 3). Kaplan and Roman (1961) note some characteristic responses in adult therapy groups to the introduction of new members: an increase in restlessness in the waiting area, notable changes in attendance (that is, increased absences) and arrival habits (increased lateness) and alterations in seating arrangements (one reason for noting where group members sit – see below). Various options on beginning the group were discussed in Chapter 3. Similar consideration needs to be given when a new member joins an ongoing group. The counsellor may say 'Welcome' or 'Welcome, Aisha' or nothing. In each case there are implications, advantages and disadvantages (see Box 4.2). Following the initial introductions and exchanges, the group tends to unfold in one of two ways: either it attempts to incorporate the new member into the group *as it is*, often some reference is made to the group rules, contracts and norms; or there is more 'milling around' and negotiation, often marked by a return to or revisiting of earlier stages of the group's development (exchange of provisional imagoes, forming, etc.), which acknowledges that this is a new group. The two responses depend on and reflect a number of dynamics:

■ The degree of threat/openness with which the new member/s is viewed or experienced. Bach's (1954) view is that every

---

Box 4.2   Counsellor options as regards a new group member

Options	Advantage	Disadvantage
Saying 'Welcome'	Is welcoming and friendly	Focuses the new member on the group counsellor
Saying 'Welcome Aisha'	Is welcoming, friendly and personal	Reveals the new member's name (not everyone checks the card) and detracts from possible interactions from other group members about 'What's your name?', 'How do you pronounce it?' 'What does it mean?', 'Who are you?' etc.
Saying nothing	Encourages other group members to react and act to the new member	May appear unwelcoming and rude
Commenting on how the group does (or does not) welcome the new member	May be useful in confronting individual and group passivity and discounting (see Schiff et al., 1975)	May detract from the individual and her/his issues about joining, attaching and belonging

---

newcomer has the potential to strengthen or weaken existing subgroup alliances and is therefore a threat to the group's equilibrium and cohesion. On the other hand, the group may be flexible, adaptable and democratic in assimilating a new member.

■ The degree of threat/openness a new member themselves brings to the group:

> the new member's reactions to the group are conditioned by his unfamiliarity with the new setting and the resultant anxiety, the self-doubt as to his acceptability, and his concern as to his status within the group. In his insecure position he may resort to such defences as role setting or role playing in order to ward off the threat of early isolation. (Leopold, 1961, p. 369)

On the other hand is the new member's ability to be flexible, to adapt and to assimilate (without necessarily being accommodating) and to participate in the group process.

■ The degree to which the group counsellor is aware and able to manage the processes of joining and acculturation, for example, the anger of existing members towards her/him for introducing this new arrival, the projected anger and hurt of the new member for having been introduced to her/him to this new, hostile environment etc. Personal, experiential as well as theoretical knowledge is especially useful in this regard (see Chapter 8).

A new leader

Occasionally, the group counsellor may not be able to make a meeting of the group, being ill or unavoidably called away for some reason. When an open group is running continuously over years, life events such as having children, looking after a sick relative, attending a funeral or the need for sabbatical leave, may extend the counsellor's absence and provoke what Gottlieb (1989), a psychotherapist writing about the effects on her clients of her pregnancy, refers to as a 'crisis of separation' (p. 298). In these instances, the therapist *and the group* have a number of choices: to cancel the group, for the group to meet on its own, or to ask another therapist to lead/facilitate the group. I emphasise 'ask the group' as I consider it not only courteous for the therapist to consult the group but, more importantly, a contractual issue. The group members originally agreed to be in a group with you as the therapist: being away, however temporarily, changes the terms and conditions of that contract and you therefore need to renegotiate the contract rather than to impose a solution. On one occasion, due to a sudden bereavement, I asked another therapist to lead a group that evening; she began by negotiating with the group about what it/they wanted; after some discussion two members left and the therapist facilitated a small (sub-)group. As regards a longer, and especially a planned, absence you also need to give a good enough period of notice – months rather than weeks. In terms of leadership, this represents responsible and affiliative leadership which, appropriately, is linked to establishing – and re-establishing – the working alliance (see Table 3.1).

As with the new member, the substitute leader, and even the prospect of having a different therapist for an evening or a period of time, evokes reactions with which the therapist needs to be prepared to work. In terms of attachment theory the parallel is that of the 'baby-sitter' or foster parent, both of which are potent metaphors. One group member initially froze when a different therapist ran the group for an evening. The therapist noticed and commented on this and, about half way through the evening, the client disclosed that as a child she had been abused by a baby-sitter, a trusted friend of her parents. The therapist and the group were able to help the client work through this: she achieved some resolution with the substitute therapist and subsequently talked about it further in the group with the group therapist.

Group norms
There are many examples of issues common at this norming stage, the negotiation, establishment, maintenance and re-negotiation of which depend much on the counsellor's attitude and theoretical orientation. Examples are given under each aspect of norming.

- *Negotiating norms* – This in particular depends on the level of responsibility and autonomy the group counsellor is willing to give to/share with/not to take away from the group. Thus the counsellor needs to be clear about their approach to negotiating as well as what is and what is not negotiable and, crucially, to be clear if and when they do not know, that is, when presented with an issue about which they have not necessarily thought or have an opinion. One example is the group asking to meet (note 'asking') without the counsellor, either in the counsellor's temporary absence or as a regular, planned part of the life of the group.
- *Establishing norms* – A major issue for many groups is that of time and the idea that each group member gets – and is only entitled to – a certain amount of (chronological) time. The counsellor's early responses and interventions (silence, 'What do other people think?', 'Ask others what they would do') will set the scene for the norm of therapy *in* the group, in which case the allocation of time is relevant, or therapy *through* or *of* the group, in which case such allocation of or bidding for time is less relevant. It is worth noting that while chronological time (from the Greek *chronos*) is one, linear view of time, there was – and is – another word for time, that is *kairos*, meaning appropriate time (see Tudor, 1999a). Knowing this helps both counsellor and group with the issue of scarcity, which often belies the issue of time.

- *Maintaining norms* – One example of this is how groups norm themselves and any group rules are passed on to new members. One client used to get angry with me for not telling the new member 'the rules' before they came into the group. In another group one member was perceived to be the keeper of the group rules, until he confronted the other members about this.
- *Re-negotiating norms* – Again, this depends much on the counsellor's attitude to negotiability. One example concerns the structure of the group. One group negotiated a different structure to the group, moving from meeting weekly to meeting fortnightly, at the same time changing the length of meeting from two to three hours.

The secondarily operative group – performing

Parallel to Tuckman's (1965) performing stage, I identify a *secondarily operative group imago* in which the individual member is concerned with clarifying and developing interdependent relationships in the context of the group which are free both from the hostility of the initial operative (storming) phase and from any adaptation based on group cohesion (as at the norming stage). In this phase, group members experience themselves and others in the group changing (as represented by the double circles in Chapter 1, Figure 1.5) and, to paraphrase Rogers, being dependably real but not necessarily consistent. Each member is increasingly differentiated both (with)in themselves, that is, from previous distorted images of themselves, and in relation to others. At this stage, the group leader's focus is both on individuals and on the group operating increasingly on their own; the leader's primary task is to let go: to encourage group autonomy and interpersonal support. Conversely, the main danger for the leader is in not letting go and in being too task-oriented. Two issues which are especially relevant at this phase of the group's development are discussed: contact, that is, the use of touch within the group; and contact, that is, socialising outside the group.

Contact in the group: the therapeutic use of touch
Understandably, the issue of touch between counsellor and client is a delicate and controversial area. In the light of childhood

sexual abuse, of the abuse and exploitation of clients by counsellors and therapists (see Russell, 1993), the increasing litigation against therapists, and the genuine concern on the part of counsellors about the danger of misinterpretation, misrepresentation and mendacious claims on the part of some clients, touch has become the latest taboo. At the same time, all sentient beings need contact and appropriate touch is a basic human need which, in our worry and defensiveness, we may ignore. In his book on *Encounter Groups* Rogers (1970/1973), his daughter and granddaughter discuss the importance of touch, offering an intergenerational viewpoint which attempts to disassociate touch from sex, viewing it as communication. As Older (1982) puts it: 'touch is not a technique: not touching is a technique'.

Traditionally, counsellors touching clients in therapy has been seen as dangerous, frightening and provocative. None the less, the importance and therapeutic value of touch and 'holding', both metaphorically and literally, is important to recognise and discuss (see Patterson, 1973; Woodmansey, 1988; Autton, 1989; Embleton Tudor and Tudor, 1994). In understanding and assessing the use of touch, distinctions may be drawn between *social touch*, for example a handshake; *occasional touch*, initiated by the client, such as 'Can I have a hug' and responded to by the counsellor (yes or no); and the *therapeutic use of touch*, either on which the whole therapy is based, as in biodynamic massage and other post-Reichian therapies, or whereby the counsellor uses touch, for example holding the client for a specific therapeutic and agreed purpose. Groups, of course, provide a space for clients (and counsellors) to explore and experience touch in a way that is subject to public scrutiny and which therefore is likely to be experienced as safer than in individual counselling. Each of the distinctions drawn are briefly explored.

■ *Social touch* – Whilst this may be the least problematic and least intimate area of touch, counsellors need to be aware of the fact that in some cultures shaking hands between a man and a woman is unwelcomed. Being open and prepared to shake hands without imposing this by proferring a hand is probably the safest option. Therapeutically, Berne (1972/1975b) makes the case for discouraging handshakes on the basis that not shaking hands establishes the serious business of therapy rather than the pupose of exchanging courtesies. If the client insists, however, then handshakes can be a source of psychological information. Shaking hands at the end of a session/meeting may indicate acceptance or comfort. The same considerations apply to cultures in which greetings are exchanged by kissing on the cheeks. Groups provide an opportunity to explore the social boundaries of touch in greeting, especially in the pre-group time, explorations which may then be processed in the counselling group itself.

- *Occasional touch* – Touch in counselling (apart from the possible social touch of a proferred handshake) generally should be initiated by the client. Occasional requests for a hug may be unproblematic, and the counsellor may respond if they feel comfortable to do this. The manner in which requests for touch are made and the experience of them provide, in Berne's terms, important information in diagnosis and treatment planning. The implications of experiencing close, physical contact and the possibility of sexual arousal on the part either of the client or of the counsellor, however, is more problematic and needs to be considered carefully both in training and in supervision and as regards the particular client. In terms of initiating occasional touch such as a hug, counsellors need to be extremely careful in this respect, especially in the current climate. When a client is particularly distressed or happy, it is natural and human enough to want to make contact. At the same time, some counsellors may be too eager to offer comfort; if you are wanting to touch clients, one safeguard of professional and ethical practice is firstly to have explored any need you may have for touch and, further, to have at least five positive therapeutic reasons for doing so. In this respect, a group provides a container in which clients and counsellors can check out these issues with others and, indeed, clients may get their need for human contact met from peers as well as or instead of the group counsellor.

- *Therapeutic touch* – Touch as therapy is discussed by Southwell (1990). Touch as therapeutic, within counselling which is essentially verbal or language-centred, is perhaps the most problematic form of touch. Although it is not prohibited in any of the principal codes of ethics to which counsellors adhere, touch needs to be carefully considered (again, having five reasons for touch is a useful discipline) and, arguably, the subject of a specific counselling contract (see Sills, 1997a).

Physically holding a client may have tremendous reparative value for someone who was abused and/or is ashamed of their body; inappropriate holding and/or the wrong timing may be stimulating and intrusive and thereby perpetuate their experience of abusive relationships. Cornell (1997) offers a discussion of touch and boundaries, encompassing ethical foundations, transference, contact and differentiation and ego development, with a view to informing the informed use of touch in therapy. The value of a group context is that any and all touch is witnessed, and that the counsellor's use of therapeutic touch, for example, holding a client, may – indeed, should – be the subject of discussion, question and review. It is certainly the focus of individual and group dynamics, as such touch commonly evokes jealousy, envy, rage, anxiety, etc. As with any other norm, touch and touching may – and, again, should – be the subject of some challenge, for instance, when a new member joins the group.

Box 4.3   Seven reasons/parameters for therapeutic touch (e.g. holding)

1. The client requests it clearly – which may be understood in terms of contact, congruence, Adult ego state, ego syntonicity etc. (the importance of assessment).
2. It is appropriate and/or understandable in terms of therapeutic relationship, e.g. a reparative relationship and therapeutic process (the importance of theory).
3. The client has no other appropriate forum/relationship/s for getting this particular need met (the relevance of context).
4. The counsellor feels congruent in their response (the importance of self-awareness).
5. The counsellor discusses the request and possible responses in supervision (the importance of professional support).
6. Client and counsellor make a specific contract/agreement about the nature of the touch, e.g. holding – how? when? for how long? who initiates it? etc. – and this is regularly reviewed (the importance of contract).
7. The holding is subject to public scrutiny, i.e. it takes place in a group (the significance of the conscious witness).

Contact outside the group

Some of the issues about group members having contact with each other outside the group, for instance, as regards boundaries and confidentiality, have been discussed and the therapeutic primacy of the group has been stressed (see Chapter 3); as one client put it: 'Anything can be fed back into the group'. Contact between group members outside the group and the group meeting as a whole (either as an alternate group meeting or socially) extends the therapeutic *temenos* (the place set aside, the sacred space, the container) into the social world in which the client's therapy/healing takes place (this argument is developed in Chapter 7). I do not have any rules about contact outside the group both as a positive statement and as I have no sanctions about this, preferring both conceptually and in practice to facilitate discussion in the group about group contracts and social contact. As a part of my research (see Appendix 2), I asked clients in two groups to comment on the nature and purpose of any social contact they had with other group members. (I distinguish between this and the contact that ensues from group members staying on after the end of a group meeting, a subject discussed in Chapter 5.)

Of eleven clients responding on this issue, only one client had no contact with anyone else and another reported that contact was rare. Two clients had some contact with one other, including one visiting a group member in hospital; three had contact with three others. Four clients reported that they telephoned other group members – mostly only occasionally, one quite regularly. Of those who did not have much contact, several commented that they liked knowing they could, the potential for support appearing more important than making contact: 'sometimes it just reminds me that there are people out there, available, who know me and care about me and who think something of me'. One group occasionally met socially as a group. The predominant reason given for such contact was support and, for some, the opportunity to explore and develop friendship: 'I am scared and excited by the prospect of contact with other group members outside the group, as there will be opportunity to have supportive, healthy relationships.' One client also identified a therapeutic value of their social contact: 'It's a brilliant opportunity for learning.' Occasionally, as the group counsellor, I make a working agreement with a client to telephone me between group meetings and may also encourage the client to make arrangements with other group members – if they wish. Generally, over the life of a group, the social contact – or the openness to such contact –

increases, reaching its zenith at this phase of the group: 'I like to feel that the group doesn't stop being a group'.

Having discussed a number of issues which are pertinent to the group in its operational or working phases, I now turn to the issue of recording groups.

Recording groups

At present there is no legal requirement to keep records or notes of therapeutic work with clients. Different professional organisations, training institutes and supervisors may, nevertheless, have particular views and requirements of the individual and group counsellor. Bond (1993) usefully reviews the issues around the keeping of written records, including their security, access to them, their possible use in court, their use in supervision and how long you should keep them. He concludes that, 'although it is not regarded as essential to good practice to keep records of counselling, the arguments are weighted on the side of keeping them' (p. 179). Recording also provides the basis and data for evaluation both for the group counsellor and for clients, thus you can monitor the number of contributions a particular group member makes and any changes in these over time (see below and Table 4.1). However, in the literature very little is written about the content or format of counselling records and even less on recording counselling groups.

Your record or notes of a group record what is useful. Foulkes (1964) offers a positional chart, which is similar to Berne's (1966) seating diagram, and comments that 'interesting dynamic observations can be made on the basis of such a form' (p. 310). However, of all the possible observations the group therapist could make, Foulkes does not indicate what is or would be interesting and it is clear that any observations are highly subjective. *What* is useful is what you think is important, that is, what is psychologically significant. This, in turn, depends on certain criteria as to *why* you think these particular aspects of groups are psychologically significant – criteria which are generally influenced by your orientation. Thus, you will note a client's therapeutic contract and how this may be modified over time if you believe that contracting is the way in which you establish what clients are wanting to change and the consequent direction their therapy needs to take. Similarly, you will note where someone sits in a group if you believe that this expresses something of significance. In drawing up his group therapy interaction chronogram, Cox (1993), for instance, emphasises the time factor in the life of a group meeting, dividing this into three phases: initial, substantial and terminal. Cox's chronogram (a circle for each patient) is thus used for recording 'dominant' events as well as interactions. In drawing up a group record sheet (below), I consider both *what* information is useful and *why*. Any record or notes also need to be concise so that you are able to record the session easily afterwards, and are able to refer to it easily before the next session or in supervision.

The next pages show and develop a group record sheet (which draws considerably but not exclusively on TA as its underlying orientation). A template showing *what* is recorded (p. 110) is followed by descriptions and explanations as to *why* the information recorded is considered significant and therefore useful; a completed version of the template, recording a specific group is shown on p. 115.

Therapy Group

Weekly, on Monday, 7.30–9.30pm   This information identifies the group and distinguishes it from any other group you may be running. The frequency – weekly, twice-weekly, fortnightly, monthly – as well as the day of the week and the time is important to note in terms of monitoring and researching the efficacy of groups of different frequency, days and times.

Seating diagram   Berne (1966) himself does not give a reason as to why he considers his seating diagram to be important. It is an easy, visual method of recording where clients sit and may provide useful information on personal patterns (one client always sits by the door, another often at the edge of the group) as well as interpersonal patterns of behaviour (one client regularly places himself opposite the counsellor, two clients always sit next to each other, another group of three often 'take over' a corner of the consulting room together). Where and how someone sits *may be* an external, behavioural manifestation of their internal state. In order to avoid the danger of insensitive comments or inaccurate interpretations, however, (one client sat by the door as she needed to go to the toilet during the group), I consider these

Therapy Group

Frequency, Day, Time
Date, no. of meeting
Ratio of clients present
Overall (ongoing) percentage
attendance

Group rules

Group contracts

Group working agreements

Individual working agreements

Group structure
– Events and change
   (external group boundary)
   Within the group
   (internal group boundary)

Group process

Group theme/key issue

Nature of the work

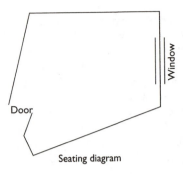

Seating diagram

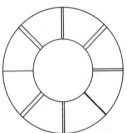

Structural diagram of group
(Berne, 1966)

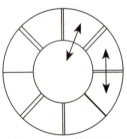

Group process/dynamics
(Berne, 1966)

The group counsellor's self-supervision-in terms of content, strategies and interventions, process and relationship, and counter-transference (Hawkins and Shohet, 1989)

Unfinished business to be carried forward

What next?

patterns significant if supported by and reflective of other con-siderations such as what they are saying (or not saying) such as:

'I can't commit myself to this group.'
'I don't feel I belong here.'
'I need to stand up to you.' ('I want you to see me.')
'We're best friends.' ('Don't get between us.')
[Silence] ('I'm furious.')

16.10.1995, 110th meeting   This information also identifies the group and provides you – and your supervisor – with a quick reference as to how long the group has been meeting. A group meeting for the 110th time will obviously be in a different phase of its development and will require different interventions than a group meeting for the 10th time.

6/6 present, 91% (695/765)   The ratio of clients present to the total number in the group provides a handy reference to the regularity of attendance and commitment. If the ratio shows that there is a number of clients not attending the group on a regular basis, then this issue needs to be addressed by the therapist. The percentage, based on the total number of attendances over the total number of possible attendances, measures group cohesion and may be referred to as the 'group cohesion coefficient'. Like the ratio, if this falls much below 90% then the therapist needs to address the issue of group cohesion and the participation in the group process. Whilst this percentage or coefficient is important in highlighting this significant factor of group cohesion or other-wise, it becomes less sensitive over time. I have therefore found it useful to consider the same percentage also over shorter time periods such as a term and to compare these. When I compared this in one group about which I had begun to feel uneasy, I discovered that the group cohesion coefficient had fallen to around 70% in the Autumn term; this lent some empirical evi-dence to my subjective felt sense. Putting this to the group led to a discussion about genuine difficulties about travel during Winter as a result of which we changed the time of the group.

Contracts, Rules, Working agreements   These – and the differ-ences between them – have been discussed in Chapter 3. I note these as they are agreed and carry them forward so that I can remind myself of them and their current status. Individual contracts are noted on the individual client's record sheet; individual working agreements are noted on both record sheets (for easy and immediate reference).

Group structure and diagram: Events and change (external group boundary); Within the group (internal group boundary)
This is the structural equivalent of the seating diagram in that it places (structures) people next to each other (single line) and identifies alliances, pairings or (sub)groupings (double line) within the group. It also allows for the noting or recording of disturbances to and intrusions on the boundary of the group from outside (externally) (for example, people leaving and coming back into the group, someone knocking on the door, noisy road works outside the building).

Group process and diagram   As regards recording this – and particularly the group process and the nature of the work (below), it is unrealistic to record every transaction or interaction in the group. It is useful at some point to do this – the web (Figure 4.1 below and Table 4.1) is a useful tool for recording the number of interactions in the group. This diagram is useful for recording the most significant transactions either between group members or between a group member and the leader. Again, what constitutes 'significant' will depend on why you consider it to be so. Thus, knowing your criteria (the *why*) for *what* is significant is not only theoretically important but is also of practical relevance.

Group theme/key issue   Based on the view, present across the range of therapeutic traditions, that the group is an entity (or organism) in itself which is more than the sum of its component members, this provides a reminder for the therapist to note what common theme has emerged in the group, for instance, 'there isn't enough time', feeling scared to express anger, sex and sexuality, etc. The key issue for the group relates to the theme and often emerges on reflection, either in or after the group, often in supervision. This might be, respectively: scarcity, safety or taking responsibility for others, and openness. I am more and more interested in commenting on the group theme/key issue *in* the group as this facilitates the group process and, by giving the group an opportunity to discuss such observations, including disagreeing with them, it provides the therapist with feedback as to their reflections and, in turn, it encourages the group to reflect on their own process, for example, 'it seems like we are all being careful with each other tonight'. The group theme or issue reflects the atmosphere of the group at a particular meeting. This may or may not relate and represent the general 'feel' or 'felt sense' of a particular group over time, for example, challenging, supportive, hard, split etc., and which is generally referred to as the group climate.

Nature of the work   As the heading suggests, this describes the nature of the work of the particular group. Reflecting on the different traditions in group counselling (see Chapter 1) and depending on your orientation and interest, you may find it useful to distinguish between work in, through and with the group.

What you record about the specific therapeutic work individuals do *in* the group again depends on why you think that work is important and on your orientation. A classical TA therapist is interested in the therapeutic operations (Berne, 1966) they use in working with a particular client which are related to the nature of the desired therapeutic outcome which, in turn, depends on the therapeutic contract and the therapist's treatment planning. A gestalt therapist working this way in a group is interested in the contact a person has with others in the group and, possibly, in noting any experiments she or he invited the individual to do.

Therapists working *through* the group note the interactions between group members, any contracts or working agreements between group members, and transactions and interventions which are usually three- (or more) handed. TA utilises a concept called a carom (or bounced) transaction whereby the therapist sends a message to one group member through another. This is useful, for example, in the case where someone finds it difficult to accept positive recognition where the therapist might say to another or, indeed, to the group: 'I like what Matt did: he's really talented isn't he?' Such an intervention/transaction needs to be used judiciously, if at all, as it can be experienced as patronising or even shaming – and is manipulative. More generally, in his writings on groups Rogers discusses the therapeutic potential of the group and especially the lay person (non-therapist) to recognise and continue to relate to unhealthy, damaged elements or pathological behaviour; 'I rely on the wisdom of the group more than on my own, and am often deeply astonished at the therapeutic ability of the members' (Rogers, 1970/1973, p. 63).

The therapist who works predominantly *with* the group, whether group-analytic or person-centred (group-centred), places more emphasis on group themes and issues and how they respond to them and the group-as-a-whole.

The group therapist's self-supervision   It is important to make time after a group both to record some notes on the group and to reflect on your own work as group therapist in that particular meeting and with that group over time. This not only benefits your professional development as a group therapist but also often provides further insight (in hindsight) on the group, for instance on the group theme and key issue; such time also helps prepare for formal, external supervision. Using Hawkins and Shohet's (1989) double matrix process model of supervision, you may reflect and make notes under the headings:

- *Content* – what happened in the group? Details about the group and group members.
- *Strategies and interventions* – what interventions I made, what options I had and have.
- *Process and relationship* – what is my relationship with the group? How do I describe it?
- *Self-awareness/self-analysis of counter-transference* – what am I feeling, what is evoked?

(The phenomenon of parallel process – between the therapy and the supervision – is, necessarily, reflected upon in supervision, and the supervisor's counter-transference, in turn, in her/his supervision and/or therapy.)

Unfinished business to be carried forward and What next? These last two questions on the group record sheet serve as an *aide-mémoire* to the therapist. For some, it gives direction, for instance, in drawing the group's attention at the next meeting to any unfinished business, incomplete transactions, etc. For others, less directive, it is an opportunity to hypothesise in preparation for the next group.

Therapy Group

Weekly, on Xday, 7.30–9.30pm
xx.yy.zz 110th meeting
8/8 present, overall 88% (667/770)

Group rules
No violence to self or others in the group

Group contracts
To attend, to respond to each other, to
speak respectfully (criticising the behaviour
not the person)

Group working agreements
None

Individual working agreement
Ed to bring his anger diary

Group structure
– Events and change (external group
boundary)
There was a certain amount of street noise
which intruded on the group this evening

– Within the group (internal boundary)
Dee's first group

Group process
Dee's new presence and the business of
introductions, curiosity and group rules; Ed
not bringing his anger diary evoked issues
about commitment to others, raised
especially by Adam

Seating diagram

Structural diagram of group
(Berne, 1966)

Group process/dynamics
(Berne, 1966)

Group theme/key issue
'Why am I here?', What does it mean to be here? Self as individual and as part of a
group. Gender dynamics: isolated women, men 'fighting'

Nature of the work
This focused on the group itself, its composition, what individuals want from the group and
what being in the group means for each – and all – of them. Most of my comments were
addressed to the group as a whole.

The group counsellor's self-supervision
I am clear about the content of the group and my interventions and my process and
relationship *to/with the group*. I am less clear about my process with and relationship to Ed
and, more obviously, to Dee. Is Ed isolating himself – take this to supervision.

Unfinished business to be carried forward
Gender issues and dynamics

What next?
No especial strategy. Stay alert!

As regards his group therapy interaction chronogram, Cox (1993) suggests taking no more than 20 minutes after the group to complete the recording (and to record events in the tripartite time phases he identifies). Clearly, any system and method of recording groups needs to be realistic in terms of the counsellor's time and the context of their work which, for instance, may include clearing up the room and de-briefing with a co-therapist.

Individual client notes

Recording the group does not preclude having records of or taking notes about the individuals in the group although, again, it is not mandatory (see Bond, 1993). Whether the group members are in individual counselling with the group counsellor or not, some similar consideration of what and why you record is necessary (see above).

Any and every group generates an enormous amount of material – therapeutic or otherwise. The group recording and note-taking discussed so far provides a framework within which the group counsellor may record or note information about the group, its structure, process, dynamics, themes, key issues etc. as well as her/his own reflections on the group. Such recording is necessarily subjective and time-consuming. Another tool in recording groups, which is more objective and which may be used in empirical research, is the group web.

The web

The web (Figure 4.1) is a visual representation of Foulkes' (1964) hypothetical web of communication and relationship in a given group. It shows the number of relationships between individual members in a group (in this case a group of eight plus the group leader). It gives a clear and immediate visual image of the network (or web), common ground and complexity of these interrelationships and is a useful means of recording and identifying them as well as the different levels of verbal (and non-verbal) contribution/s of group members. In terms of recording, an observer sits outside the group (this may also be done by an observer or by the group leader after the group with the aid of audio or video recording) and marks on the appropriate line each time an individual speaks (or has a non-verbal interaction with another group member).

Box 4.4 Group member's individual record/notes

Date of group
xx.yy.zz

Name
Ed

How long in group
47/110 (i.e. just over one year in a group which has been running for three years)

Contract/s
To express his anger.

Working agreements
(From last week) To keep an anger diary for a week (and to bring it to the next group)

Nature of work
Ed did not bring his anger diary (although he reported that he had kept it for some days of the past week) and was confronted about this. He avoided contact and spoke little – when he did speak, he sounded resentful. Other group members got angry with him. I facilitated some of this communication and I reflected on this process, i.e. his passivity and the group's involvement.

Assessment/Stage of process/Treatment planning
Ed seems to have taken a step backwards this week: he is expressing his feelings less, appears more fixed and remote in terms of his experiencing, is clearly anxious and reluctant to communicate about himself, etc. – stage two to three in Rogers' (1961) stages of process. (In terms of TA treatment planning, Ed is at the decontamination stage.)

Self-supervision/Issues for supervision
I don't think I worked well with Ed this evening and think, on reflection, that it was not a good idea for him to agree to someone else's suggestion to keep an anger diary. I think this was too soon and it frightened him. What do I mean by 'too soon'? Am I being overprotective? I don't know. I do know that I get irritated with him when he goes helpless and passive. I feel like I swing from one extreme to another – like others do in relation to him – and did? – and like he does internally? Questions to take to supervision.

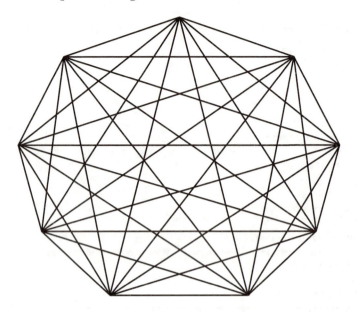

Figure 4.1 *The web*

The recording may be made more sophisticated by use of numbers to indicate the order and number of transactions and the use of S to represent the initial stimulus and R for the response, thus S_1, R_1, S_2, R_2, S_3, R_3, R_4, etc. Obviously it is too time-consuming to use this method of recording for every group or even for the whole of one group; it is nevertheless useful to do this from time to time and to note if contributions and patterns change.

Using the web, in a small group (of 4 people) the pattern of (numbers of) interactions shown in Figure 4.2 was recorded over 20 minutes.

From this web, or what I refer to as a sociomatrix, the contributions of group members, their interactions with each other (and lack of them) and the patterns these create may be easily seen. This may confirm or challenge the perceived dynamics of a particular group.

However, whilst visually and empirically useful, the web does not show the relationship between one or more group members and neither the web nor the sociomatrix shows relationships

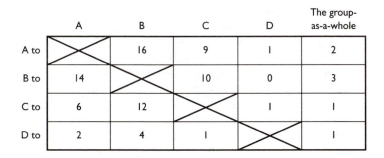

Figure 4.2 *Sociomatrix of communications in a group*

between more than one individual group member or, indeed, relationships with and between other relationships.

The elements of a group

In any group, there are a number of relationships and inter-relationships. What I refer to as the six *elements* of a group thus comprise:

1. *The number in the group*, say, nine, including the group therapist.
2. *The number of relationships between each, individual member* – in a group of nine, eight plus seven, plus six and so on (giving a total of 36).
3. *The number of relationships between one member and a pairing or perceived pairing of two other group members*. Barrett-Lennard (1984) discusses this relationship in terms of a person-centred systems view of families. Thus, in addition to having a relationship with each of say two parents/carers, a child also relates to the relationship between their parents/carers. As regards groups, in this and the remaining elements, the calculation increases geometrically as the numbers increase arithmetically.
4. *The number of relationships between one member and, depending on the size of the group, a (sub-)grouping of more than two other group members*. This is an important phenomenon in all groups, especially in existing groups, and one which, in my view, is often overlooked. Group members Penny, Florian and Mark know each other outside the group, often arrive together and sit next to each other in the group;

theirs is an intense friendship which has its ups and downs at which times they address these in the group. Shileen has difficulties with this strong sub-group: she is jealous and envious; at times wants to 'break in' to this group and, at other times, withdraws from engaging with them *as a group*, although she maintains contact with them as individuals. Thus, in addition to having some relationship with each, she has a clear relationship with their relationship (as do other members of the group).

5. *The number of relationships between more than one member and other members, pairings and groupings of other group members*. This extends the previous element to the situation in which two people are relating (or not) to two others and their relationship. Again, this is noticeable in all groups and particularly so in a couples group (a group comprising only of couples) in which their relationships and interrelationships are very much the focus of the group therapy.

6. *The number of relationships between one or more members and the above relationships* (as identified in 3–5 above). This identifies the element of the group represented by the reaction of a group member to the relationships and interrelationships identified above. Taking the example above, Shileen's relationship to Penny, Florian and Mark has an effect on Frank who says:

> [*looking into the group, somewhere in between where all four are sitting*] God, I just wish you'd sort your relationship out. You know, Shileen [*looking at her*], at times I feel really supportive of you trying to break in to these guys and sometimes I just feel like screaming 'Leave them alone': if they don't want to include you, what are you doing banging your head against a brick wall? And at those times [*looking at the others*] I want you to be just, I don't know, more open to her . . . [*pause, sighs*] and I guess all this reminds me of my family and me being just desperate to be accepted.

In addition to these elements, there is the distinct and unique *quality* of a particular group, the 'feel' of the group *(or group climate)*.

To give an idea of the complexity of a group and the exponential increase of such complexities and potential dynamics, whilst in a group of three the total number of elements is ten, and in a group of four there are 31 such elements, in a group of five this number rises to 231!

Having reviewed various aspects of the working or operational group, my consideration of the developmental life of the group concludes with the next chapter, which focuses on issues of ending in groups and the ending of the group itself.

5

Ending the Group

This chapter concludes the discussion of the developmental phases/stages of groups begun in Chapter 2 by considering the ending of groups, that is, the clarified group imago (Clarkson, 1991) or the adjourning stage (Tuckman and Jenson, 1977) and what I identify as the *historical group imago*, parallel to the mourning phase. These are used to frame discussions about endings, about group members leaving – and the ultimate leaving of a group member or the group counsellor dying, and about what happens after the group meeting and what happens after the group itself ends. I conclude with some reflections on time-limited groups and on evaluation.

The clarified group – adjourning

Although Berne (1963) identifies only four phases of people's subjective experience of groups, Clarkson (1991) takes Berne's comment that 'the real aim of most dynamic psychotherapy groups is to *clarify* the group imagoes of the individual members' (Berne, 1963, p. 241, emphasis added) and suggests a further phase/stage as the clarified group imago in which 'its clarification and differentiation is part of facilitating individuals and groups to live more in terms of their current needs and to reduce or eliminate anachronistic interferences in intimate relationships, whether in the therapy group or life' (Clarkson, 1991, p. 46). This phase is characterised by such clarification and differentiation and by the process of ending. The leader's focus and tasks for this and the post-group phase of the historical group imago are summarised in Table 5.1.

In the therapeutic literature in general comparatively little attention is paid to ending therapy and, with the exception of

Table 5.1 *The group leader's focus and tasks/attitude in relation to phases of group development and common issues – Part III*

Group imago (Berne, 1963)	Stages of group (Tuckman, 1965)	Common issues	Leader's focus	Leader's tasks/attitude
Clarified group imago (Clarkson, 1991)	Adjourning (Tuckman and Jenson, 1977) Termination (Lacoursiere, 1980)	Clarification, differentiation, remembering and recycling	On termination	To 'hold' group's ambivalence, to encourage reminiscing, to facilitate learning, to accept feedback especially criticisms, to end appropriately
Historical group imago	*Mourning*	(In working with individual ex-group members) Separating, distance, maintaining contact/ letting go, denial, anger, regret, hope	On learning, integration and self-support	To accept and encourage mourning

Piper and Klein (1996), this is no less the case in the literature on group therapy – Yalom (1995) devotes less than two pages to it in his otherwise comprehensive work. Elsewhere, I discuss ending psychotherapy from a transactional perspective, drawing a parallel with the psychological literature on attachment and bereavement as, fundamentally, such endings represent a loss of attachment and are a separation (Tudor, 1995). Extending his questioning of group development, Yalom (1995) speculates whether fixed views of developmental stages and especially those based on stages of dying (Kübler-Ross, 1973), represent an avoidance on the part of the therapist of death anxiety – a flight into structure. Nevertheless, there are useful parallels between stages of dying outlined by Kübler-Ross (1973), the phases of mourning as described by Parkes (1972) and Bowlby (1981), and the tasks of mourning as identified by Worden (1983). From these, I suggest a number of tasks in the ending phase of group counselling (see Table 5.2). Again, as with the respective tables in Chapters 3 and 4, although these are formulated as tasks, I do not view them strictly as therapeutic work which *has* to be done, rather as considerations and attitudes on the part of the group counsellor.

As far as these stages or coping mechanisms are concerned, Kübler-Ross (1973), from her study of terminally ill patients, identified five stages of dying (which, although originally derived from the dying, also have resonances and parallels for the friends or relatives involved in and witnessing this process). In addition to these five final stages of life, hope is included as an attribute which persists and indeed which nourishes the person facing death. The (fourth) task of disinvestment which Worden (1983) identifies is put in parenthesis (in Table 5.2) as this is the subject of some debate and dispute in more recent literature on attachment and grieving (see Klass et al., 1996). It is no longer considered necessarily pathological for a survivor to remain attached to their loved one. More humanistic, existential, phenomenological and cultural approaches take account of a survivor's need for continued attachment, the experience and essence of the relationship, the person's subjective experience of attachment, as well as cultural beliefs about and expectations of the survivor, for instance, to hold the personal and collective memory of the departed. A counselling group – fixed term or open – provides an opportunity for members to understand both the process of ending and themselves in this process as well as for working

Table 5.2 *Comparative stages, phases and tasks of death, dying, mourning and ending in group counselling (developed from Tudor, 1995)*

Final stages of life (Kübler-Ross, 1973)	Phases of mourning (Bowlby, 1981; Parkes 1972)	Tasks of mourning (Worden, 1983)	Therapeutic 'tasks' in ending group counselling
Denial and Isolation (partial acceptance)	Numbing	To accept the reality of loss	To remind the group of the ending (and of the beginning)
Anger (rage, envy, resentment)	Yearning and searching	To experience the pain of grief	To accept and facilitate the expression of the group's feelings, to deal with any unfinished business
Bargaining			To understand and confront bargaining (e.g. re. postponement)
Depression	Disorganisation and despair		To accept the group's feelings and to maintain contact with it and them
Acceptance	Greater or lesser degree of reorganisation	To accept the reality of loss, to adjust to an environment in which the deceased is missing	To affirm this acceptance, to encourage remembering and reminiscing and the recycling of issues
Hope		(To withdraw emotional energy and reinvest it in another relationship)	To affirm the client's reorientation, to facilitate and process the learning from this ending, to affirm relearning and self-support strategies
			To finish at the arranged time, to end appropriately

through the establishment, maintenance – and ending – of particular attachments. In a fixed term group, ending is on the agenda from the beginning and group members all experience the ending at around the same time – in a termination (or clarification) phase of the group. In an ongoing, open group, the issue of endings arises each time a member leaves and, because this often evokes strong feelings, is a good reason for group counsellors to require that members give a specified period of notice of their intention to leave the group. Although this appears to be a group rule, it is ultimately not enforceable and you have to rely on the goodwill of the individual to keep to this agreement or contract (see Chapter 3).

The termination phase for the group

Whitaker (1985) identifies certain special features of the termination phase of a group, including the sense of 'time is running out'; experiences of separation and mourning; and opportunities for self-assessment, review and planning. That there is a limited amount of time left can have the effect of the group 'getting on with the business'. The group may avoid the impact of the ending by not referring to it or by decreased attendance – the group cohesion coefficient (see Chapter 4) is useful in monitoring this – in which case the group counsellor's task is to remind the group of the ending. This phase is often characterised by group members recalling other endings and separations and losses, and by beginning to mourn the loss of the group. In this sense the group may provide an important experience of working through 'anticipatory grief' (Lindemann, 1944), which helps the subsequent process of mourning. One important task for the group counsellor at this stage is to facilitate members' evaluation of their time in the group and their learning – this often takes place through reminiscences of earlier phases of the group. For the group counsellor, too, this is a time for reflection and evaluation. Finally, this is a phase in which group members look to the(ir) future and often need to identify strategies for supporting themselves beyond the group. Rice (1996) places all termination or endings in an imaginary four-dimensional matrix, comprising four continua:

- *A continuum of endings* – from dropouts, through early, good-enough and late endings to ''till death do us part' endings.
- *An unconscious–conscious continuum* – from unconscious 'acting out' to conscious choice about endings.
- *A continuum of group events* – which relate to phases of the group which may enhance or precipitate endings.

■ *A continuum of effective to ineffective endings* – based on an assessment about the ending as regards those leaving, those remaining and the therapist.

'Premature termination' is generally applied to individual group members (see next section); however, some counsellors may terminate the group prematurely for a variety of reasons:

■ External factors, such as the counsellor's changing circumstances due to moving home or work, accidents or unforeseen additional responsibilities etc.
■ Personal factors, such as a bereavement or stress or burnout on the part of the counsellor.
■ Interpersonal factors, such as serious disagreements between the counsellor and the group which may occur particularly when a counsellor comes into an existing working group or team (a commonplace in consultancy is that a group may need to get rid of its first consultant).

Individual members leaving

In an ongoing, open group issues about ending are evoked by individual members giving notice and/or leaving. The parallel with experience of loss and bereavement is most pronounced, especially as regards the relationship between the group members: the more ambivalent the relationship, the harder it is for group members to acknowledge the impact of the loss and to process this. Group members generally have two initial reactions to someone announcing that they are leaving the group: one supportive and the other surprised. These reflect their evaluation as to how 'ready' the individual is to leave the group which, in turn, reflects some assessment on their part as to whether the person leaving has completed what they set out to do or to achieve, or is 'better' or 'cured'.

> *Eddie*: I've decided that I'm going to leave the group so I'm giving my notice tonight.
> [*Pause*]
> *Freda*: Oh, that's great. I'm really pleased for you.
> *Gil*: Well, I must admit, I'm surprised. I didn't think you were ready to leave. I always thought Ian would leave before you or me.

Helen: Yes. I feel a bit the way Gil does. Only the other week you were saying how down you felt and that you wanted to get through your depression.

Ian: I don't know what to say. I suppose 'Good luck' is the order of the day and, at the same time, I'm slightly worried about what you'll do without the group.

Eddie: Well I don't know what to say either. I didn't know that my leaving would cause such a fuss . . .

Counsellor: It appears that people have different reactions to you leaving and that you are surprised by their concerns.

These composite responses are not untypical: each is a response to Eddie's announcement; each reflects something about the respondent's relationship to Eddie; and each reflects the respondents' own issues, respectively: pleasing others, competition, being judgemental, rigidity.

The counsellor's response to an individual leaving will vary, partly on the basis of their theoretical orientation and to what extent they link this ending to the beginning through a therapeutic contract or some defined goals of counselling. A transactional analyst will tend to make this link explicit and confront any discrepancy between the agreed therapeutic contract and a premature chosen outcome, whilst a person-centred group counsellor will tend to trust the process of a person leaving on the basis of their belief in the actualising tendency and the proposition that all behaviour is needs-driven and goal-directed. From his research, Yalom (1995) identifies nine major reasons for clients to 'drop out' of group therapy:

1. External factors – physical reasons or external stress.
2. Group deviancy – feeling isolated as the most different from the rest of the group in some way, for example angriest, quietest, most 'ill'.
3. Problems of intimacy – from emotional withdrawal to unrealistic demands for intimacy.
4. Fear of emotional contagion – being adversely affected by others.
5. Inability to share the doctor (counsellor).
6. Complications of concurrent individual and group therapy.
7. Early provocateurs.
8. Inadequate orientation to therapy.
9. Complications arising from subgrouping.

Yalom views the first four reasons as more to do with selection and the last five more about therapeutic technique.

Despite the care with which groups are prepared and established, with or without selection, there is a consistent and relatively high drop out rate in group therapy. In his review of drop out rates amongst sixteen groups across the range of public and private practice and short-term and open-ended groups, Yalom observes group therapy attrition as between 17 and 57 per cent – and an average amongst the groups reviewed of 35 per cent. The negative effect on the person concerned, the others remaining in the group, on the morale of the therapist and on the group's cohesion cannot be underestimated and must be addressed. In an attempt to minimise premature terminations, Bernard (1989) reviews a number of factors:

- The therapist's motivation for referral – which needs to be clear and open.
- The composition of the group – to be mindful of those with a potential for narcissistic injury in the face of being placed with others whom they experience as more seriously disturbed than they are.
- Preparation (see Chapter 2) – which establishes the therapeutic alliance.
- The importance of the early phase of treatment – to include striking a balance between giving and receiving, dealing with conflict, and exploring 'negative' feelings.

Members returning
In an open group, whether drop-in/drop-out or replacement, there is the logical possibility, although rare in practice, of members returning. Returning to a group with its familiar rules, contracts and agreements is a bit like returning home after you have left and still knowing your way around the kitchen – and may well have some developmental therapeutic benefit. Some clients, prior to leaving, may seek reassurance that they can return to the group and the counsellor needs to decide whether this is part of a bargaining phase of ending or, following acceptance of their ending/leaving, a genuine enquiry about future support. In any case, the group counsellor needs to decide in advance how open the 'open' group is and then, in conjunction with the client, what the therapeutic advantages and disadvantages are to their possible return.

The death of a group member

Increasingly, counsellors are becoming more involved in working with clients who are dying, whether this is due to working in particular client groups such as with people with AIDS or the elderly, or in particular settings such as hospitals and hospices, or working with people who are vulnerable and/or at risk of self-harm or suicide. Even if counsellors choose not to work with such groups or in such settings, existing clients may develop serious illnesses and death may occur through accidents.

> Death belongs to life as birth does.
> The walk is in the raising of the foot as in the laying of it down.
>
> (Rabindranath Tagore, 1917 *Stray Birds*)

'Death is psychologically as important as birth and, like it, is an integral part of life' (Jung, 1931/1968, p. 46).

It is a well-founded generalisation that post-industrial Western societies have become protected – and even defensive – against the experiential reality of death (at the same time as the body count escalates on television both in fiction and in reporting fact). Low infant mortality and the breakdown of the extended family mean that children and many adults until mid-life do not experience personal bereavement; the loss of ritual around death and mourning means that we hardly pause to appreciate the breath we draw; the lack of community and interconnectedness (explored in Chapter 7) mean that 'we' do not have a sense of 'our' collective loss: 'any man's death diminishes me, because I am involved in Mankind; and therefore never send to know for whom the bell tolls; it tolls for thee' (John Donne, *Devotions*, 1624). In a rare book exploring dying and creating, written from a Jungian perspective, Gordon (1978) reviews social attitudes to death as well as stories and rites about death drawing on traditions across a number of cultures.

Although, in the usual course of the lifetime of a counselling group it is rare for a group member to die, it is common for group members to be affected by death or the threat of death. When a group member talks about or reports harming themselves or others, or reports the death of a person they know, whether an adult, a child or a baby (still birth, abortion, miscarriage), or when a person in the public sphere dies: all not only affect the person concerned but also evoke responses in the other group members which may be based on their feelings, beliefs and their own personal histories. In the case of a group member threatening to harm themselves or others, in addition to their usual response to and assessment of the client and the situation, the group counsellor needs to be aware that any and every response they make is under the microscopic gaze of the rest of the group and impacts on other group members. In the specific instance of someone in the group dying, some consideration needs to be given to issues involved in and the impact of a member of the group dying and their death.

In the case of it being known that someone is dying, there are two areas of issues: confidentiality and the group contract, and planning. First, there is the question of who knows? Respect for the dying client's wishes and individual confidentiality, especially in circumstances in which they may experience some stigma attached to the cause of their illness, needs to be balanced with the needs of the group in being able to work through its feelings and be in a position to support the group member who is dying. This is especially important in an open group in which new member/s will not have all the information shared by existing group members, a situation that can lead to a sense of there being 'family secrets'. Soon after Viv joined a counselling group a long-established member went on sick leave from the group (with the perceived intention that she would return). For a number of months there was an 'empty chair' left for the absent member whom, it transpired, had a fatal illness from which she later died. Viv got the distinct impression from the other group members – and the group counsellor – that it was inappropriate for her to enquire after the other member. Even after the member's death, although this was acknowledged, neither the circumstances nor the impact on the group and its dynamics were fully explored. Psychologically, this reflects a lack of empathy on the counsellor's part; technically, it was – and is – a problem of clarity in group contracting and rules about confidentiality. It is important to discuss the impact of death not only in order to acknowledge the dead person but also to surface feelings about death in the group, commonly, fears of death and fears of death as a contagion.

The second area of issues concerns the planning with the client and, in this context, with the group, the client's therapeutic care. In the situation in which a group member knows that they are dying and all concerned know this, then some consideration needs to be given to the therapeutic value and effect of the

client's continuing in counselling. Depending on their circumstances, the nature of their illness and the course it takes, it may
be most therapeutic for them to remain in counselling for as long
as they are able. This may help to overcome the emotional
isolation of the dying person (see Eissler, 1955). It may not,
however, be possible for the client to continue to attend counselling and this raises the issue of the counsellor's willingness to visit
and the therapeutic and practical parameters around such arrangements. Equally, given this stage of their life, it may be more
therapeutic for them to withdraw and disinvest from this form of
help and these relationships. At this stage, individual counselling
may be more preferable or appropriate. In all of this, the group
counsellor also needs to take account of the impact – and the
extent of the impact – of this process on the rest of the group,
especially in a closed and/or time-limited group.

In the case of death being unexpected, as with any sudden
death (accident or suicide), the grief reactions on the part of both
group members and the group counsellor are more complex
(Worden, 1983). A sense of unreality, guilt, blame and helplessness
on the part of survivors is often associated with sudden death; in
addition, in the case of suicide, shame, anger, fear and distorted
thinking are common reactions. In both instances of unintentional
and intentional death the need for survivors to understand and
make meaning of the death is often paramount and is the focus of
the group counsellor's work with the group. The counsellor needs
to be especially alert to their own needs and to have good
personal and professional support, for example, through supervision. The counsellor may be involved in additional work with
the relatives and close friends of the deceased and in relation to
medical and legal authorities, such as the Coroner's Court, and
will need to decide what and how much they say in court (see
Bond, 1993, pp. 91–2). Sam had been a member of a closed, fixed-
term counselling group and had attended regularly up until his
death by suicide. Although his death was unpredictable, the
counsellor felt guilty. This was exacerbated by Sam's GP saying, in
retrospect (although with no reference or evidence) that she was
not surprised. In the absence of information and meaning both
the counsellor and the group focused initially on their anger and
then the fragility – and even danger, as they saw it – of counselling, blaming Sam's suicide on the process of counselling itself. In
supervision, the counsellor initially focused on practicalities (of

notes he had from Sam, the status of records, the forthcoming inquest) and on issues of protection for group members between and outside the group. Following this, another group member left and the counsellor noted an avoidance of expressing feelings. Subsequently, in supervision, he reviewed her assessment procedures and the timing and structure of the group as regards holiday breaks, length of meeting, etc. as well as her willingness to disclose more of her own process in order to facilitate the exploration of feeling in the group.

When someone dies there is usually some ritual – a funeral, a memorial/thanksgiving service, a period of mourning. When a client dies, given the confidential nature of the relationship, sharing in the ritual is more complex both for the counsellor and, in the case of a group client, for the other group members. Murphy and de Smith (1997) discuss their involvement with clients who died, their attendance at their respective funerals, and the fact that their maintenance of boundaries such as confidentiality, even after death, led them not to join in or to attend the gathering afterwards as they would otherwise have done. Whilst the maintenance of such boundaries is the counsellor's responsibility, it is less clear that other group members have the same level of responsibility (see Chapter 3), and attending a funeral may help their process of grieving. It is also likely that the group will want to acknowledge the passing of one of its members and make its own ritual.

The majority of counselling textbooks assume the counsellor is well – and alive. Given the increasing number of older practitioners – and counselling and psychotherapy is an activity which you may continue to practise into old age – issues associated with a counsellor dying will become more common. Traynor and Clarkson (1992) review some of the practicalities involved when a psychotherapist dies, including the need for therapists to nominate a professional executor or psychological trustee who, as a part of their duties, will oversee the deceased's professional estate, inform clients and make appropriate referrals. In the case of a group counsellor who dies – and Foulkes died whilst conducting a group – I suggest that it is a part of the executor's role to facilitate or to organise the facilitation of the group. In this way, the group itself may be helped to come to terms with the group counsellor's death and to decide its own future.

The end

Whilst end*ing* is a process, the end is a specific point in time. Whilst increasing attention is paid to the process of ending (and dying), very little is focused on the moment of the end point (or death). Often, in hospitals, whilst excellent care is taken of the dying person and their relatives and friends; once the person dies, however, some medical and nursing staff treat 'it' simply as a body. Especially given a variety of religious and spiritual beliefs about death and the relation of body to mind and spirit, more care and consideration needs to be given to the moment of this end and after. Similar attention needs to be paid to the moment of the end of the group. How does the group counsellor say 'Goodbye'? Do you even say 'Goodbye?'

> *William*: [*Silent, close to tears*]
>
> *Xena*: Well I want to thank you all for being such a great group. I'm going to miss you.
>
> *Yvonne*: In a way I don't believe that this is happening and that we're not going to meet again. It's hard to accept.
>
> *Zoë*: I agree . . . and at the same time it's also right . . . we've come to an end, at the end of the year.
>
> *Counsellor*: Thank you. I wish you all '*Tante buone cose* – All good things'. . . . That's it.

'Acceptance of death is truly the final test for the acceptance of life' (Gordon, 1978, p. 25).

One group ended, after five years of meeting regularly, with a poem read by one of the group members.

> *A Ritual to Read to Each Other*
> If you don't know the kind of person I am
> and I don't know the kind of person you are
> a pattern that others made may prevail in the world
> and following the wrong god home we may miss our star.
>
> For there is many a small betrayal in the mind,
> a shrug that lets a fragile sequence break
> sending with shouts the horrible errors of childhood
> storming out to play through the broken dyke.
>
> And as elephants parade holding each elephant's tail,
> but if one wanders the circus won't find the park,
> I call it cruel and maybe the root of all cruelty
> to know what occurs but not recognize the fact.

And so I appeal to a voice, to something shadowy,
a remote important region in all who talk:
though we could fool each other, we should consider –
lest the parade of our mutual life get lost in the dark.

For it is important that awake people be awake,
or a breaking line may discourage them back to sleep;
the signals we give – yes or no, or maybe –
should be clear: the darkness around us is deep.

William Stafford, 1977, *Stories that could be True*

The historical group imago – mourning

The historical group imago is the image/s a person has of a group once she or he has left the group. Although this only emerges and may be worked through after a person has left a group, perhaps in individual counselling or in a subsequent group, as with the provisional group imago and the pre-forming stage, it properly belongs to consideration of groups. It both represents and affects, for instance, how an individual experiences their withdrawal from the group, their ability to separate and distance themselves from the group – or not, and their ability to disinvest their emotional energy from the group and reinvest it in new relationships (see Figure 5.1). In Chapter 1, I described the historical group imago in relation to Alpha (see Figure 1.7).

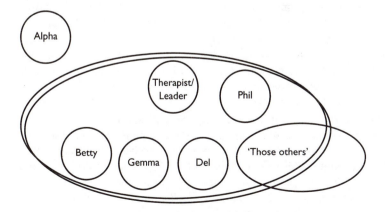

Figure 5.1   *Alpha's second historical group imago*

Figure 5.1 shows another historical group imago – again Alpha's – making the point that our historical imago, like any other, changes over time: 'those others', some known and some unknown, have moved further into what is now their group. This is as useful a description of our relationship with family and work groups as it is of counselling groups of which we have been members. We all have historical imagoes of many groups; the issue is what we do with them. In talking with one person about a group to which I had belonged I 'forgot' that she was a current member. Having apologised for overlooking her in this respect, I drew on this concept of the imago and considered what this oversight might mean about me, her, my relationship with her, and my relationship with the group and its members, historically or currently. In working with groups and with individuals, it is inevitable that they and we deal with their (and our) historical group imagoes.

Postlude I – after the group meeting
A third area for my enquiry after the pre-group time and what happens outside the group (see previous chapters and Appendix 2) was on the time after the group meeting, after I, the therapist, have left. The group may spend some time together as a whole or break up into pairs and small groups; some may leave, others may stay. The length of time varies: one group disbands and leaves quickly, another stays together for 20 minutes, one group stays regularly for a further hour – and once stayed on for two hours (the equivalent length of the therapy group itself). Although pre-group time is not strictly an alternate group meeting (see Chapter 3), clients may well experience the therapeutic value of 'staying on', which is discussed here as regards the nature and the purpose and value of this time.

The nature of post-group time   From their reports, how long group members stay on appears to depend on whether the discussion is of interest or importance to them. The main differ-ence from the group meeting itself, from the alternate group and from the pre-group time, is that the group members spend this time predominantly in pairs or small groups, with often two or three conversations conducted at the same time. Some clients experienced this time as more interactive, with more movement (people changing places) than during the therapy group. One client said there was 'less of an audience' in this time. What group members experience as the confrontation, encounter, 'optimal anxiety' or 'safe emergency' of the therapy group itself is replaced by a lighter, 'hands off' atmosphere in which 'not everything we say matters in quite the same way'. Most group members responding to the research described this time as more casual, more comfortable and more relaxed – 'it's more like being with an understanding group of friends' – in which they felt more support, less challenged and less pressure 'to get it right'. Some compared this time with the pre-group time, in which generally people talked in/as a group, experiencing each other after the group as more relaxed and connected and less reserved and superficial than before the group. Clients in different groups reported different experience of how the post-group time had changed over the life of the group or of their membership of the group. For members in one group the nature of the time had not particularly changed since the group had stayed on after the first group meeting; in another group a pattern emerged: for the first two years the group or some of the group used to go to one of the local pubs but since tended to stay in the consulting room 'without props . . . and stay connected'. In another group this time had developed over time: initially the group had disbanded immediately the therapist left the room, then occasionally it began to remain together for a while until there was an increasing trend to stay on after the group. One client, talking about this time, wrote : 'there is a small, umbilical link after the group . . . even with people who I am not so friendly with outside the group'. As the group sees its ending and/or members leave, such contact tends to dissipate.

The purpose and value of post-group time Respondents identified a number of purposes for the post-group time:

- A continuation of the group, both
  - Socially, in having more social contact, 'getting to know more about people', and
  - Therapeutically, in giving more details or additional feedback, several group members commented that it sometimes continues as therapy, almost formally – although

　　　　another commented wryly that 'I leave if it gets thera-
　　　　peutic'.
■　Reinforcing individual relationships.
■　Ending – by 'finishing off anything I want to say to another
　　　group member', having time to celebrate the group, and
　　　saying goodbye.

The principal value of this time appears to be time itself: a
number of group members valued the fact that they had more
time for themselves and each other due to breaking up into pairs
and smaller groups. The second value is a therapeutic one in that,
as with the pre-group time, it raises issues which may then be
worked with: one group member reported that they felt lonely
during this time, another acknowledged that they were tempted
to be more polite. Several discussed departure time: one did not
like to be first to leave, a number commented that ending and
leaving were harder than leaving at the end of the formal group.
One client made the link back to therapy: 'as my relationships
with the members of the group develop, I want to stay on more
and then take any difficulties back into the group'.

Postlude II – after the group
These reflections on ending were written two weeks after I had
finished a psychotherapy group which I had facilitated for five
years, on the evening and at the time it usually met.

> I am sitting here on Xday . . . two weeks after the last group. I spent
> last Xday going out, I felt quite liberated: the first time apart from
> holidays (and only recently) that I'd been able to go out in the evening
> on an Xday for years. In some ways I am only now just – or fully –
> realising the commitment, and the extent and personal cost of that
> regular commitment. I wonder about the therapeutic value of such
> continuity. I know that as a group member myself there was something
> enormously important for me, knowing that the group was there and
> was reliable – and that it had a history going back before I joined and
> that it continued after I left. With this group I know – by the fact that
> the numbers had dropped over a period of time, by the withdrawal of
> energy and commitment (reflected in the decision to meet fortnightly
> rather than weekly), and by a lack of interest in the form of new clients
> – that it had run its course. On the other hand if I/we had kept it
> meeting weekly, maybe that would have generated more – or, at least,
> different – interest. I think there's an issue here – maybe for me, maybe
> a general one – about how to sustain interest, energy and commitment
> in an open group over a long period of time. The other possibility is to

run probably closed groups over a fixed period but then I would have to put more time into publicity and recruitment. I miss the people I have worked with over years as a group. I sometimes wonder about having a recall group meeting, a day perhaps, of all the people who have ever been in the group – like the reunion of a band! What will I do with my time? What will they do with their time. The (my) temptation is to fill it. Rather I want to have more unstructured time. How was the group? Was it a success? What do I mean by that? I think most people left well – so that's a criterion for success?. Most had achieved what they wanted from the *group* (another criterion), although not all had got what they wanted from *therapy* and some went into and some continue in individual therapy. I think the limited evaluation shows that the group members experienced a number of therapeutic factors. Is there a way of making this process more intense? Yes. Is such intensity desirable or does this promote a quick plunge into the psyche rather than the integration of understanding and change over time? I don't know. I do know that I have favoured continuity over time. Do I want to do it, to set this kind of group up again? Not at the moment. I want a rest and then to think about how I want to work – probably in intensive group situations, perhaps more in groups than with individuals, with created (that is, therapy or work-shop) groups but also with existing groups (families, households, teams, organisations, communities).

Time-limited groups

This brief discussion of time-limited groups is appropriately placed here as the end of the group is built in to the structure, understanding, experience and imago of the group. Time-limited individual therapy ranges from the one-off session (whether plan-ned as such or not) to around sixteen sessions; for a review of the literature, see Feltham (1997b). Equally, time-limited groups may run for one session, for example, a marathon, through anything from six to fifteen sessions, to a group which meets for a year, that is, around forty meetings. Yalom (1995) suggests that inpatient groups may be regarded as having the lifespan of a single group.

There is a substantial literature on time-limited individual ther-apy informed predominantly, although not exclusively, by rational emotive behaviour therapy, multi-modal therapy, brief solution-focused therapy and cognitive analytic therapy (see Feltham, 1997b). Although, traditionally, these focus more on individual rather than on group therapy, these approaches may be applied to group settings (for example, Scott and Stradling, 1998). There are a number of reasons for offering time-limited groups:

- *Context* – Therapists working in agencies may only be able to offer time-limited/short-term contact.
- *Economics* – Time-limited and especially short-term therapy is more economically viable both for private clients and for funders/managers in the public sector.
- *Efficiency* – Time-limited groups may be more efficient in effecting change, cure etc. than long-term individual or group therapy. Marcovitz and Smith (1983) review patients' positive perceptions of curative factors in short-term psychotherapy; Yalom (1995) comments, however, that research in this area is rudimentary and equivocal.
- *Client preference* – In time-limited individual therapy there is some evidence that many clients do not take up all the allocated sessions. Similarly, given the drop-out rate from groups (discussed above), many group clients are in effect choosing a briefer therapy than the therapist intended.
- *Group cohesion* – Setting the time limit on a group may help to foster group cohesion, expecially if the group is homogeneous (Klein, 1985), and less drop out amongst clients or fatigue on the part of the therapist.
- *Flexibility* – Time-limited groups give both client/s and therapist greater flexibility in suiting the structure of therapy to the client's process, for example a series of time-limited groups, different forms and combinations of therapy.

There is a danger that time-limited groups are viewed as a truncated form of 'real' group therapy; this is not the case and there are specific considerations in establishing and facilitating time-limited groups – developed from Yalom (1995) and MacKenzie (1996):

- *Selection* – To take account of clients' suitability to the format of the time-limited group.
- *Type of group* – A time-limited closed group increases group cohesion.
- *Preparation* – Yalom warns against any 'finessing' of the group therapist's preparation and emphasises the importance of the pre-group individual meeting which helps focus the client.
- *Focus* – The group leader needs to maintain the focus and task of the group, including reminding the group of its time-limited nature and existence, especially at the beginning of the group

and in the last half of the group. Both Yalom and MacKenzie suggest that the therapist provides focused inverventions.

- *Leadership* – The role of the leader of time-limited groups appears more active and interventive. Yalom asserts that the group leader needs to manage time, maintain the focus of the group, encourage the transfer of learning, and to clarify that the treatment is not complete. MacKenzie argues that the leader is responsible for forestalling premature termination. Dies (1985) expresses some concern about the role of the leader in short-term group therapy, which may be experienced as manipulative rather than facilitative.
- *Themes* – MacKenzie also argues that the leader needs to reinforce certain common termination themes such as deprivation, resentment, anger, rejection, grief and loss.
- *Final session* – The group therapist needs to decide whether or not this should be structured.
- *Follow-up* – A follow-up session may encourage the continued application of what has been learned in the time-limited group, the value of which continues beyond the limited lifespan of the group.

Evaluation – an environmental framework

Although there are a plethora of procedures based on empirical research methodology by which you can research and evaluate clients' – and therapists' – experience of group counselling, it is significant to note that Yalom (1995) is sceptical about outcome research and Corey (1995) comments that he ultimately relies on subjective measures such as self-reports, as represented by my own research. Here I offer a framework by which to understand clients' experiences of group counselling and within which specific research may be located with specific reference to the group as an immediate environment.

The group as a space set aside   At one level, a counselling group provides a physical and psychological *temenos*, a space set aside or 'marked off from common uses' (Liddell and Scott, 1901) (see Adler, 1979; Embleton Tudor and Tudor, in preparation). This space is bounded, marked, psychologically, by such boundaries as confidentiality. It may be experienced as a container in which the client can feel, say and do what they cannot, or believe they cannot in the rest of their lives. For clients abused as children, a group may be more safe than individual counselling or individual counselling alone. The *temenos* as vas (Adler, 1979) or crucible represents the transformative nature of therapy. In this space, the group focuses on working as a group, forging a bond with the group counsellor and each other around common and agreed goals and tasks, however loose.

The group as a microcosm of other groups and group situations
Most people live and work in groups. Our experiences in and reactions to such groups inform our subsequent experiences and behaviour. Thus, a counselling group may be viewed as a forum in which we can replay our actions and reactions, analyse them and make decisions about changing negative or unhelpful patterns. In comparing individual and group psychotherapy, Berne (1966) describes groups as an opportunity for clients 'to exhibit a wider repertoire of spontaneous behavior' (p. 43), which is then open to transactional analysis – literally, the analysis of transactions between group members. Many clients find it helpful and easier to explore and to make changes first in a group and later to generalise these and to experiment outside the group in the rest of their lives, in other group situations.

As a part of this, the group counsellor offers a unique opportunity for clients to explore issues of leadership and authority. One of the differences between counselling groups and other groups is that the former are explicitly set up and, in some way, *led*. This acknowledges the ultimately unequal therapist–client relationship and, by implication, the inequality of other relationships in life. This leads some, such as Masson (1989), to reject therapy. Others consider issues of power, authority and influence an essential part of the human social condition and, therefore, the opportunity to explore these in a safe, therapeutic group environment essential to people's development.

The group as a reparative environment   Given people's individual histories and experiences in groups, the prospect of joining – and, indeed, their experience of – a counselling group will vary. For some it will be frightening or worrying: one client expressed his ambivalence about 'getting lost in the crowd'. For others it may be easier than being in individual psychotherapy: another client found it easier to 'hide in the open'. For yet others, counselling groups are an opportunity to (learn how to) make contact or connections with others and to become social: another client described the loneliness and isolation of individual therapy. In all these instances a therapy group offers a reparative experience. Perhaps the most significant difference between working individually and working therapeutically in groups is that the work is witnessed by a group. Given the issues of abuse and shame which many clients bring to counselling, the role of such witnessing is a crucial one.

The group as an equalising experience   This is almost an opposite reason to that of working with issues of power, influence and authority. It is based on the value of providing an environment in which people may explore the possibility of and experience mutual and equal relationships, especially across differences such as gender, sexuality, culture, race, class, disability, age etc. Some clients want to work exclusively in homogeneous groups of women, gay men, lesbian and bisexual people, black people etc. in order to counter-balance their predominant experience of patriarchal, heterosexist and racist influences. Some male clients with whom I work are or have been in individual psychotherapy with a female psychotherapist and want to balance this experience with (a) working with a man and (b) being in a men's psychotherapy group.

From time to time, the group may be experienced as in some sense beyond the individual and even the group itself. For some, the experience of interacting (or transacting) with others and of being in a group becomes, over time, more an experience of belonging in a deep way. Groups can be a matrix in which being, becoming and belonging are all experienced both by individual members and by the group itself. For some, groups are a powerful, a transforming and even a transpersonal experience.

This framework reflects Gelso and Carter's (1985, 1994) components of counselling relationships – the working alliance, the transferential and the real relationship – with the subdivision of the transferential into the transferential and the reparative and the addition of the transpersonal 'moment' (see Clarkson, 1990, 1995b; Tudor, 1999b). During their lifetime, therapeutic groups may offer possibilities for experiencing all these therapeutic relationships and, as such, this component model offers itself as an integrative organising framework for the evaluation of clients' experiences of group counselling.

Having discussed practical aspects of the group through its life cycle, the next three chapters consider groups in residential settings, the wider social context of groups and the education, training, personal development and supervision of the group counsellor.

6 *Groups in Residential Settings*

Jenny Robinson

This chapter considers the implications of groups in residential settings – which constitutes a particularly intense psychological environment. Not only does the residential context affect the group, but what happens in the group creates ripples within the home or institution as a whole. Thus, in addition to doing the work within the group itself, the group leader has to attend to the interaction between the group and the immediate – and wider – environment. In this chapter, drawing on my experience as a psychologist in a prison and now as a psychotherapist in a therapeutic community, I discuss the significance of the residential context as regards contracts, the use of groups in a therapeutic community, the therapeutic implications of working with clients with different diagnoses, the importance of group dynamics, and, finally, the example of a specific therapeutic community: the Trident Housing Association Therapeutic (THAT) Community.[1]

The significance of the residential context: contracts

Every group takes place within a wider context and this context is always important. This is both physical (that is, the building and room within which the group meets) and psychological. The psychological context is determined in the first place by the group's task, for example, training, assessment, psychotherapy. It includes the authority structure which supports the group, the relationships group members may have outside group meetings, as well as the reactions of family, friends and colleagues to each member's involvement.

English (1975) points out that people running groups within any organisation are subject to a three-cornered contract (Figure 6.1). The leader(s) has a contract, either explicit or implicit, with group members to provide them with a service, for example, training or counselling. The leader also has a contract with managers (the 'great powers') who have engaged them to provide this, or at least agreed that this service be provided. Thirdly, the managers and, say, employees, students, patients also have explicit (and implicit) contractual obligations and expectations. It is important to note that the goals of these two sets of people may be somewhat different and that an unwary group leader may find themselves trying to juggle two different and not very compatible contracts. So, for example, an employer might expect that a group set up for training will improve performance on the job, whereas the employees who make up the group may see it primarily as a chance for a break from routine. A college may engage a counsellor to set up a group to assist students who are experiencing emotional distress in the *hope* (often the sign of an implicit contract) that this will improve their performance academically.

Figure 6.1   *The three-cornered contract (English, 1975)*

The counsellor, however, may find themselves assisting a student in a decision to leave the college because their focus is on the psychological well-being of each individual.

This concept of a three-cornered contract is especially useful in a residential context and helps to highlight and clarify the issue of running groups within a residential establishment where the focus of work within the group may differ from that of the institution as a whole. One important element in the psychological environment of a group is the support which it receives – or fails to receive – from the powers of the residential management. It is essential that backing is provided at a high enough level to supply the necessary resources, protection and encouragement, otherwise the whole enterprise may be sabotaged by staff who either see it as unimportant or are hostile to the idea. In a prison, for example, a group or group programme needs official recognition and support from the governor downwards. Only then can the leader be sure of being provided with a room on a consistent basis, that the prisoners involved in the group will be brought together at the right time and that only a real emergency will be used as a reason for cancelling a particular meeting.

Not only does the residential setting affect the group in terms of demands that the group fit in with the overall schedule, needs and philosophy of the home or institution, but the group itself will also affect the rest of the institution, particularly in that it is likely to set up some psychological dynamics, among both residents and staff. In prison, those involved in a group may be seen as soft, crazy or sucking up to the authorities; there may be anxieties amongst the inmates that other group members will reveal information to the authorities by way of the group; they may be scapegoated, or envied as having gained a privilege. No matter what happens, an emotional climate will be created *around* (as well as within) the group, the complexities of which both members as well as the leader have to deal with and manage.

Managers of residential settings are invariably well aware of this interaction between a group and the surrounding psychological environment. Even when enthusiastic advocates of groupwork, they may be cautious about introducing someone from the outside to run a group for residents or staff or of supporting one of their own staff in setting up a group. They recognise that, no matter what benefits flow from a group, it is also likely to 'rock the boat' at some level, to create more work for staff at times and often likely to cause hassle and anxieties for the managers themselves. As part of their contract, managers will expect group leaders to be sensitive to the overall residential task and to communicate to residential staff any information about group members relevant to that task. This, in turn, has implications for the contract between the leader and group members, particularly with regard to confidentiality.

It is part of the responsibility of the leader of any group to establish a boundary around the group and create a safe space within which members can do the work they have come to do (see Chapters 2 and 3). Unless they feel secure they will not allow themselves to be vulnerable enough to use the group productively. This boundary will be concerned with time and place but also, very importantly, with confidentiality. The establishment and maintenance of such a boundary is particularly vital in a residential setting because institutions can often be intrusive and also wary about demands for privacy. Residential institutions tend to care for people who are the most vulnerable members of society in terms of age, illness or disability or to contain those who are most at risk of harming themselves or others. It is understandable that such institutions become anxious about internal boundaries which may restrict the flow of information between a group and the rest of the establishment. Also, confidentiality is a particular issue because opportunities and invitations to gossip outside the group will be so readily available.

In such a setting the duty of a group leader to pass on certain information is inescapable. If a group member leaves the group upset and vulnerable, then the leader needs to consider not only the needs for protection and support of that individual but also the need for information of those responsible for caring for, and managing that person outside the group. The contract between the leader and the residential authorities – and other colleagues – therefore needs to be very clear concerning the leader's responsibility for communicating information outside the group. The need for communication is obvious when safety is the issue. Group leaders, particularly of groups for people who are disturbed or potentially volatile, have to assume some degree of responsibility for group members. If the leader believes that a member is likely to do damage to themselves or someone else it is clear that she/he has a responsibility to pass on this concern to relevant care staff.

Sometimes, however, residential authorities expect the leader to share other information from within the group with those outside. This is either a legitimate need (that is, one relevant to the overall residential task) or an understandable, but illegitimate desire to benefit from any disclosure of personal information which occurs within the group. The leader needs to accommodate the authorities in the first case, while resisting invitations to become some kind of psychological 'spy' on management's behalf. In a prison, the authorities are not only concerned about individual *safety* but also expect the group leader to communicate any information with implications for *security*. In the case of a penal institution, the third side of the triangle in the three-cornered contract involves a contract with 'society-at-large' (represented by the government through the Home Office) for and to whom the Governor and staff are providing a service of containment. In this case, although there is a duty of care for and protection towards prisoners, elements of the contract on the management–public side of the triangle take precedence over any contract(s) between the prison authorities and the prisoners themselves. The complexities involved in this kind of example may be seen as a series of overlapping three-handed contracts (see Tudor, 1997a).

Of course, the members of any group need to know what information from within the group the leader will give to people outside and to whom it will be given and in what circumstances. It is rare for any group to have a confidentiality boundary which is totally inviolable: leaders of counselling groups take group material for supervision and group members need to know the limits of confidentiality (see BAC, 1997, B.2.3.). Members of a prison group need to know in advance that not only will the leader need to act on information concerning the safety of individuals but also that if they talk about escape plans or drugs being smuggled in the leader will also have to pass on this information.

It is part of the responsibility of the leader to demonstrate that they understand and respect the tasks of the institution as a whole and provide reassurance to all that they will support these appropriately. All staff involved need to be confident that the group leader will keep their contract with the institution as assiduously as their contract with group members – and, for group members, this is true probably with the emphasis the other way around.

The most important thing about the boundaries around the group is not how tight they are in terms of how little information is allowed out but that they are clear and that, once established, they are rigorously maintained. This does not mean that they cannot be amended – sometimes this is necessary in the light of experience – but that any process of re-negotiation is also clear. It does mean that boundaries need to be explicit and that there needs to be a demand made on all concerned to take them seriously. Members of institutional groups understand implicitly that a group leader has responsibilities to the management as well as to them and will be suspicious if this seems to be discounted and, ultimately, may not feel safe. They may not like that the group leader passes on to care staff that a group member talked about having suicidal impulses, for example, but will expect and respect that they are consistent about keeping all the contracts they have made.

The use of groups in a therapeutic community

In this section, I consider a residential environment where groups are an inherent and central part of the overall regime: that of a therapeutic community (TC), although the implications are relevant to other settings such as a psychiatric hospital or a boarding school.

A therapeutic community, a termed first coined by Main (1946), is an extreme example of the residential use of groups; as such it is virtually impossible to imagine such a community where groups are not an essential element. In his book *Community as Doctor*, Rapoport (1960) includes democracy as one of four ideological guiding principles of the Henderson Hospital TC (for a discussion of which see Chapter 7); again, the idea of a TC that does not have at least community meetings is almost unthinkable and most have other types of groups as well.

The way in which a TC differs from every other residential setting is that the main confidentiality boundary is round the community as a whole, rather than any individual group subsumed within it. In a hospital, for example, all staff may have access to patients' records and confidential personal information is likely to be discussed in case conferences. However, in a therapeutic community residents share a great deal of personal information with one another and with all others who are included within the community boundary: staff, volunteers, trainees etc. There is an expectation that residents will support and help each other with the problems which have brought them there and in order to do this they need to know and understand these problems. This contract – explicit or implicit – of mutual help between residents is one of the features which distinguishes a TC from a residential home with an in-house psychotherapy programme.

Another is the fact that the therapeutic community aims to provide a milieu which is therapeutic in itself. Every aspect of the regime is designed to provide safety and opportunities for learning and change for the particular client group for whom the community caters. Therapy almost always takes precedence over anything else other than safety or physical illness: to take a common example from THAT Community, if at the end of a meal it becomes clear that people are upset, scared or angry, then holding a group to find out what the problem is and what needs to be done to solve it takes priority over the washing up. (For more about the design of such a therapeutic milieu and how the different components fit together, see below.)

Here it is sufficient to note that different types of groups are likely to be part of this therapeutic structure. Typically these are likely to include community meetings, staff meetings and therapy groups. Community meetings are business meetings where matters of communal interest are discussed. These might include planning a party, sorting out a problem about laundry and/or deciding how best to deal with a disruptive resident. Staff meetings and groups not only provide an opportunity to discuss the needs and problems of residents, both as a group and individually, and to deal with staff business, they need also to be a forum where staff dynamics and interpersonal difficulties can be sorted out and where staff get support, supervision and in-house training.

Therapy groups come in different shapes and sizes. In a small community such as ours everyone attends the same therapy group, but this is by no means always the case. Some communities have a mixture of large marathon groups which meet for, say, half a day, and shorter, smaller, more intimate therapy groups where a few residents form very close therapeutic relationships with their therapist and with one another. The latter tend to be the places where the more sensitive problems are addressed. Most TCs also provide specialist groups focusing on a particular method (for example, art therapy, bodywork, psychodrama) or a particular type of client group or issue (newcomers group, leavers group, eating disorders group).

Communities differ about how far they make use of individual therapy alongside groups. Some communities, such as the Arbours Crisis Centre, appear to offer formal psychotherapy only in individual sessions (Berke, 1990; Berke et al., 1995); the Henderson Hospital, on the other hand, does all therapeutic work exclusively in groups (see Rapoport, 1960). At THAT Community we offer a mixture of both groups and individual therapy sessions for our residents, which has some advantages. Often when new people join they are scared at the idea of talking about their problems in a group. Providing individual sessions as well gives us flexibility to create a personally tailored programme for each new resident which can be reviewed and amended as their therapy proceeds. However, the relationship between groups and individual sessions needs to be managed carefully otherwise it can create some problems of its own (see Chapter 2).

One of the strengths of our community is that our therapeutic approach is a dual one: we have a strong group culture and at the same time offer individuals the opportunity to make and work within attachments with particular members of staff (their 'attachment person'). The reason that we offer both is because of the nature of the client group with whom we work: they are confused, fragmented, regressive and dependent. Often they have no secure sense of self and do not know whether they and other people are real; invariably they have a history of disturbed attachments; usually they have been given a psychotic or borderline diagnosis. They need the experience of having a new, close, healthy, therapeutic relationship within which they can build up trust and can receive some of the nurturing which was missing in their past (see Rawson et al., 1994; Robinson, 1998). Bowlby (1981) talks about such a relationship in terms of a secure base: this describes very accurately what we aim to provide. Nevertheless, this is difficult and risky work which can only be done safely within a supportive and protective environment, which is where the group and community culture becomes important. Because of their past difficulties in forming and maintaining relationships our clients have learned survival strategies which include bullying, threatening and manipulation. Often their expectation is that they will be rejected sooner or later and so they will reject before they can be rejected. Both they and their attachment person need a lot of support if their work is to have a chance of reaching a satisfactory conclusion. It is part of the role of the community as a whole to challenge dysfunctional relationship strategies and psychological games. It is another part to provide comfort and reassurance when the going gets tough and, for example, a resident runs off or hurts themselves. Safety and protection are the main reasons that we have community values about openness and truthfulness in communication (Rapoport's 'communalism'). Sometimes a resident needs the chance to talk about a problem they are ashamed of until they find enough courage and get enough reassurance to take it to group. Sometimes staff too will decide to keep a particular worry to themselves, and that it is their job to hold that particular anxiety and not to pass it on to residents. Both these situations are understood and seen as acceptable, although in general the rule is 'no secrets'; the supporting beliefs which go along with this are 'That nothing is so bad that it can't be talked about' and 'That problems, no matter how awful, can be faced and solved'.

Implications of working with clients with different diagnoses

There are differences between TCs in terms of what kinds of group meeting they include in their regime and whether or not they use a combination of individual and group therapy. These and other differences are determined to a large extent by the clients for which they cater. In this section I discuss the necessity of using different types of groups to respond to the needs of different clients, identified by diagnosis, using the example and my experience of differences between working with clients with personality disorders and those with psychotic structures. In talking (and writing) in these terms I am aware of adopting a particular frame of reference about diagnosis, psychopathology and reality. In doing so, I am concerned that all clients deserve and receive the best possible therapy and care for them, *and* this must be of a type and method which responds to their particular needs with counsellors or psychotherapists skilled at using these methods.

Earlier, I cited the TC at the Henderson Hospital; the reason that all the therapy there is conducted in groups is that it specialises in treating clients with personality disorders. Such clients have serious problems in relating to people in authority and will attempt to seduce or threaten anyone they perceive to be in this position. A favourite strategy is 'making fools of parents', that is, setting up people whom they see as being in a position of authority over them, such as staff members, to look foolish. People with personality disorders will also try to cause dissension amongst staff. In saying this I am not ascribing blame or bad motivation to them or anyone else: people with personality disorders are no more responsible for having grown up with this personality deficit than psychotic clients are to blame for their psychosis. Catching and confronting these psychological games is an important part of working therapeutically with such clients. It means that it is desirable that all therapy is done publicly with plenty of witnesses. Of course, the real experts at spotting and responding to such strategies will be other clients with similar problems, so, in groups, it is often other residents who make the most telling interventions. Also, because of their mistrust of authority figures, residents with personality disorders often take more notice of what their peers say to them than of any pro- nouncements by staff.

By contrast, people with a psychotic disorder want and expect staff to be in charge. They are generally scared if they manage to catch staff out (rather than triumphant as is the person with a personality disorder). In a therapy group it is important for such residents that the therapist is in control and that the group time is structured and predictable, for instance, that people take turns to do their 'work' while others listen and respond to them. They tend to seek, accept and make use of parenting and reparenting from staff (see Robinson, 1998). As was noted earlier, these residents, for example those who come to THAT Community where I work, are regressive and dependent and usually desperate for someone to tell them what to do and how to do it, with the hope of finding a way of making their lives work instead of failing all the time as they have in the past. Residents who are psychotic will feel safe with structure and predictability.

This will not work with residents with a personality disorder. In this type of situation they will be quick to 'learn the ropes' and find ways of using them to their advantage. What helps a resident with a personality disorder to feel safe is to be understood and not allowed to get away with manipulating others. Invariably they will test and re-test staff to find out whether they can be conned or persuaded to break the rules. One implicit question they always ask of counsellors is 'Are you quick enough and smart enough to catch me?' Another such question is 'Do you really mean you are honest?' If a staff member does agree to something they should not agree to or lies, then the resident will have confirmed yet again a pathological belief that everyone is basically corrupt or corruptible and that those in authority are no better than they are. In the conversation of most prison inmates, for instance, all police officers and judges are 'bent'.

From time to time, the resident with a personality disorder will catch out a member of staff who will, in turn, in effect fall flat on their face. A staff member in this situation has to recognise that this will happen and be prepared to get up, dust themselves down and carry on. What helps is to acknowledge in advance to residents that this will be the case. As they are masters of manipulation there is no therapeutic disadvantage in acknowledging this fact; thus a staff member might say 'Sometimes you will lie to me and I will believe you and will be taken in, and sometimes you will tell me a truth which sounds like a lie and I will doubt you and again you will have got me. However, this won't make me believe I've failed.'

Up to now, we have been considering the differences between these two client groups with regard to their relationship with authority and what they need from staff. Another important difference concerns the way in which they get stimulus – one of the six human hungers identified by Berne (1970/1973). Psychotic residents will get this from other people in terms of recognition and comfort. Stimulation from contact with others is unlikely to mean much to those with personality disorders because, in general, their relationships are experienced as shallow. Their stimulation comes from drama and excitement which they will create if it is not provided for them. Again this difference has implications for the therapeutic environment and the kinds of groups required by each, and what happens in them. Psychotic clients need to form attachments and work within them. They seek security and get this from being in an environment which is familiar and compact enough to be manageable; they wish to feel 'held' by the psychological environment and to have help in containing what they often experience as internal chaos; they find any change difficult to cope with and respond with what we describe as 'loss of structure' – a heightened level of anxiety which persists until they have adapted to the change. Invariably, they are fearful of being abandoned and rejected and, through confrontation and care, recognise their need for contact with other people, for love and attention. They need a therapeutic milieu that is predictable and where staff are both firm and nurturing. A structured day and week with rules about what should be done and how will assist them in functioning and help them feel secure; change needs to be planned in advance. They need groups with clear boundaries and which are reasonably small and intimate otherwise they will not feel safe enough to engage therapeutically.

In working with people who have personality disorders it is quite another story. In his book on working with such clients, Midgley (1994) recommends eliminating predictability as part of the therapeutic stance: if their environment becomes too stable they will start to become bored and will begin to look for excitement; unlike people with psychosis, they thrive on change. Residents with this disorder need a variety of different groups within their regime. S. Schiff used to say that any therapist working with these residents needs to have mastered at least two very different kinds of therapy and be able to switch from one approach to the other whenever the group starts to get too cosy (personal communication, 1976). A useful guideline for the leader of a group of residents with personality disorders is to avoid taking a parental stance. It is likely to be more productive to play and joke with them and invite them to do this with one another; tough confrontations can be made in this way with light words but a serious intent. Serious talking about behaviour should be done from an adult position focusing on consequences rather than 'should's or 'shouldn't's: 'Violence is wrong' is likely to lead, at best, to a fruitless argument; on the other hand, 'If you go around hitting people, some of them are likely to hit you back', will usually lead in a more productive direction. People with personality disorders have trouble learning from experience and so tend to sabotage themselves in the same way again and again. Part of the solution to this problem is for them to learn that their behaviour has consequences and that they need to take these into account.

Finally, moving from the level of the group to that of the institutional or therapeutic community regime, it is important to recognise that people with personality disorders will create drama for themselves if this is not provided. It is one of the tasks of management and staff to see that they are in charge of the drama most of the time and that it happens on their terms and not those of the residents. A fire drill at 2.00am may well create enough excitement to last a few days but then something else will need to be arranged, otherwise the level of acting out among residents is likely to increase. In working with people with personality disorders in a residential setting there is a continuous struggle between staff and residents as to who is going to control the drama; at times the residents will grab control and then it is the job of staff to find an elegant and therapeutically interesting way of grasping it back again – which brings us to the important subject of group and community dynamics.

The importance of group dynamics

In this section I comment on the dynamics set up both within groups in a residential environment and within the institution as a whole and its management; again, while I refer specifically to therapeutic communities, these intra- and extra-group dynamics are relevant to other settings.

Bion is the father of group dynamics theory. When using groups to treat victims of shell shock after the Second World War he became aware that a group is more than a collection of individuals and, rather, may be regarded as an organism in its own right. He recognised that it is possible to describe the behaviour of groups as a whole and moreover that our understanding of this group behaviour, from the inside, can be an important learning experience for those involved in it (Bion, 1961). While I do not find the details of his theory particularly useful in my day-to-day work, I agree with him wholeheartedly that no counsellor or psychotherapist can afford to ignore what is happening in the group as a whole. When working in any residential setting, the group counsellor needs also to attend to dynamics within the whole institution.

I commented earlier on the dual nature of the therapeutic approach in THAT Community. However, if it becomes clear to the therapist that there is something serious going on in the group as a whole then this will take priority. Some of the reason for this is that we work with clients who are high risk in terms of their propensity to hurt themselves and others; and negative dynamics in our setting can get out of hand quite quickly with potentially destructive consequences. What is likely to happen is that one resident will experience that they are unable to tolerate the level of feeling in an emotionally charged atmosphere and will escalate, that is become acutely upset or angry then act out in some way by, for example, becoming threatening or running out of the room or house. This may trigger similar upsets and escalations in other people. The therapist in this situation needs to be able to maintain control and hold the group together until everyone has calmed down. This takes a great deal of energy and skill, and the consequences of dynamics at this level can be serious. For example, a resident may run off in a situation like this and not come back. We may then have lost them because if they stay away too long they may not be able to return even if they want to because the funding for their therapy may have been withdrawn. Obviously it is better if we can anticipate and defuse this kind of trouble while it is still brewing, and this is always our aim. Even if the level of feelings and discomfort in the group does not seem particularly high or ominous, in our setting the therapist will usually stop the individual work and pay attention to the group dynamics. Residents with psychotic problems need to feel secure and comfortable in a therapy group in order to be able to make productive use of it, and if there is an uneasy atmosphere then our residents will not feel safe to make themselves vulnerable in the way that is a prerequisite for effective therapy and change: hence the priority given to group dynamics.

A common example of a particular group dynamic in our TC is what we call a 'Get-rid-of' game – for more on psychological games, see Berne (1964/1968), and for more on the 'Get-rid-of' life position, see Ernst (1971). This is a serious dynamic with potentially serious consequences and we always take it very seriously. At the first indication that this is going on we are likely to stop everything and call a dynamics group. We will then stay together either until the reason behind the dynamic has been identified and dealt with satisfactorily, or at least until we have got to a place where it seems safe to leave it for a while. The belief behind a 'Get-rid-of' game is always about scarcity: the group members will have become frightened that there is not enough of something to go round (love, attention, food, time, therapy) and, therefore (they believe) they have to compete with one another to get it. In their frame of reference, the solution would be for someone to leave, that is, to be 'got-rid-of', so that those remaining will then have sufficient. From our experience, it appears that anyone's leaving will satisfy the group and individuals will often offer to 'get-rid-of' themselves as the sacrificial victim for the good of the group. All this is usually out of awareness and the task of the dynamics group is to bring it into consciousness so that the underlying problem can be identified and resolved. Residents need to have permission to talk about their wish to get rid of particular individuals and their sense or fantasies that other people want them to go. In order to be able to do this safely, we begin by asking everyone to make a commitment to stay. Once the reason for the dynamic becomes clear it is usually reasonably easy to respond to it. It may be that it is about a new, demanding, resident being due to arrive or a particular member of staff going on holiday. It is then possible to make plans and give reassurance that, in fact, everyone's needs can and will be met.

Another example is of what we refer to as a 'manic' dynamic. Its symptoms are a lot of commotion and agitation within the group with often a lot of laughter, but with a jarring edge to it: people do not listen and talk over one another; there is a general sense of people believing they have to compete with one another to get heard and get attention. One way of responding to this is again to call everyone together, staff as well as residents, and have a particular kind of 'feelings check'. As part of the need underlying this dynamic is for people to get heard, each person in turn is invited to say what they are feeling without anyone else being allowed to interrupt, comment or respond. Invariably what emerges is that there is some anxiety in the group which is not being expressed or listened to. Once it is clear that staff are listening and responding then everyone starts to calm down.

Of course, it is not only residents who get caught up in group dynamics. Staff get drawn into them also and the staff group can and does have dynamics of its own. Certainly, in THAT Community we have had manic dynamics in staff meetings and occasionally have had a 'Get-rid-of' game amongst the staff. Staff dynamics are taken at least as seriously as dynamics within the resident group, if not more so. While it is true that staff are less likely to act out on the basis of their feelings, if the staff are at odds then residents quickly start to feel insecure and the whole situation within the community starts to become unstable. Residents need to know that staff will be responsible about sorting out their own problems; if told that a staff meeting is being called as a priority they will know that staff need to do something about setting their own psychological house in order and, by and large, will trust that we will do so. They may well be curious but are generally reassured rather than alarmed.

Often transference and counter-transference issues will be involved in community dynamics. For example, a very heated argument will blow up out of the blue which makes no sense in terms of anything going on in the here-and-now. We will then realise that what is happening is that we are acting out the dynamics in someone's family. Each new resident will, at some point, project his or her family on to the community and try to get us to react in similar ways to their original family members. When we can catch this projection and feed it back to the resident it can be very enlightening. It seems as though sometimes people need to put their family dynamics out so that they can stand back and see the whole picture of their interactions. At other times they themselves will be involved in the dynamics and then usually what they need from us is a different response from the one they got originally (see Yalom, 1995).

In THAT Community we see it as one of the most important parts of the manager's role to monitor community dynamics and initiate any action that needs to be taken. Other staff and residents do this as well as there is, in practice, a general expectation that people be aware of what is going on at a psychological level and be active about drawing attention to anything that seems wrong. Nevertheless, testing the emotional atmosphere requires a certain degree of experience. The person doing it needs to be in touch with their own feelings and fantasies and be prepared to give credence to them even when they seem bizarre. For example, I have, at times, had a strong sense that one of the residents in the community wants to kill me; sometimes I have chided myself for being melodramatic but have nevertheless checked it out and almost invariably my fantasy has turned out to be correct. However, the person monitoring dynamics also needs to be able to separate enough from their own feelings to be able to look at, and think about what is going on in the community as a whole. It is sometimes easier for the manager to see the overall picture than for other staff who are working more closely with residents and therefore more at risk of becoming entangled in whatever dynamics are happening.

An example of a therapeutic regime and the groups within it: Trident Housing Association Therapeutic Community

In this section I briefly describe the regime in THAT Community – for further descriptions of which, see Rawson, Buddendiek and Haigh (1994) and Robinson (1998), and for another description of regime, roles and issues in TCs, see Kennard (1988). THAT Community draws on transactional analysis (TA) as our main theoretical frame of reference and finds this a particularly useful model in working with residents and clients who come to us (see particularly Schiff et al., 1975). All our therapists are either trained in TA or are in TA training.

Community meetings are the vital element in the regime of every therapeutic community and ours is no exception. It is chaired by one of the residents and is the main forum where staff and residents consult together and make decisions about matters which are of importance to the TC as a whole. More unusual are the *peer group meetings* held at the start of every day except Saturday. These are meetings of residents and non-resident clients without staff, although a staff member can be called in for support if necessary (see Chapter 3 on the alternate group). They deal with various matters, including monitoring feelings, menu planning and allocating household jobs. The peer group is responsible for the running of the house including the cooking. These are followed by different kinds of *therapy groups*: one is devoted to art therapy and another includes an opportunity for residents to read and get feedback on the notes they have made of their week's work. On Saturday mornings we have what is called the *safety and security meeting*. This is an opportunity to talk about fears that could give rise to the kind of negative dynamics discussed above. Our hope is that by providing a place where such fears can be aired and responded to we can avoid some of the upsets and escalations with which we might otherwise have to deal. Weekly *staff meetings* are given a high priority; they include a training session and are protected from disruption as far as possible. We also have plans in hand to set up an additional and regular fortnightly staff group where staff working in attachments can get support, conflicts between staff members can be disentangled and tensions within the group can be defused before they have the chance of developing into full-blown dynamics. *Dynamics groups* (discussed above) are one response to an impending crisis; another is a *structure meeting*. Any member of the community, resident or staff, may call one of these at any time. It is a way of gathering together all residents and staff on duty in order to respond to an urgent problem. A fairly typical example would be that someone has found a sharp knife left out of its drawer. A kind of inquest follows in an attempt to find out why: Was this a simple mistake? Is someone upset and acting out on an unconscious level? Is it a warning from someone who is angry? Is it a plea for protection from someone having impulses to hurt herself? We know from experience that we cannot afford to ignore this kind of low level signal because if we do, the person having the problem will, without doubt, present it again at a higher level so that we have to take notice.

It is always our goal to pick up potential trouble at the lowest possible level. There is a strong expectation within the community that people be aware of what is going on with one another and that if a resident is becoming distressed this be drawn to the attention of staff immediately. This is probably the main reason that we have a good safety record. We also have regular times in the day for monitoring how people are doing so that we can catch any potential problems with individuals or in the group dynamics at an early stage. These are the 'feelings checks' which are held in the peer group meeting and after lunch and dinner, meals that we all eat together. It was residents who introduced the after-meals feelings checks, which have proved themselves to be an invaluable safety net within the overall structure.

These are the regular groups which fit together and complement one another: some are for carrying out the main task of the community (therapy groups); some are devoted to providing a safe environment within which this may be done (safety and security meetings, feelings checks); others are where different sections of the community can attend to their particular concerns (peer groups, staff meetings), while matters of common concern are brought together and major decisions made as a community (in the community meeting); finally there are groups which can be called together as necessary to respond to a possible impending crisis (dynamics groups, structure meetings). It is worth noting that in such a group culture organising a group or meeting tends to be a way of dealing with anything which needs to be done or decided. Almost always there are other groups going on set up for specific purposes. We may organise a group to talk with visitors, make plans for a forthcoming holiday or festivity, or meet with a resident who has been hostile and wishes to apologise. Currently there is a group of staff and residents looking at the use of space within the house; this group will report back to community meeting in due course. One particularly rewarding type of group is a seminar, held when we perceive a need to review some aspect of our philosophy, theory or methods; the creativity which is unleashed when residents and staff get together in this kind of discussion is usually impressive and deeply satisfying. An important factor in drawing together the numerous groups into a coherent regime is that we have a particular (TA) model and theory to which we adhere. A recent visitor from a psychiatric unit commented on the fact that this gives us a sense of direction and confidence in what we are doing which he experienced that he and his colleagues were lacking. We do also make use of other approaches when we think this will be useful, for example, bodywork, hypnotherapy, gestalt therapy, but they need to be consistent with our philosophy and fit with our methods.

Finally, how do our groups fit with other aspects of the residential context in our situation? This is an interesting question because for those of us who live and work here the question almost never arises. For us, therapy is going on all the time whether in groups or out of them. Groups are a part of a whole structure for living which is designed to be therapeutic in itself. However, sometimes this question is asked by visitors and the fact that our residential TC also includes some members who are non-resident means that the difference between group and community is more pertinent. Our legal status is that of a registered residential home; Social Services inspectors, for example, sometimes want us to make a distinction between residential care and therapy, as do agencies providing funding for residents. This does not make sense within our frame of reference, and when we are forced to make such a distinction it is always quite arbitrary.

Conclusion

It seems that people have an in-built need to belong to and to form communities. In his book *A Different Drum* Peck (1987) uses the word community to define a clearly identifiable level of development within the process of a group characterised by cohesiveness amongst members. In his terms any group could develop into a community while a community set up as such might never become one psychologically (see Chapter 7). Peck sees achieving community as an important and worthwhile goal for any group. He has now set up an organisation – The Founda- tion for Community Encouragement (FCE) (see Peck, 1987) – to foster the development of communities, believing that the mutual caring and creativity engendered within them could help amelior- ate some of the conflict in the world.

However, I am also conscious that the culture of a community can be subverted and used for destructive ends. One has only to look at the warring communities in some of the world's 'hot spots' such as Northern Ireland, the former Yugoslavia and the Middle East and at the suicide pacts entered into by members of certain cults to be reminded of this. Communities can be powerful forces for good or ill. When set up to serve a positive end, for example, to provide a place of healing or to teach people how to relate to others in healthy ways, the positive dynamics (of mutual support, involvement, commitment) can create an environment which is therapeutic in itself. The use of groups within this context can both accelerate the healing and learning and serve to strengthen the community as a whole; alternatively, they can lead to splitting and internecine warfare.

There is a need to build in safeguards, first to ensure that groups within a residential setting support the overall task and goals and do not sabotage it. One of the things I appreciate about working in a therapeutic community is that, most of the time, residents are just as committed to the work as the staff. It is rare for us to find ourselves in an 'us and them' situation and when we do we know we have a problem. We respond to this, like any other dynamic, by sitting down together and talking until we understand what is going on and can start making a plan to respond to it. However, there is an even greater need to make sure that the residential setting remains true to its purpose and supports the groups and individuals within it. Whole organisations can lose sight of their goals and engender a culture within them that is, for instance, cynical and time-serving. This can be even more disastrous in a residential institution where a lack of direction and slipping standards can lead to abuses of power by staff in their dealings with residents. Sadly, there is no shortage of examples of this – it is only necessary to read the newspapers, especially on the abuse within so-called childcare homes and institutions.

A healthy institution has several features which make it virtually impossible for an abusive culture to take root. Here, I identify four requirements:

1. *Clarity about its purpose and task which is known and understood by all staff and residents.* Usually, in order to make sure this is explicit, it is written down in, to use the current management jargon, a mission statement.

2. *A set of values and/or a code of practice which is also known and understood by all.* This maybe drawn up by the institution or community and may also be affected by its organisational context and governing bodies (housing association, social services etc.).

3. *A commitment by staff to putting these values into practice.* There need to be ways of checking within the residential setting to ensure that this is happening. One of the most useful ones which we have in the THAT Community is a confrontation contract. Every member – resident, day attender, staff member, student, volunteer – makes a contract with the community 'to confront and be confronted from a caring position'. This is taken very seriously and means that everyone in the community has a responsibility to challenge anyone else who is behaving inappropriately or acting in ways that make others uncomfortable. Also, everyone is equally responsible for listening and responding appropriately when confronted.

4. *External monitoring.* It is important that any residential institution be open to receiving visitors from the outside, although this has to be balanced against the need for residents to be able to relax within the privacy of what is their home. Fortunately, nowadays, most residential establishments are subject to formal inspection and this adds another dimension to the monitoring process. In addition to such formal monitoring, other formal and informal monitoring needs to be

undertaken by people who visit regularly, get to know the establishment, its staff and residents, and are qualified professionally to assess the work that is being done and the general morale. A wise manager will make use of such visits to get feedback on the overall performance of the institution through a fresh pair of eyes.

Not only do all groups occur within a social context, so too residential institutions and TCs exist within a wider societal context. As such it is important that we do not become isolated from the surrounding culture and the wider society and people which we serve – issues to be taken up in the next chapter.

Notes

Jenny Robinson is co-director of Connect Therapeutic Community, Birmingham. She is a certified transactional analyst, registered with the UKCP and qualified to train psychotherapists under supervision. Previously, she was principal psychotherapist in the Home Office Prison Department. Jenny acknowledges the work of Jacqui Schiff and her colleagues at the Cathexis Institute, California.

1 As this book went to press, Trident Housing Association Therapeutic Community became independent and changed its name to Connect Therapeutic Community Ltd.

7

Social Psyches: Groups, Organisation and Community

If groups represent the individual-in-context, then consideration of groups-in-context takes us into the contextual fields of inter-group relations and the wider social locations of groups and applications of 'group'. Through discussions of the large group, inter-group relations, organisation and community, this chapter reflects on the movement from the therapeutic to the social sphere: from the psychotherapeutic to the *socio*therapeutic.

To what extent small, median and large groups reflect and represent community – and, indeed, society – has been the subject of much debate in the field of psychology and philosophy. De Maré (1975) suggests that 'if we are to survive at all we can no longer put off the day when the psychological, the politico-economic and the socio-cultural context must meet operationally in a unified field' (p. 145). Historically, psychoanalysis has always been concerned with such context/s and the application of psychoanalytic concepts to understanding the social world. The problems of being an individual and of society were discussed by Freud in *Civilisation and Its Discontents* (Freud, 1930/1985b); one of Jung's central interests was the collective unconscious connections between peoples across cultures and time; whilst in *The Mass Psychology of Fascism* Reich (1933/1975) applied his theories of character structure to the body politic. More recently, the journal *Free Associations* has, for the past fifteen years, considered issues in and connections between psychoanalysis, groups, politics and culture; Samuels (1993) has developed an analysis of political issues (such as the market economy, environmentalism and nationalism) and of personal issues (as regards fathers and the male body); and, generally within psychotherapy and counselling, the interface between the social/political and personal spheres is increasingly the subject of debate within the psychotherapeutic literature and in training (see Embleton Tudor and Tudor, 1994; Tudor, 1997e). Finally, in an innovative book, Alford (1994) argues that the group and not the individual is the most fundamental reality in society and that political theory needs to draw on the insights of group psychology and leadership.

Large groups

Whilst there are no precise definitions of small, median and large groups, as indicated in Chapter 3, their respective ranges may be said to be: between three and eight, fifteen to thirty and anywhere from thirty to sixty up to 200 or 300 – the democratic forums in ancient Greece had 2,000 participants. Over the past twenty-five years there has been an increasing interest in the phenomenon of the median and the large group: 'whatever one's orientation . . . there can be little doubt as to the contribution that the large group can make to any therapeutic régime' (Kreeger, 1975, p. 14). The median group applies the principles of group analysis to groups larger than the traditional small analytic group. The median group is considered small enough for people to speak and have dialogue and yet large enough to promote discussion connecting the group to the outer world (see de Maré, 1972; de Maré et al., 1991). Although most of our experience in life may be in small groups at home and at work, there are occasions when we are in larger and indeed large groups: on a street, in a park, at a school or work meetings, at a sporting event, at a cultural festival or religious gathering. Most political decisions (beyond the parish council) are made in and by large groups of people. We only have to remind ourselves of the destructive power of mass psychology to understand that we ignore the phenomenon of large groups at our peril.

Although some therapists and facilitators report similar group characteristics and group dynamics in large groups (of fifty to seventy-five) as in small groups (Hopper and Weyman, 1975), for others the sheer size of large groups shifts the experience and definition of such groups from therapy to a more general experience – which we may equally gain through specific social events in life such as family gatherings, concerts, workshops, a shared crisis, community-building etc. Kreeger (1975) discerns three types of large groups:

- *Problem-centred* – concerned with the problem of inter-relationships, and in which the principal vehicle of operation is verbal communication between members with the leaders facilitating this.
- *Experience-centred* – the principal purpose of which is to provide an experience of the large group in which often there is a minimum of structure and 'leadership'.
- *Therapy-centred* – meeting with the express purpose of doing therapy, for instance, in the context of a psychiatric hospital/therapeutic community, and marked by the therapeutic approach of the leaders.

Two important debates, especially regarding large therapy-centred groups, are around the nature of the large group as compared with the small therapy group, and the issue of whether particular psychotherapeutic analysis, methods or attitudes may be usefully applied to working with the large group.

From the psychodynamic perspective, the large group is viewed, with few exceptions, as having a distinct purpose, function and role. De Maré (1975) compares the psychodynamic approach to the small group with the group-dynamic approach to the large group. Kreeger (1975) states that individual interpretation is particularly inappropriate in large group settings and concludes that the conductor or, preferably, a team of conductors should act as moderators, 'to keep anxiety and tension at a tolerable level for constructive work' (p. 55). The objective of psychodynamic or group-dynamic groups may be considered to be 'outsight', 'looking out at the surrounding culture and society from a perspective of openness to understanding' (Sturdevant, 1995, p. 70). Following Edelson (1970), Whiteley (1975), then Director of the Henderson Hospital Therapeutic Community argues, that the large group – with the inevitable formation of subgroups and rival factions and individuals and sub-groupings demanding, dominating and retreating – lends itself more to the examination of *social* than intra-personal dynamics, and defines such activity as sociotherapy. From his research conducted at the Henderson, Rapoport (1960) identified four *sociological* processes pertinent to the *socio*therapeutic community:

- *Permissiveness* – whereby the community allows the individual to be themselves.
- *Communalism* – through which everyone shares in the exploration of, experimentation with and experience of community life.
- *Democracy* – by which everyone has the right to determine community policy.
- *Confrontation* – the technique of constantly putting before the individual what they are doing.

Whilst permissiveness and confrontation may be considered as *psycho*therapeutic as well as *socio*therapeutic methods, communalism and democracy have their roots in the large democratic forums of ancient Greece and of other cultures.

Within the person-centred approach (PCA), whilst large groups are often experienced as therapeutic, their initial aims are often problem-centred in, say, resolving intercultural tensions and conflict (see McGraw, 1973; Rogers, 1978) or experience-centred in providing an experience of large groups and the forms of social interaction and communication which take place usually in a cross-cultural context. The first large group – community for learning – took place in 1973 and the PCA now draws on a rich history of experience and research into the phenomenon of the large group (see Bozarth, 1981; Wood, 1984, 1995a, 1999; Lago and Macmillan, 1999). Given the emphasis in the PCA on the facilitative conditions for growth and change (Rogers, 1957, 1959), which, in a group context, are reflected predominantly by the therapeutic attitudes of the group facilitator/s and the group, the large group is viewed essentially in a similar way to the small group: the principles are consistent, the application varies with the context:

> what a person-centered approach taught us about community was that a large group, in a creative state, can resolve crises, find solutions to complex problems, intelligently co-ordinate its activities without plans, legislation, or parliamentary procedures, and even transform its culture

in a compassionate and efficient process that involves, respects, and benefits each of its members and itself (Wood, 1984, p. 311).

Within this approach, facilitators are also participants and fully involved in the group (Rogers, 1970/1973), the difference from other participants being that the facilitators are 'conscientiously participating' (Macmillan and Lago, 1993). Often, there are no designated facilitators, the initiators/organisers of the event usually resigning their administrative/leadership function at the beginning of the first gathering – sometimes to the frustration of the group!

Interestingly for two very different and mostly differing theoretical orientations, the psychodynamic and person-centred approaches share a conceptual interest in and practice in the forum of the large group and its application in the social world of work and conflict resolution. Both account for the intrapersonal and, especially in the large group context, the interpersonal; both emphasise communication and dialogue which provide continuity through disorganisation, chaos, fear, conflict to build community; both require empathy or 'outsight'; both advocate flexible structures and responses. Combining the insights of Eastern philosophy, modern physics and Jungian psychology, process-oriented psychology (Mindell, 1992, 1995) has a similar focus (especially to that of the PCA) in facilitating large group transformation, conflict resolution, community building and 'deep democracy' (Sturdevant, 1995).

This brief reflection on the phenomenon of large groups, which are in many ways *created*, sets the scene for the application of large group dynamics to *existing* groups, through consideration of intergroup relations, organisation and communities.

Intergroup relations – the meeting of cultures

One practical way of viewing groups in context is to bring two or more groups together; indeed, one of McDougall's (1920) conditions for groups (see Chapter 3) is that the group should be brought into interaction with other groups. Often, when a therapist or a trainer runs two or more groups, each group expresses some curiosity, jealousy and/or envy of the other/s. One way to work with and through this is to bring the groups together from time to time – person-centred conferences and training courses, for instance, have a tradition of the large learning community meeting. When two individuals form a partnership they bring, at some level, their families into the relationship. The therapeutic adage that 'six in a bed is too crowded' (a couple and both sets of parents), and that a successful relationship needs to exclude said parents from the 'marital' bed, informs couples counselling and sexual and marital therapy. If and when families meet, traditionally at births, deaths and marriages or commitments and at other family occasions, in effect two groups or groupings are meeting. The same is true when one family adopts members of another family. The strain and stress of such occasions and situations bears witness to the complex dynamics of *inter*group relations. In the political sphere, peoples, cultures, tribes and nations have been dividing, uniting, partitioning, merging, separating and unifying from since the first invasion took place, topical examples of which are in Germany, the island of Ireland and the geographical area referred to as 'the former Yugoslavia'. The history of immigration control in Britain and in other countries and the attitudes it fosters reflects a hostile, defensive and negative attitude to new, incoming members and 'acculturation', which Klein (1968) views as one of the basic functions of a community. A more positive attitude and one which acknowledges differences comes from the musician and founder of *Talking Heads*, David Byrne: 'there's no point zero. When two cultures clash, that's where the heat and energy come from'. As an example of this, I trace the development of intergroup relations – in effect and explicitly *intercultural* relations.

Encounter, development and relatedness
In considering the meeting of cultures, I draw on two models of development: one about minority identity (Atkinson et al., 1989) and the other about white racial consciousness (Helms, 1984). The models are taken to apply to groups and group development (see Chapter 1) as well as to individuals. The groups concerned may be notional groups representing, for instance, black and white culture; groups that come together with the express purpose of resolving intercultural tensions and difficulties (see Rogers, 1978); or specific groups, organisations or communities (see Levitan, 1998). Here, the minority identity development model and the white racial consciousness model and their stages are paralleled and interleaved with comments on what I identify as stages of intergroup relations with examples. Although these

models were developed specifically regarding minority identity and white consciousness, they are, in my view, applicable to any minority-dominant cultural axis such as class, disability, gender, sexuality etc. In the examples I use 'black' in the political generic sense to refer to members of minority cultural/racial groups.

Stage 1

Minority identity development

Conformity – identification with values of dominant culture, lack of awareness of an ethnic perspective, exhibition of negative attitudes towards self and others, acceptance of dominant group stereotypes of self and others.

White racial consciousness

Contact – unawareness of self as a racial being, tendency to ignore differences, awareness that minorities exist, resolution of any conflict through withdrawal.

Intergroup relations

Unconscious co-existence – At this stage, precisely because of the lack of awareness in both groups and their implicit acceptance of the dominant culture, there is often little or no explicit tension. There may, however, be a general sense of vulnerability to the possibility of anxiety or disorganisation such as a potential threat to a group's cultural identity, as in the example of the merging teams (above) or in the vague unease groups may have in relations to other groups which are identified as different in some way. This is only the case, however, if groups are founded on or suppose that difference is problematic or threatening rather than interesting, stimulating, even exciting. This possibility of anxiety is one of Rogers' (1957) three process elements of incongruence elaborated by Singh and Tudor (1997) as regards cultural conditions of therapy.

Stage2

Minority identity development

Dissonance – confusion and conflict about previously held values, awareness of issues involving racism, sexism, oppression etc., feelings of anger and loss, search and identification with history of and role models from personal cultural group.

White racial consciousness

Disintegration – awareness of racism with resultant feelings of guilt and depression, feeling caught between internal standards of human decency and external cultural expectations; responses: overidentification with black (minority) people, paternalism, or retreat into white (dominant) culture.

Inter-group relations

Conscious unease – It is at this stage where much of the heat and energy comes from two cultures clashing. In many ways each group is experiencing a similar process of cognitive and emotional dissonance and disintegration of previous certainties. Whilst black people may be angry, if white people allow their feelings of guilt to render them passive, black people may get more angry, in response to which white people may feel more guilty, passive and stuck, and so on. The movement and outcome for the two groups at this stage is different. For the minority group, prefiguring the next stage, it is the beginning of a re-orientation to its own cultural heritage, whilst for the white (dominant) group there is often a movement towards minority cultures – expressed through increased interest in different cultural traditions (festivals, food, music, fashion, etc.). Such movement and learning may be genuine but is more likely at this stage to be overidentifying, for example some white Rastafarians, or patronising, for example, viewing black people and black cultures as exotic. As far as personal and intergroup relations are concerned, and depending at which stage the minority group may be identified, such overtures may be welcomed, accepted or rejected – which, in turn, may lead white people to adopt a psychological Victim position – 'What (more) can we do?', 'We can't get it right' etc., and to a retreat into (rather than an exploration of) white culture. For some, affirmative action and positive discrimination (illegal in Britain) represent misguided attempts to counteract dissonance and disintegration.

Stage 3

Minority identity development

Resistance and immersion – active rejection and mistrust of dominant culture, greater identification with cultural group, immersion in cultural group history, traditions, language etc., activism geared to challenging oppression, possible separation from dominant culture (separatism).

White racial consciousness

Reintegration (accommodation)[1] – hostility towards minorities, positive bias in favour of own racial group.

[1] I refer to stage 3 of the white awareness model as accommodation (in the Piagetian sense), rather than reintegration, in that it is a stage of unresolved and undigested emotions, beliefs and behaviours (rather than a re-integrating process of assimilation).

Intergroup relations

Polarisation – As distinct from the previous stage, this is a time of polarisation and often bitterness and resentment between the two groups. While the minority cultural group focuses more on itself and its cultural heritage, the dominant cultural group is often hostile to minority cultural initiatives and demands and biased in favour of its own culture. This is a stage characterised by explicit and, at times, explosive tension over issues on the macro political level such as immigration controls, disputes about history, landrights and the 'ownership' of cultural artefacts, and, on the micro political level, about separatism and autonomy, for example over policies about equal opportunities, education and religion, support for separate minority groups – in response to which there is often a dominant cultural backlash: 'The Council is spending too much money on minorities', 'We don't want to send our children to a Moslem school where they don't celebrate Christmas', 'Why can't we have white only groups?'.

Stage 4

Minority independent development	**White racial consciousness**
Introspection – a questioning of rigid rejection of values of dominant culture with resultant conflict and confusion over loyalty to own cultural group, struggle for self-awareness.	*Pseudo-independent* – increasing interest in racial group similarities and differences, intellectual acceptance of other groups, limited cross-cultural interaction with 'special' black people.

Intergroup relations

Re-evaluation and encounter Between groups, this stage is characterised by an ownership of issues, problems and histories, greater self-responsibility, a relaxing of defensiveness, threat and tension, and a tentative reaching out and meeting. The interest on the part of the dominant cultural group is genuine and comparative – and based on a genuine enquiry into and developing awareness of its own culture. The movement and communication between groups is more equal and reciprocated. It is at this stage that there may be some tentative meeting and encounter between groups and cultures, with openness and learning often initiated by the oppressed (see Freire, 1972). Drawing on his own experience of resolving intercultural tensions, Rogers (1978) discusses the necessary attitudes of the facilitator/s of such encounters, including freedom from a desire to control the outcome, respect for the capacity of the group/s, skills in releasing individual expression, and the ability to listen respectfully to *all* attitudes and feelings.

Stage 5

Minority independent development	*White racial consciousness*
Synergetic articulation and awareness – resolution of many conflicts, fulfilment as regards personal cultural identity, appreciation of other cultural groups as well as a critical selection of values of dominant culture group, motivation to eliminate all forms of oppression.	*Autonomy* – acceptance of racial differences and similarities with respect and appreciation, perception which does not perceive differences as deficits or similarities as necessarily enhancing, active seeking of cross-cultural interactions.

Intergroup relations

Mutual respect – Positive and growthful intergroup relations are based on mutual respect, acknowledgement of differences and similarities and a critical evaluation by both groups of values, beliefs, history, customs etc. This is based on a strong, felt and lived sense of identity – and identities. In terms of groups working through conflict and working together, at this stage they are often able to integrate contradictory values (see Wood, 1995a). This is the stage at which it is possible to offer genuine and respectful criticism across cultures without this being experienced as threatening or received defensively on sensitive matters such as arranged marriages, legal and judicial systems, corporal and capital punishment, human rights, political prisoners – all of which cut both ways in that they are issues in and for both minority *and* majority (dominant) cultures.

Having discussed intergroup relations between existing groups and intragroup and intergroup relations with groups that come together for an explicit purpose to resolve particular problems, to have the experience of being in a large group or of creating community, or to do therapy (for further discussion of which see Brown, 1988 and the new journal *Group Process and Intergroup Relations*), I now explore the interface between therapy and organisation and community. This informs a discussion of the movement from therapeutic groups and communities to groups and communities which are therapeutic, a movement in which the sociotherapeutic counsellor can facilitate.

Organisation

I have already referred to the impact of groups and intergroup relations within an organisation (above). In this section I explore the purpose and role of group counselling and group counsellors as it and they impact on the sphere of work and organisation.

Historically, the interest in therapy and organisation can be traced back to the convergence of two distinct traditions – psychoanalysis and social science. Mosse (1994) traces the historical roots of consulting to institutions through the Tavistock Clinic (founded in 1920) and the Tavistock Institute of Human Relations (TIHR) and three influential projects:

1. The examination of unconscious group processes at work, through six 'industrial fellows' seconded from industry to the TIHR.
2. The study of organisation as a 'socio-technical system', research which, from its origins in the coal mining industry, came to be applied to social organisations in which the technical system is largely human, notably in nursing (Menzies Lyth, 1959/1988).
3. The study of internal relations of a manufacturing company, which led to the recognition that social systems in the workplace defend workers against unconscious anxieties inherent in the work (primary anxiety) or created by the organisation of the work/place (secondary anxiety) – for an application of this to a Social Services Department see Embleton Tudor and Tudor (1995).

Whilst it is undoubtedly the case that for the past eighty years psychoanalysis and analytic psychology (see Stein and Hollwitz, 1992) have dominated our understanding of dynamic processes at work, the humanistic/existential tradition has made some – and increasing – contributions to the analysis of and interventions in organisational life (see, for example Berne, 1963; Merry and Brown, 1987; Clarkson, 1995a).

Despite the development of new technology and the increase in people working from home, most people in employment still work in groups and at work identify in and with those work groups (teams, project groups etc.). However, although the organisation of work is predominantly in groups, the organisational response to problems is predominantly individual and individualising. The growth of counselling at work, for instance, in the form of Employee Assistance Programmes (EAPs), may reflect a positive response to individual needs; it is also an individual response to what may be a collective, organisational problem. A counsellor may receive a steady stream of referrals through an EAP or directly from an organisation and, indeed, some organisations are employing counsellors. Without detracting from the impact on individuals of dis-stress and their need for help, organisations need to analyse and address the levels of stress and secondary anxiety they themselves create. Unfortunately, this individualising and pathologising perspective is one which is supported by government policy and initiatives (see Tudor, 1996a). Learning from the legacy of the TIHR projects and maintaining the focus on the 'work group' – in both the organisational sense and the conceptual meaning (Bion, 1961) – the group counsellor/consultant is in a good position to work *in*, *through* and *of* the organisation just as we work in, through and of/with the group.

- *Counselling in the organisation.* This is the traditional approach to individual counselling in organisations taken by management, personnel and counsellors whereby employees are referred to the counsellor for, usually, a fixed number of sessions. The counselling may take place outside the organisation through an EAP, but it is nevertheless with*in* the aegis of the organisation that finances the EAP. Due to the way the three-handed contract is established and to boundaries of confidentiality, there is, with rare exceptions, no feedback from the counsellor to the organisation. I know of no examples of counselling *in* the organisation taking place in groups.
- *Counselling through the organisation.* Counselling *through* the group focuses not only on the relationships between group members themselves and between them and the counsellor but also, importantly in this context, on relationships between the group members and the group and the organisation. Examples include working with work groups, teams, support groups and specific focus groups etc. Counselling through the organisation can only be effected – and effective – working through groups and is a way of responding to what may be presented and viewed as a series of individual issues

such as stress or absenteeism. In my view, counsellors working within or on behalf of EAPs have, by virtue of their work with individuals who are *employees*, a wider responsibility – a responsibility to the community and in this case the organisation – to act in a consultative role, for instance, in helping people to confront particular work practices within the organisation which are causing undue stress on them, other individuals and groups (secondary anxiety). Obviously this needs careful negotiating and clear contracting and, if the organisation is not too defensive, may be welcomed as a creative and effective way forward to meet the needs of both employees and the organisation.

■ *Counselling of the organisation.* Following Bion (1961), in the same way as the counsellor treats the group-as-a-whole, this focuses on the organisation-as-a-whole with interventions directed at the whole or total organisation, traditionally through working with groups of managers and/or decision-makers. Whilst this is a strategy and role familiar to internal and external consultants, it may be less familiar to the group counsellor. Nevertheless, group counsellors working of/with groups have, based on their systemic view of groups, directly transferable analysis and skills to work with organisational systems. Following the references made to stress, examples of this strategy are programmes designed to confront stress at a systemic, organisational level and to promote workplace well-being (see Tudor, 1996a). The difference between working *through* and *of* organisations is that, whilst the focus in the former is on facilitating and enabling work groups within the organisation, the focus of the latter is on the organisation itself, its structures, objective features, tasks, technology, social defences, etc.

In some ways these three ways of relating to the organisation in terms of groups echo Kreeger's (1975) three types of large groups: the problem-centred, experience-centred and therapy-centred. Perhaps the greatest task is to find a *people-centred* approach to the health of groups, organisations and communities.

Although I have used the term counsellor in these contexts, these perspectives, strategies and attitudes may be employed by any competent consultant. The two traditions mentioned by Mosse (1994) – psychoanalysis and social science – have given rise to two sets of consultants with backgrounds, respectively, in psychoanalysis, psychology (e.g. occupational psychologists), psychotherapy and counselling, and in social science, management and industrial relations. From whatever background, working knowledge and experience of groupwork is essential to the development of organisation through groups.

As an example of working with groups in organisation and continuing the theme and development of intergroup relations, the following case study describes and comments on the meeting and facilitation of two work groups coming together.

Merger, meeting and mediation
Following a change of management a reorganisation took place in a social services department, as a result of which two mental 'health' teams were required 'to merge' (the management's phrase) under one team leader (the other took early retirement). Prior to the date by which the two teams would become one administratively and managerially, the team manager, being aware of existing discontent and potential problems, asked a consultant to work with the two teams during the period of transition. The consultant met the two teams initially as they were constituted, separately and then facilitated two 'team-building' days which, whilst initially seen as problem-centred, soon became experience-centred and even therapy-centred (see Box 7.1).

The consultant then worked with the new unified (if not united) team as the two previous teams began to work together under the one manager. The consultation took place over two separate days, six weeks apart with, respectively, 94% and 75% attendance out of the total new team of 33 members (the lower attendance on the second day was the result of the team deciding to cover duty and three people's absence on sick leave). On the first day issues of separateness, joining, merger – and the reality and feelings of submerger of team Y into team X – surfaced strongly. Members of the previous team X experienced the process as one of 'moving over', of accommodation (rather than assimilation) and of re-formation. Members of the previous team Y were very clearly mourning their loss of identity as well as certain practical losses, for instance, of 'their' duty system, and were, generally, in a state of confusion (see Kübler-Ross, 1973). Alongside some negotiation, there was a lot of reminiscing, remembering and (re)claiming of their separate histories and what the two

Box 7.1

Team X – with team manager (16 people)	**Team Y – with no manager (17 people)**

What emerged from this meeting was that the team fluctuated between resentment and 'making things all right'; some felt safe(r) when Neil, the team manager, was not wearing his manager's hat but when he was more part of the team. Generally, they perceived that in the organisation as a whole hierarchy and hierarchical decision-making was valued and that consultation with workers was not; within the team some did not feel able to say what they wanted and most felt safe(r) in small groups. As for their work in the mental health/illness field, they felt defensive about potential exposure. In terms of the context of their work, they were not based in the area they served, a situation they experienced as a loss ('we're deprived'); a number of colleagues had recently left, they were 'thin on the ground' and wanted to 'concrete over the gaps' of people leaving.

Team Y had a strong team identity with a sense of continuity and togetherness, having previously worked together to achieve a clear personal and collective philosophy and purpose regarding their work, also in mental health/ illness. When the consultant met the team there were a significant number of absences. The team were very much focused on the other team and expressed some concerns about the style of the manager of team X who would become their manager. During the meeting the team quickly identified two key issues of attendance and joining, and saw the task of the consultant 'to take them into the Team' (as into the lion's den).

separate teams had done well; there was also some acknowl-edgement of each other's strengths, although at that stage not of any weaknesses. On this first day Neil, the team manager, alter-nated between almost taking over and hanging back, echoing the developmental crisis of initiative vs. guilt in Erikson's (1968) epigenetic formulation. The second day was characterised by some apprehension, initially a certain amount of 'them and us' feeling, thinking and behaviour and, ultimately, by moving for-ward. There was more expression of feelings both of ambivalence and of satisfaction, explicit identification of differences, dealing with 'unfinished business' left over from the previous day and from what had happened at work in the weeks between, and discussion of practicalities – this was especially marked by the contribution of specific ideas and systems from the members of the previous Y team who had produced a list of questions about 'where things were'. The result of this was an agreement to produce a team booklet covering policies and negotiated 'customs and practices' as well as a shared team philosophy. As the 'them and us' view held along the lines of the previous teams dissipated, other subgroupings formed within the team (in this case along the lines of professional identity, affiliation and support) – a common process observed in median and large groups. At this second meeting, the consultant's role changed from facilitating the group to mediating and helping mediation between group members and emerging subgroups. The consultant supported the team manager in being and becoming the team leader and using his role and authority appropriately.

This case study may be understood in any number of ways, depending on your orientation and, as with any such study, warrants further analysis. The principal point and process descri-bed in this brief report is the movement from individual (two separate) teams with their separate and individual concerns, problems, perspectives and solutions to (the beginnings of) a unification through acknowledging the commonality of shared concerns and problems as well as diversity. In terms of Rapoport's (1960) processes, whilst the first consultation day had been one of permissiveness and communalism, the second was characterised by confrontation and democracy. This also reflects the process which occurs when two groups, families or cultures meet and how each accommodates, assimilates or rejects the other – at times precisely because it is 'the Other'.

Having explored the application of our understanding and experience of groups to organisation/s, I now review some therapeutic – and political – concepts of community.

Community

> What life have you if you have not life together?
> There is no life that is not in community
>   (T.S. Eliot, 1934, *Choruses from 'The Rock'*)

The *Shorter Oxford English Dictionary* defines community as 'the quality of appertaining to all in common, common ownership'

(1973, p. 379). However, over forty years ago Hillery (1955) identified ninety-four different sociological definitions of community and no one definition would be agreed, or indeed desirable. More recently, using paradigm analysis, I elaborated four ways of organising different and differing definitions and ideas of community – functionalist, interpretive, radical humanist and radical structuralist (Tudor, 1996b), the third and fourth of which are based on notions of radical change. Hillman (1993) recognises community in three ways:

- through work
- an alert sense of social justice, and
- fellow, social or community feeling.

All three have implications for psychotherapy and sociotherapy.

Work implies community (as discussed above) and many workplaces such as hospitals and large organisations are communities in themselves. As far as social justice is concerned, as noted above there is a renewed level of interest in the counselling and psychotherapy community about social responsibility and social justice and the application of therapeutic insight – and outsight – to community and the social and political sphere. This has found voice in the network and organisation Psychotherapists and Counsellors for Social Responsibility (PCSR), founded in 1995 – although, given that almost everyone supports the concept of social responsibility, it is a pity that PCSR did not take up the challenge to include the more discerning and critical concept of social *justice* in its title. Citing the work of the Spanish poet Lorca, Hillman (1993) views social justice as furious, passionate and compassionate. Righteous anger and anger about social injustice and oppression has an important place in the therapeutic arena and should not, by default, be interpreted as some unresolved, archaic defence or seen as a 'negative' feeling. Anger, along with political analysis and critique (feminism, black and cultural critiques), has fuelled many of the critical developments in counselling and psychotherapy, for example, on access to therapy and training, the exploitation and abuse of clients, issues of power, authority and influence, and oppression in therapeutic sphere. The third component of community Hillman recognises is 'fellow feeling' (Adler's *Gemeinschaftsgefühl*) or, more broadly, social feeling or community feeling. It is this sense of community which is at the heart of therapeutic and social initiatives to build 'community'.

Community-making

One example of the application of the large group experience (which is both problem-centred and experienced-centred), is the practice of community-making. Based on the ideas of Peck (1987), this involves often large groups of people coming together with the purpose of building community. Peck (1987) proposes four stages of community-building which groups experience:

- Pseudocommunity
- Chaos
- Emptiness
- Community

Comparing these stages with Tuckman's (1965) stages of group development, pseudocommunity is akin to a false or forced norming, and chaos to storming. It is the concept of emptiness which lies at the heart of Peck's contribution to building community: 'there are only two ways out of chaos . . . one is into organization – but organization is never community . . . the only way from chaos to community is into and through emptiness' (Peck, 1987, p. 94). Some years ago I remember attending a five-day training workshop – significantly, perhaps, on the subject of chaos theory and quantum group dynamics – in which I had an overwhelming sense of needing to empty myself – of thoughts, feelings and the general business of my life. For the whole workshop I (unusually) took no notes, did not 'take in' any of the theory, therapeutically did some cathartic work and gave out very little and, I remember, ate little; and yet experientially it was one of the highlights of my training. This is the sense of what Peck means by emptiness which he describes as an emptying of the barriers to communication (expectations, preconceptions, prejudices, solutions, the need to control), a facilitator of which is silence. Many people who have experienced community-building groups take this process of 'letting go' of barriers to communication into the rest of their lives after a particular community-building – or therapeutic – event: De Marignac (1984), for instance, describes experimenting with the PCA in her neighbourhood and Stockwell (1984) describes an attempt at community living, also informed by person-centred principles. Peck's ideas have given rise to the Foundation for Community Encouragement (FCE) based in the United States and to an international network of people interested in community-building with contacts in many countries, including Britain.[1]

Community-making and community feeling, of course, also depend on the context of what is happening in the immediate and wider social/political world, outside the external boundary of any group: 'there is little doubt that the 1980s saw an acceleration in the disintegration of social solidarity and of communities. During this period, virtually all forms of collective institutions became weakened' (Furedi, 1997, p. 140). I now briefly turn to the political world for a critical analysis which has impacted on the theory and practice of community.

The psychopolitics of community

In addition to his more famous economic analysis and theories, Marx developed a theory of alienation which is central to a Marxist approach to individuals and which may be applied to class-conscious therapeutic practice (Tudor, 1997b). Marx (1932/1975) proposes a political (and psychological) communism:

> the positive supersession of private property as human self-estrangement, and hence the true appropriation of the human essence through and for man; it is the complete restoration of man to himself as a social, i.e. human being . . . it is the genuine resolution of the conflict between man and nature and between man and man, the true resolution of the conflict between existence and being, between objectification and self-affirmation, between freedom and necessity, between individual and species. (p. 348)

This may be read as a humanist/existential view of personal goals, being 'that self which one truly is' (Rogers, 1961), resolving conflict and increasingly being open to one's experience, trusting in one's organism and being willing to be a process – in short: being, becoming and belonging. For many, such a restoration of human essence *in relationship* is a desirable outcome – for our societies as well as our psyches. The communist notion that all property should be invested in the community and labour organised for the common benefit may also be viewed by many as equitable and even desirable. However, over the course of this century, the regimes which have purported or attempted to apply Marxist theory have for the most part failed miserably, presiding

instead over chaotic (rather than planned) economies, estrange-
ment, with the breakdown of communities, families, individuals
and relationships, appropriation and state bureaucracies – mock-
ing the ideas and ideals of Marx and his early followers. None the
less, communism, communitarianism (the practice of commu-
nistic theories) and communalism (a theory of government which
advocates the widest extension of local autonomy for each locally
definable community) are still influential. Kingdom (1992) traces
the history and examines different expressions of our instinct to
communal, mutually supportive life, arguing that 'the sense of
community is necessary to fulfilment' (p. 103), and, in doing so,
reviews political theory which views the state as organism.
Similarly, although from a different direction of enquiry, Alford
(1994) argues that groups (rather than individuals) are the state of
nature.

In practice, such ideas have influenced various forms of societies as well as common living arrangements, whether through
some form of *cooperation*, such as the Co-operative Society, or
cooperative living or settlement, such as the Israeli *moshavot*, or
different forms of *collective* and even *communal* living, such as
the *kibbutzim*.

Cooperation literally means working together. The following
passage shows how cooperation works amongst geese – from
which humans have much to learn.

> Next fall, when you see geese heading south for the winter, flying
> along in 'V' formation, you might consider what science has discovered
> as to why they fly that way. As each bird flaps its wings, it creates an
> uplift for the bird immediately following. By flying in a 'V' formation,
> the whole flock adds at least 70% greater flying range than if each bird
> flew on its own.
>
> People who share a common direction and sense of community can
> get where they are going more quickly and more easily, because they
> are travelling on the thrust of one another. When a goose falls out of
> formation, it suddenly feels the drag and resistance of trying to go it
> alone – and quickly gets back into formation to take advantage of the
> lifting power of the bird in front. If we have as much sense as a goose,
> we will stay in formation with those people who are headed the same
> way we are.
>
> When the head goose gets tired, it rotates back in the wing and
> another goose flies at point. It is sensible to take turns doing demand-
> ing jobs, whether with people or with geese flying south.
>
> Geese honk from behind to encourage those up front to keep up
> their speed. What messages do we give when we honk from behind?

Finally – and this is important – when a goose gets sick or wounded by gunshot and falls out of formation, two other geese fall out with that goose and follow it down to lend help and protection. They stay with the fallen goose until it is able to fly or until it dies; and only then do they launch out on their own or with another formation to catch up with their group. If we have the sense of a goose, we will stand by each other like that. (Source unknown)

A *collective* is formed by a number of individuals acting together with some purpose, usually to work together (for example, a workers' coop) and/or to live together (in a collective household for example, or a spiritual community such as the Buddhist *sangha*). The boundary around this number and purpose defines and distinguishes the collective from isolated forms or incidents of cooperation. The difference between this and some form of communalism usually centres around the degree of sharing – of resources, income and distribution (respectively, less and more). In a collective, members tend to view themselves as individuals collecting together around a specific purpose, whilst retaining a strong sense of individuality and individualism in the rest of their lives. In a collective house, for instance, it is common for people to enjoy and retain their different incomes whilst sharing a proportion of their money and other resources, such as time, by discussion as regards issues such as housework and childcare.

By contrast, a *communal* workplace, house or community is one in which the members have and hold more of a life in common. The commune often forms around a particular ideology (political, social, spiritual, ecological). There is generally more sharing of *all* available resources and collective discussion and agreement (rather than individual decision-making). There are numerous examples of communal movements and experiments over time and across cultures – five living communes are described by Rigby (1974), at least one of which is still thriving today, nearly a quarter of a century later.

The relevance of these different ideas of and influences on community for group counsellors is:

■ That they broaden our views and appreciation of community and of culture.

■ That some clients – and counsellors – may be involved with such ventures. The Local Economic Trading Schemes (referred to in Chapter 2), for instance, are examples of cooperation.

■ That as group counsellor you may be invited in to work in or with groups, cooperatives, collectives or communes and their intragroup and intergroup dynamics.

> The transformation, through the development of labour, of personal powers (relations) into material powers . . . is not possible without the community. Only in community [with others has each] individual the means of cultivating his gifts in all directions; only in the community, therefore, is personal freedom possible. (Marx and Engels, 1846/1970, p. 83)

From therapeutic community to communities which are therapeutic

Finally, in concluding this chapter, I sketch out the logic of the focus on groups and on the context of groups which this book and this chapter describes – moving the therapeutic from the individual to the group and from the group to intergroup relations and into the wider social sphere of organisation and community. As Rogers puts it: 'while my whole approach to persons and their relationships changes but slowly (and very little in its fundamentals), my interest in its applications has shifted markedly. No longer am I primarily interested in individual therapeutic learning, but in broader and broader social implications' (1975, p. 144).

Context

Rogers (1986) writes: 'there is one *best* school of therapy. It is the school of therapy you develop for yourself based on a continuing critical examination of the effects of being in the relationship' (p. 135). Paraphrasing Rogers, I suggest that there is one best school of group therapy and that is based on critical examination of the effects of being in relationship *and in relationship-in-context*.

Just as you cannot not be in relationship, so you cannot not be in context. The point is to be aware and intentional about context – the counsellor's, the clients' and the group's: this is cultural psychology, and good counselling – in practice. Figure 7.1 represents the context and relationship of the individual and individual therapy to group/s, community/ies and society. This parallels Kreeger's (1975) diagram of concentric circles, representing the relative degree of analytic components: self-analysis and psycho-analysis (individual), group analysis (group), open air psychiatry (community) and life – although I view 'life' as present equally in all contexts (see Figure 3.1).

Unlike the commonplace 'time is a great healer' (which, whilst reassuring, may encourage a fatalistic passivity), the aphorism '*life is the great healer*' represents a positive statement about the potential of life as a healing or therapeutic experience. In the context of therapy, life may be viewed as the great co-therapist. Indeed, some schools of therapy recognise not only the limitations of formal (and usually individual) therapy but also acknowledge life as part of the process. Rogers (1951), for instance, notes that what he identifies as the final of seven stages of process, a process of fluidity of feeling, experiencing, etc. 'occurs as much outside of the therapeutic relationship as in it' (p. 151). Yalom (1995) acknowledges the therapeutic factors outside the group and the impact of internal changes on the patient's interpersonal environment – as a positive 'adaptive spiral' (p. 103).

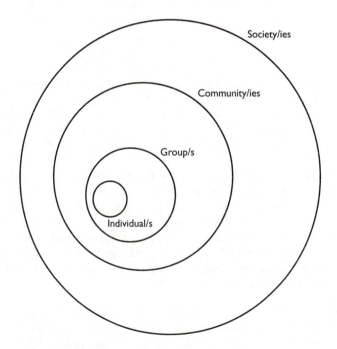

Figure 7.1   *The individual-in-context*

Relationship in context

Given that I am in relationship, I am who I am in all contexts; who I am is differentiated only by the particular *role* I am in at any one moment: husband, father, writer, employer, consultant, customer (and that's just today!) (see Tudor, in 1999b). This whole (holistic) view of who I am draws on a number of psychological traditions, including: holism, which affirms the complexity of persons and events; the person-centred *approach*, which applies its principles and extends to relationships and events outside the consulting room as much as to those within it; and social action psychotherapy, which focuses on the social context in which client and practitioner are located (see Holland, 1990).

> If therapists and clients truly form an endogamous community, then the boundaries between personal problems and social problems vanish; the personal and the social become merely polar points on a spectrum, and therapy can deal with the whole spectrum by working to transform the individual and his surroundings at the same time. (Castel et al., 1982, pp. 160–1)

This has enormous implications for the counsellor and the group counsellor in managing the transition between individual therapy and more collective, sociopolitical forms of therapy – implications which are not popular in the current climate of defensive therapy and worries about qualification, accreditation and registration. From a person-centred perspective, for instance, Barrett-Lennard (1990) suggests that, as no transference is being cultivated, client–therapist contact outside therapy 'may further the anchorage between in-therapy experience and outside life experience and behavior' (p. 151).

Macmillan and Lago (1996) and Schmid (1996) trace the history of the person-centred approach as a group therapy – whereby the group is the interface between the person and society. It seems to me that a number of group therapeutic initiatives represent this interface and the possibility for group counsellors to take therapy into the community and to be part of making communities more therapeutic or healing places in which to live. Here I refer briefly to three such initiatives.

Conscientizaçao   Conscientisation, a kind of two-way, collective and political consciousness-raising, comes from the work of Freire in South America who, drawing on his experience of teaching adult literacy, describes an egalitarian educative process – a pedagogy of the oppressed (Freire, 1972, 1974). In his writing on education, Rogers acknowledges Freire and their similar, shared philosophy. More recently and also from a person-centred perspective, O'Hara (1989) describes the need for social consciousness-raising. Although, for many, consciousness-raising is associated with the early days of the women's movement and self-help groups, for instance, in the mental health/illness field, there is still a need for community groups to be facilitated in ways that encourage their members to take social action for themselves (see Holland, 1990).

The alternate group meeting   This meeting (see Chapter 3) is one way of democratising the process of therapy whilst, as a group counsellor, still retaining an interest in the process. The logic of people meeting on their own, in each other's homes, talking with the partners and friends of group members, all combine to undermine dependence on the group therapist and, positively, to take therapy literally out into the community. I know of a number of examples of fixed-term therapy (and training) groups which decide to meet on their own, a process which continues long after their 'official' end. One group recently negotiated to meet for a weekend and, after some discussion about the pros and cons of facilitation, asked a group facilitator if he would be willing to 'stand by' on the second day in case they wanted, needed or in any case decided to involve him in the group process.

Sharing life therapy   This is based on the work of Stamatiadis (1990), who describes this as a personal and extended way of being with clients in which the ways and means of working developed from the process of therapy. These include what Stamatiadis refers to as: verbal tools – the 'standard' therapeutic interview or meeting, taping sessions for the client and telephone calls; body tools – physical touching and holding (see Chapter 4), focusing, wrestling and walking; art tools – drawing and painting; dream work; and giving gifts. This takes place in a variety of time structures, including extended meetings, and in various settings outside the consulting room. The work is constantly negotiated with clear therapeutic limits, mainly to do with the therapist's commitment. It is an unusual, demanding, creative, intensive and, judging by client reports, successful form of therapy. Drawing on these traditions, my partner and I developed a group form of sharing life therapy, which we ran over three years and which we viewed as essentially providing the possibility for a non-residential therapeutic community (Embleton Tudor and Tudor, 1997).

Having discussed the developmental life of the group and its wider context, in the final chapter I now turn to issues in the education/training, personal development and supervision of group counsellors.

Note

1 The FCE may be contacted via its internet web page http://www.fce-community.org/. The Community Building Network in Britain may be contacted through Anthony Kirke, 125 Greenham Road, Newbury, Berkshire RG14 7JE.

8

The Group Counsellor: Education, Training, Personal Development and Supervision

By way of concluding this book, this chapter reviews the current organisation – state and status – of training in Britain as regards group counselling/psychotherapy/analysis. With reference to the theory and practice of group therapy as discussed throughout this book, the implications for the professional training and personal development of counsellors as well as for ongoing supervision of the counsellor's groupwork practice are considered. Education/ training in therapy is generally considered to comprise three elements: the formal training or 'taught' course, personal therapy and/or development and supervised practice. In training the group therapist Yalom (1995) adds the component of observing experienced clinicians and subdivides personal therapy into personal group experience and individual therapy. These, however, are all predicated upon the necessary qualities and attitudes of the group counsellor which are therefore explored first.

The qualities of a group counsellor

The person of the group counsellor

For Rogers (1961), the person of the counsellor is expressed in their attitudes (as discussed below). Berne (1966) discusses the person of the therapist in terms of presentation, suggesting that 'he will do no harm by presenting himself as a reasonably courteous, alert, interested, and enthusiastic person . . . [although] a certain reserve should be maintained . . . His conduct should be guided by aesthetics, responsibility and commitment' (pp. 72–3). In discussing personal characteristics, Aveline (1988) suggests that the good leader will be characterised 'by an abiding interest in people, a fundamental conviction that people have it within them to change and to grow and, significantly, that group members can assist each other in this endeavour' (p. 318). In a political and organisational climate in which increasing emphasis is placed on measures and outcomes in education and training, it is worth noting that these are largely based on different concepts of learning to those which place an emphasis on personal and social values and attitudes.

A facilitative attitude

In a chapter on the training of counsellors and therapists, Rogers (1951) comments on the importance of 'the attitudinal orientation of the counselor' (p. 432). For the person-centred group counsellor in particular it is essential to have and to be constantly developing a facilitative attitude. In terms of the person-centred approach (PCA) this entails: being in contact with the client, being genuine, and experiencing unconditional positive regard towards and empathic understanding of the client/s, although these qualities are a matter of degree at any given moment rather than absolutes. As an integrative statement about the group counsellor's facilitative attitudes, these may be expressed as follows.

1. Being in psychological contact with the individuals in the group and with the group as a whole, making a difference in the experiential field of the group. In this the leader/facilitator

has an important climate-setting function which relates to the preparation work considered in Chapter 2. In many respects, because of the numbers involved in group therapy greater attention is paid to the here-and-now contact. In discussing the selection of therapists for training (as individual therapists), Aveline (1996) offers his impression that individual therapists

> seem to have a greater interest in the vertical or historical axis of *there-and-then* exploration into the childhood origins of adult problems and their re-creation within the therapy relationship, as opposed to the horizontal axis of *here-and-now* interactions which is central to the focus of the group therapist'. (p. 373)

2. Being aware of the clients' and group's incongruence – in terms of the PCA this refers to discrepancies between their experience and self and the group picture. In other terms, this might involve assessment and diagnosis of the presenting person and their problems as well as of the group (see Chapter 1).

3. Being genuine. Rogers (1958/1990b) identifies some of the characteristics of a helping relationship, including being trustworthy, being 'dependably real' (rather than rigidly consistent), being expressive enough to communicate unambiguously, and being strong and secure enough to be separate from others. Another important aspect of this quality is the positive side of not being defensive: freeing myself from external threat so that if and when a client or clients or the whole group are, say, angry with me, I am able to listen, understand and respond from a position/attitude of clarity rather than, clouded by my own issues, reacting from hurt, blame, embarrassment, a belief about unfairness etc. All this involves group counsellors in a commitment to being in process ourselves (see Rogers, 1961). There is some evidence to suggest that the genuineness of the facilitator in the context of the group *as a whole* has more impact on an individual's outcome than their receiving the facilitator's genuineness directly (see Wood, 1995b).

Being genuine is not an excuse for indiscrimate self-disclosure; it is an argument for active self-involvement in the process of the group. Within the PCA more than many other approaches, and especially in groups in which the facilitator is also a participant, it is more common for the facilitator to share more of themselves, which may include self-disclosure. This is based on the philosophical value of mutuality, reflects personal presence in terms of intervention style (Lietaer and Dierick, 1996), and often has the effect of helping clients or the group to share more of themselves – universality, identification, instillation of hope, existential factors in terms of therapeutic factors (Yalom, 1995). Given the current climate of competence-based learning and accreditation, it is interesting to note that the current competencies for qualification in social work do not include specific reference to the use of self or to genuineness (Central Council for Education and Training in Social Work, 1995).

4. Being fully accepting or 'confirming the other', both of individuals and of the group as a whole. Rogers (1970/1973) likens the group to an organism and talks about trusting the group and its process 'to develop its own potential and that of its members . . . [with] a sense of its own direction (pp. 49–50). In their study of encounter groups, Lieberman, Yalom and Miles (1973) found that leaders who were providers, specialising in caring and the attribution of meaning – who, in effect, gave love – produced positive changes and minimised negative outcomes (see Chapter 1).

5. Being understanding of the individuals and the group by perceiving as accurately as possible others' 'internal frame of reference', doing so with sufficient sensitivity so as not to be perceived as threatening, and in doing so helping them to free themselves from the continued external threat of the way they have internalised distorted perceptions. A key aspect of a person's frame of reference is their culture (discussed below); and empathy also entails appreciating issues of power and how they affect people's lives, position and participation in a group (see Chapter 3). Empathy is often associated and (wrongly) equated with the 'technique' of reflection. Bozarth (1984) helps move our understanding of empathy beyond reflection to emergent modes of empathy, including evocative reflection such as metaphors, personal reaction etc. and idiosyncratic empathy, which may involve unexpected responses. This active, responsive, intuitive, expressive and creative way of being is especially important in a group where there are multiple interactions and exponential dynamics.

Importantly, this attitude also involves the counsellor in facilitating group members' empathic understanding of each other – which is viewed as a crucial variable in group therapy (Giesekus and Mente, 1986; Mente, 1990). In this respect, Rogers' question 'Can I be strong enough as a person to be separate from the other?' (Rogers, 1958/1990b, p. 121) applies equally to group members in developing their empathy as it does to the group leader and, in turn, is something which the leader needs to facilitate.

6. The sixth condition in this schema requires that the communication to the client/s of these last two conditions is achieved; hence the importance and value of research into helpful events and therapeutic factors (see Chapter 2).

Any subsequent techniques developed by the group counsellor may be viewed as 'an implementation of attitudes' (Rogers, 1951, p. 433).

Ability to use our senses

Berne (1966) discusses the requirements of the group therapist, summarising them as an ability to 'ideally use all five senses in making a diagnosis, assessing the situation, and planning the treatment: sight, hearing, smell, touch and taste' (p. 65) – although he acknowledges that the sense of taste is seldom used (except when the client offers the counsellor a sweet which may be sweet, sour or bitter!).

1. *Visual observation.* This is 'the basis of all good clinical work, and takes precedence even over technique' (Berne, 1966, pp. 65-6). Berne's detailed comments on this are worth noting and quoting at length:

    Any well-read student or properly programmed computer can make correct interpretations, given properly weighted findings; the real skill lies in collecting and evaluating data. Observations in group treatment should be made on a physiological basis, although their interpretation will be psychological. The therapist should be aware of the probable physiological state of every one of his patients during every moment of the session. He should know when to look directly at a patient, when to be content with peripheral vision, and when to sweep the whole group with his gaze. He should note not only overt blushing, palpitation, sweating, tremors, tension, excitement, rage, weeping, laughter, and sexuality, but should also be able to detect each of these in their incipient stages before they come out into the open. In order to do this he must observe carriage, posture, movements, gestures, facial mimicry, twitches of single muscles, arterial pulsations, local vasomotor and philomotor phenomena, and swallowing' (p. 66).

Berne pays particular and detailed attention to facial expressions and pasimology, the science of gestures. This is not to suggest that the therapist comments on all that he or she observes; it is to suggest that all this is available to their awareness. Observing in such detail has direct implications for the training of therapists in general and of group therapists in particular.

2. *Listening*. Listening is applied or focused hearing. Berne discusses several kinds of listening: listening to the content of what is said; to auditory clues (coughing, wheezing etc.); to pitch, timbre, rhythm and intonation; to inconsistencies; and listening to vocabulary. Berne identifies three types of vocabulary which correspond to different ego states: borrowed (Parental), learned (Adult) and rebellious or compliant (Child). Fleming (1998) identifies seven levels of listening, some of which supplement Berne's discussion. What Fleming refers to as passive listening is 'a combination of meditation and listening which aims to blank the mind and let in the other person whole and complete without the interference of the listener's thoughts, assessments, diagnosis, programmes and ideas' (Fleming, 1998, p. 8). One way of developing passive listening skills is to close your eyes while listening to someone and to focus inward on your listening rather than outwards on them. Other levels include: listening to the therapist's own emotional response to listening (the equivalent of developing congruence or being aware of countertransferential reactions); and listening to goodwill, that is, to the client's willingness to consider the possibility of change.

3. *Smell*. Although learning about smell theoretically, let alone experientially, does not form much (or even any) part of most counselling training, this is an important and underrated sense. How a person or a group smells is a part of our experiential field. Most people smell quite strongly, for instance, when they are afraid; most of us also wear artificial smells in the form of perfumes and deodorants. The different smell of a room after someone has been very angry and the different smells of different groups are all part of the field.

Acupuncturists educate and train their sense of smell and, using the Chinese five elements system of diagnosis, are able to identify different smells which are diagnostic (see Table 8.1).

4. *Touch*. The relevance of the discussion in Chapter 4 is that there needs to be more input on counsellor training courses and in supervison on the implications of touch, close physical contact, sexual arousal and attraction, as well as the therapeutic use of touch (see also Hunter and Struve, 1997).

Professional and personal education: training and development as a group counsellor

Although these elements are often separated – for instance, as professional training and personal development – the present discussion takes these together as inextricably and inevitably interrelated as it is one person who is undertaking education/training. Although, in his ideas and writing about education, Rogers is generally against 'training' and 'teaching' – 'one cannot "train" an individual to be a *person*' (Rogers, 1970/1973, p. 152) – and *for* the facilitation of learning, he does identify six elements of a 'desirable preparatory background' for the (generic) therapist (Rogers, 1951), which I expand as regards a necessary knowledge base for the group therapist.

An experiential knowledge of the human being in their cultural setting

This prefigures more contemporary concerns about being an effective multicultural group counsellor (see Corey, 1995). Whilst it is interesting to gain knowledge of other cultures, it is most important to develop awareness of and insight into your own culture and the impact this has on you and how you are as a counsellor (see Singh and Tudor, 1997), including any attitudes which are not facilitative of pluralism – whether cultural, racial, sexual or social. In this sense all counselling is and should be culturally located and all counsellors culturally intentioned (see Ivey et al., 1993) and socially intentioned (Tudor, 1997d). Cultural setting extends to the context of culture, groups, subcultures and communities. A necessary part of any group counsellor's knowledge base, then, includes the experience of median and large groups, intergroup dynamics, organisation and community (see Chapter 7).

Table 8.1 Some characteristics of the Chinese five element system[1]

Seasons	Winter	Spring	Summer	Late summer	Autumn
Characteristics	Fallow time, generation of seeds	A time of new growth, birth (rebirth)	A time of warmth	A time of harvest and harvesting	A time for pruning
Element	Water	Wood	Fire	Earth	Metal
Colour	Blue, black	Green	Red	Yellow	White
Odour	Putrid (e.g. stagnant water)	Rancid (e.g. fresh grass)	Scorched	Fragrant (sickly sweet)	Rotten (e.g. rotting leaves and compost)
Flavour	Salt	Sour, sharp (e.g. lemons, vinegar)	Bitter (e.g. chocolate, spinach)	Sweet	Spicy
Emotion	Fear, awe	Anger	Joy	Sympathy	Grief
Sound	Groaning	Shouting	Laughing	Singing	Weeping
Life cycle	Old age	Childhood/adolescence	Young adult	Middle-aged adult	Retiring adult

[1]My thanks to Pam Gegges for her contribution to this chart.

As regards training in group therapy, Yalom's (1995) component of observed group therapy may be viewed as enabling the trainee group therapist to gain experiential knowledge of the human being in the particular cultural setting of the group. Some of Yalom's strategies for facilitating this – trainees observing the group through a one-way mirror, observers sitting in the group room outside the circle of the group – will be unacceptable to some; and Yalom's presentation of this to clients, being beneficial to unknown future patients, somewhat stretches and indeed may influence the therapeutic factor of altruism. Nevertheless, having practice upon which to reflect is essential to training and Yalom makes a number of points about including the group in the training process (giving it/them feedback and even inviting the group to the post-group discussion with trainees). Another way of gaining this experiential knowledge is in therapeutic and/or personal development groups *as a part of* the training course. Whilst these are invaluable in terms of learning through experience and reflection, the issues involved are complex and are well discussed by Yalom (1995) and by Dryden and Feltham (1994) – Who runs such groups? Is participation voluntary? Is there any component or sense of assessment? Is the training group a therapy group? A useful distinction in this context may be made between a *therapy* group and a *training* group whose effect is *therapeutic* (Yalom, 1995). Both in facilitating and participating in this, it is important that the primary and secondary purposes of any group, as reflected in the contract, are acknowledged and maintained:

> in a therapy group, the intensive group experience, the expression and integration of affect, the recognition of here-and-now process, are all essential but secondary considerations to the primary goal of individual therapeutic change. In a training group of mental health professionals, the reverse is true. (Yalom, 1985, p. 523)

Empathic experiencing
This is discussed above.

A basic personal philosophy
This requires the counsellor having thought through some of the basic questions regarding human life, its nature, development, how people change etc. and especially how we deal with difference/s and with people who do not share and are even antagonistic to our personal philosophy and world-view. The point made about pluralism (above) is a case in point. This is based as

much on a personal philosophy of mine which welcomes and celebrates difference and diversity as it is on a scientific (biological) and psychological appreciation of human development through differentiation (see Rogers, 1959). In my view the study of philosophy and its implications for therapeutic practice (see Erwin, 1997) should form a larger and more central part of counselling and psychotherapy training courses than it does currently.

Experience of personal therapy
See the next section.

A deep knowledge of the dynamics of personality
Again, Rogers stresses the empathic and experiential aspects of this knowledge and a preference that these should be gained before the theoretical knowledge – for similar reasons as Dierick and Lietaer's (1990) objections to a priori categorisation. A deep knowledge and understanding – comprehension, application, analysis, synthesis and evaluation (Bloom et al., 1956) – of the dynamics of groups comprises:

- Knowledge and understanding of the chosen therapeutic approach in its application to working in, through and with groups.
- Knowledge and understanding of therapeutic or helping factors of groups, of developmental processes in groups, of group dynamics, and of issues of leadership/facilitation.
- Knowledge and understanding of the practical and practice issues involved in preparing for, establishing, maintaining and ending groups.
- Knowledge and understanding of other approaches to group counselling/psychotherapy/analysis.
- Application of theory to group therapeutic practice – and of practice to theory.
- Analysis of the chosen approach and its application to groups (for example, within the PCA the concept of the group as organism).
- Synthesis of different parts of group theory and practice, for example, of the relation between group development and group process (see, for instance, Tables 3.2, 4.1, 5.1).

■ Evaluation of theory and practice as a reflective practitioner, critically evaluating experience and learning, including assumptions about groups and groupwork, context and culture, assimilated – or accommodated – during training and in practice, for example as regards 'check in' time which is different from 'group time', 'group process time' and 'community meeting' (see Chapter 3).

A knowledge of research and research design (see Chapters 2 and 5 and Yalom, 1995).

Personal development and therapy

It has long been a requirement of most psychotherapy training and is for all such training leading to United Kingdom Council for Psychotherapy (UKCP) registration that the student/trainee is themselves in personal therapy. Further, this requirement usually specifies that its form (orientation), intensity (frequency) and duration parallels that which the therapist is training, and expects, to practise. Although many counselling training courses also have this as a course requirement, it was not until 1998 that the British Association for Counselling (BAC) stipulated a minimum personal counselling requirement of forty weeks for counsellors seeking BAC counsellor accreditation – a contentious decision which has led to fierce debate from a number of perspectives, reflected in the pages of the BAC's journal, *Counselling*.

There are a number of rationales for this requirement. Alongside formal training/learning and supervised practice, personal therapy and development is arguably the most personal and potent means of learning about therapy and, especially when your therapist shares the orientation in which you are training, of internalising your understanding of the approach – as applied to yourself. Therapy also supports the trainee therapist in terms of understanding their own issues, their motivations to do this work, and with any personal issues which arise in the course of working as a therapist with clients. Being in therapy also provides an equitable frame of reference of empathy for clients: 'I know what it is to be a client, over time.' There is also an argument based on mutuality: 'I don't ask people to do something I haven't done or which I'm not prepared to do.' In his references to this Rogers (1951) talks about the *desirability* and *opportunity* for personal therapy, placing no requirement on it or on the timing of it; arguably any such requirement may be viewed as antithetical to this particular approach. Indeed, one of the problems of making this a requirement is that it sets up trainees – and their therapists – with the issue of involuntary attendance: 'I have to be here because it's a course requirement.' Although such a presentation provides fuel for the therapy and, in any case, is easily addressed by reminding trainees that their participation on the course itself is voluntary, it is nevertheless a source of contention amongst some trainee therapists.

Different courses and orientations place differing emphasis on the relationship between the three – or four (Yalom, 1995) – elements of the course. In psychoanalytic training the training analysis is classically viewed as very much part of the course with progression dependent on reports from the training analyst. In some psychodynamic circles and in transactional analysis (TA) the roles of trainer and supervisor (and sometimes therapist) are combined – which conflicts with perceived wisdom and with current BAC codes of ethics and practice about dual relationships (see Tudor, 1999b). Within the PCA and some other humanistic/existential schools, personal development on the course itself is viewed as an essential part of training: developing the person 'heralds the true challenge of person-centred training: the enormous personal development work which is necessary to win a sufficient degree of self-acceptance which will allow the counsellor to feel consistently unthreatened, accepting and open to the experiencing of her clients' (Mearns, 1997, p. xi). In many ways personal and professional development *on* the training course, through group time, working in small and large groups, in community meetings etc., is the best way of integrating the total learning experience: 'personal development for professional working is so crucial to the person-centred approach that it cannot be left to the vagaries of individual therapy' (Mearns, 1997, p. 35) (also see Appendix 1). It is ironic that, although the majority of counselling training takes place in groups, the implications of this training experience for practice *as a group counsellor* are not often reflected upon or applied. Of course, as regards the experience of personal therapy for training *group* therapists and in terms of parallelling the process they are offering, such experience needs to be in a group. The Institute of Group Analysis (IGA), for example, which offers a specialist Diploma in Group Analysis and is a qualifying course leading to UKCP registration, requires trainees to be in personal group analysis throughout its four-year course.

In practical terms, the group counsellor with experience of being in groups themself has experiential knowledge of a range of issues: beginning a group, joining a goup, being in a group when new members join, leaving a group, ending a group etc.

Supervision of group counselling

Despite the increase in interest and publications on supervision over the past ten years and the fact that supervision often takes place in groups, there is surprisingly little in the literature specifically on the (individual or group) supervision of group therapy. Here I consider issues regarding supervision both in the context of training and of ongoing practice and development.

The setting

Whilst it is possible to receive individual supervision of your practice as a group therapist, there are distinct advantages to group supervision in this context. First, it parallels the process offered. Secondly, group supervision provides a container which holds the helping relationship, especially so when this involves another group. Thirdly, the supervision group provides a source of process on which to reflect and from which 'live' learning may be derived and which, in turn, often reflects a process parallel to that of the therapy group. A supervision group thus also provides a forum for more and creative options for supervision (role plays, sculpting, etc.) as well as simply more responses. Finally, depending on the level of experience and interest of its members, such a supervision group offers a context for the training of supervisors.

The group

In the context of training, the supervision group generally comprises a peer group of trainees, 'led' by a supervisor who may or may not be a member of the training course staff. More experienced practitioners may form their own leaderless peer group. Hawkins and Shohet (1989) review the psychological and practical aspects of establishing group, team and peer group supervision. More attention has been paid in the past ten years to developmental perspectives of practitioners in supervision (and in training) whereby supervisors (and trainers) match the structure and process of supervision (and training) to the practitioner's level of development (for example, Stoltenberg and Delworth, 1987); Holloway (1995) notes eighteen different developmental models. Table 8.2 offers a summary of a developmental approach to supervision, integrating various elements including Hawkins and Shohet's (1989) process model. I place this here as, in forming a supervision group, both facilitator/s and participants need to consider its composition: some prefer to meet with peers in terms of the level of their experience, others may choose a mixed economy of experience and, for that matter, a mix and/or balance of orientation – theoretical and sexual – culture, gender, class and ability.

The supervisor
In addition to having the qualities of a counsellor (as above), the supervisor should themselves be experienced in facilitating groups and in the supervision of groupwork practice and, where appropriate, in the supervision of trainee therapists – which offers its unique complexities and challenges and (as with the training of therapists at the beginning of their training courses) should not be left to beginning supervisors (or beginning or 'apprentice' trainers). Igwe (1997/8) elaborates the requirements and qualities of an effective supervisor for cross-cultural counselling and includes welcoming diversity, which he equates with unconditional positive regard.

Supervision in training
Supervised practice in the context of training is an essential element in the development of the group therapist. Rogers (1951) argues 'that the practice of therapy should be part of the training experience from the earliest practicable moment' (p. 433). Yalom (1995) cites some of his own research with colleagues (Ebersole et al., 1969), comparing group leaders who received training and supervision with others who received neither, commenting that the results indicated that 'not only did the trained therapist improve but the untrained therapists . . . were *less skilled than at the beginning*' (Yalom, 1995, pp. 515–16), concluding that ongoing supervision is essential in 'reinforcing' training. Yalom also argues for the practice of supervisors observing groups. Aveline

Table 8.2 A developmental approach to supervision (developed from Stoltenburg and Delworth, 1987)

	Level I	Level II	Level III	Level IV (Level III integrated)
Supervisee–supervisor relationship	Supervisee dependent on supervisor	Supervisee fluctuates between dependence on supervisor and autonomy	Supervisee is more separate and dependent on supervisor only in relation to specific issues/situations	Supervisee has personal and professional relationship with supervisor, the relationship is more collegial
Analogy with stages of human development	Childhood	Adolescence	Early adulthood	Maturity
Metaphor (in relation to medieval craft guilds)	Novice/apprentice	Journeyman/woman	Independent craftsman/woman	'Master' craftsman/woman
Supervisee's focus	Self-centred	Client-centred	Process-centred	Process-in-context-centred
Supervisee's concern	'Can I make it in this work?'	'Can I help this client make it?'	'How are we relating together?'	'How do processes relate to each other?'
Supervisory tasks	To provide: – A clearly structured environment – Positive feedback and encouragement – 'Balancing support and uncertainty'[1]	To help the supervisee focus on the client. To be less structured and didactic	To help the supervisee focus on the process of their work. To 'let go' of the supervisee	To be senior peer/colleague
Relationship to the process model[2]	1 Reflection on content of the therapy session 2 Exploration of strategies used by the therapist	1, 2 and beginning 3 Exploration of the therapy process and relationship	1, 2, 3 and 4 Focus on therapist's counter-transference 5 Focus on supervisory process and relationship	1, 2, 3, 4, 5 and 6 Focus on supervisor's counter-transference 6a Focus on fantasy relationship between supervisor and therapist's client 7 Focus on organisation context of supervision

[1] Stoltenberg and Delworth, 1987.
[2] Hawkins and Shohet, 1989.

(1988) briefly discusses supervised practice as an element in a balanced training and argues that supervised experience of being both a solo and co-leader is preferable.

Theoretical orientation
Although it appears obvious that consistency in theoretical orientation is preferable and 'a good thing', this is the subject of much heated debate. In the light of comparative research which does not prove the effectiveness of one therapeutic approach over another and, indeed, research which estimates the contribution of *technique* (although not approach) to outcome as only 15% (Lambert, 1985), Aveline (1988) reminds us as trainers to be cautious in singing one song. Recently, Feltham (1997a) has, at least conceptually, challenged the BAC requirement for the accreditation of training courses to have a (one) core theoretical model – the logic of which is, of course, that courses based on such philosophical and ethical objections would not seek BAC accreditation. My own view of counselling and psychotherapy training courses is that the core model is generally not core enough – or, preferably, integral – in terms of the structure, content, process and organisation of the course and that it is possible to advocate the integrity of one approach whilst recognising, being interested in and even studying other approaches and world-views. After all, one of the learnings we take from living and working in groups is that we live in a plural and pluralistic world.

As regards supervision, the issue of orientation is also linked to development. At the beginning of training (Table 8.2. Level I) trainees are often great advocates and sometimes dangerous proselytisers of what they may view as *the* approach. Some either come in with or develop criticisms or even an antagonism to the approach (Level II). As they become more experienced in and more familiar with the therapeutic world – adult learners are, of course, experienced adults in the wider world (a point some supervisors, trainers and courses overlook) – they often become more interested in other approaches and in comparing their chosen approach with these (Levels III and IV); indeed, a comparative component is a requirement of BAC accredited counselling courses. It is at this stage that practitioners may want to be in a supervision group with therapists from other orientations and to undertake further supervision and training with practitioners of other orientations.

What all this requires of the supervisor is to be clear in their own theoretical orientation and their experience and knowledge of and competence in supervision and groupwork and that the(ir) process of supervision reflects their orientation.

The organisation – state and status – of group counselling in Britain

For the past hundred years, since Freud first coined the term psychotherapy in 1896, the whole issue of accreditation, registration and the professionalisation of counselling and psychotherapy has been the subject of much debate, although these debates have become more intense since the founding of the British Association for Counselling (BAC) in 1976, the coming into being of the United Kingdom Council for Psychotherapy (UKCP) and the establishment of the first National Register of Psychotherapists in 1993 and the United Kingdom Register of Counsellors in 1996. Whilst (UKCP) wants to move towards statutory regulation of psychotherapy in order to give protection to the public, the argument that registration does this is not substantiated. The case against psychotherapy registration is well made by Mowbray (1995), as are arguments for maintaining pluralism and autonomy in counselling and psychotherapy (House and Totton, 1997). In the absence (as yet) of national and international legislation, alternative networks of practitioners are on the increase, for example the Independent Practitioners' Network which, together with other independent-minded therapists and theorists, keeps open debates about assessment, accreditation and accountability. In a challenging address to the American Psychological Association (APA) in 1973, Rogers asked if they (we) dared to develop a *human* science, to be whole people, to be designers rather than repairers – in all spheres of life – and to do away with professionalism: 'as soon as we set up criteria for certification . . . the first and greatest effect is to freeze the profession in a past image. This is an *inevitable* result' (Rogers, 1973/1990a, p. 364). In his ideas about education in general Rogers (1983) challenges traditional theories of 'top-down', 'banking' theories of education and training. Rogers' regret at his involvement in establishing a board of examiners within the APA is paralleled by Thorne's (1995) more recent concerns about the vicious circle of accountability and losing the soul in counselling. All these issues have been echoed in debates about the location and organisation of counselling and psychotherapy training – initially within medicine, later in academic settings and, more recently, in private organisations and institutes.

In terms of the present organisation, training, qualification and accreditation/registration of therapists in Britain there is no legal mandatory requirement to have completed a training in groupwork in order to facilitate a counselling group. Moreover, the BAC's current accreditation criteria (BAC, 1994) apply only to counsellors working with individuals and couples and specifically not to group counselling; thus counsellors running groups may not count those hours towards the 450 hours counselling practice requirement for BAC accreditation. This appears to be an historical anomaly and is (to date) unchallenged custom and practice rather than a deliberate policy of exclusion. Unlike its British counterpart, within the American Counseling Association there is a division concerned with groupwork: the Association for Specialists in Group Work (ASGW), with its own code of ethics as well as professional training standards (ASGW, 1989, 1992) and best practice guidelines (Appendix 1). There are a number of member organisations within the various Sections of the UKCP which are by definition specifically concerned with training in group therapy: within the Family, Couple, Sexual and Systemic Therapy Section, all organisations; within the Humanistic and Integrative (HIP) Section, the British Psychodrama Association; and within the Psychoanalytic and Psychodynamic Section, the Association for Group and Individual Psychotherapy and the Institute of Group Analysis. In addition, other member organisations run training courses in group therapy (see Appendix 4). Within the HIP Section the Association of Humanistic Psychology Practitioners (AHPP), which offers a route to UKCP registration, has a full membership category of group counsellor. The requirements for full membership of the AHPP and therefore UKCP registration as a group counsellor/therapist reflect the three elements of training and currently involve the following:

■ *Supervision* – Trainees and inexperienced practitioners at the rate of one hour's supervision with an experienced practitioner or trained supervisor to every eight hours' practice and in any case not less than one and a half hours a month.

- *Personal counselling* – At least forty hours of personal counselling, consistent with the counsellor's core theoretical model and in the same length and depth as the counselling they are offering, the implication of which is that the counsellor would need to have had experience of group counselling (see discussion above).
- *Practice* – At least 450 hours of supervised groupwork counselling practice and, during the two years prior to application for membership/registration, at least six clients maintained with the same supervisor.
- *Orientation* – Applicants must demonstrate their group counselling work has a humanistic orientation (AHPP, 1997).

As has been indicated, current training in group counselling is either (more commonly) generic or specialist.

Generic training
The majority of counselling and psychotherapy training is generic, that is, training which prepares the practitioner to work as a counsellor and/or psychotherapist:

- With a range of clients with a variety of presenting problems or issues and across a physical and psychological spectrum of illness–health.
- In a variety of modalities (individuals, couples, families, groups).
- In different sectors and settings:
  - statutory (NHS, social services, therapeutic communities).
  - voluntary/independent, for example, counselling agencies and projects.
  - private practice.

In practice, however, generic training predominantly prepares trainees for working with individual adult clients. Practitioners, employers and sometimes courses assume that learning and skills are transferable to working with groups, the only safeguard being the individual counsellor's commitment to monitoring the limits to their competence (BAC, 1997; UKCP, 1996). There is no requirement on generic courses – from either the BAC or the UKCP to have either a theoretical or practical component on groupwork. Aveline (1996) strongly favours that a required element in the training of individual therapists should be some experience of running groups such as a small group over 18 months: 'a degree of competence in group therapy, or, at the very least, a favourable familiarity with the approach should be part of the skills of an individual therapist. This can only be gained through direct experience' (p. 382).

Specialised training

The primacy of training as an individual therapist perhaps reflects the primacy of the individual over the group or the collective in many Western societies and, indeed, the primacy of individual therapy over group therapy (see Chapter 2). This also means that training in group counselling/therapy/analysis is seen as additional, specialised and even postgraduate, that is, after a graduating course in (individual) therapy. Given the current cost of training – as a counsellor, with training fees, supervision and the requirement to have personal therapy, this can easily cost £6,000, whilst training as a psychotherapist can cost £15,000 or more – requiring therapists to complete a full postgraduate training in group therapy is unrealistic, if not exclusive. The consequence of this in terms of training is that there are:

1. A number of specialist training courses in group therapy/ analysis which are, in themselves, qualifying courses leading to registration such as the IGA's Diploma course and the Westminster Pastoral Foundation's Diploma course, and
2. A number of short courses in groupwork, group counselling or group therapy which provide additional, supplementary training, which are generally shorter and which lead to a qualification but not accreditation or registration.

A number of courses in groupwork are listed in Appendix 4.

Conclusion

To paraphrase T.S. Eliot, there is no life if not in groups. Groups provide us with examples of the highest aspirational qualities of human beings in society with each other as well as the nasty, brutish and short side of humanity. The aspiring and culturally intentional counsellor may wish to add conceptual, theoretical and experiential understanding of groups to what they offer and contribute to individuals, groups and groups-in-context in organisations and in the community. This book has aimed to stimulate and facilitate such contributions.

Appendix 1

Best Practice Guidelines for Groupwork

Association for Specialists in Group Work (ASGW) Best Practice Guidelines
Approved by the ASGW Executive Board, 29 March 1998
Prepared by Lynn Rapin and Linda Keel, Co-Chairs, ASGW Ethics Committee

The Association for Specialists in Group Work (ASGW) is a division of the American Counseling Association whose members are interested in and specialize in groupwork. We value the creation of community; service to our members, clients, and the profession; and value leadership as a process to facilitate the growth and development of individuals and groups.

The Association for Specialists in Group Work recognizes the commitment of its members to the Code of Ethics and Standards of Practice (as revised in 1995) of its parent organization, the American Counseling Association, and nothing in this document shall be construed to supplant that code. These Best Practice Guidelines are intended to clarify the application of the ACA Code of Ethics and Standards of Practice to the field of group work by defining Group Workers' responsibility and scope of practice involving those activities, strategies and interventions that are consistent and current with effective and appropriate professional ethical and community standards. ASGW views ethical process as being integral to group work and views Group Workers as ethical agents. Group Workers, by their very nature in being responsible and responsive to their group members, necessarily embrace a certain potential for ethical vulnerability. It is incumbent upon Group Workers to give considerable attention to the intent and context of their actions because the attempts of Group Workers to influence human behavior through group work always have ethical implications. These Best Practice Guidelines address Group Workers' responsibilities in planning, performing, and processing groups.

Section A: Best Practice in Planning

A.1. Professional Context and Regulatory Requirements
Group Workers actively know, understand and apply the ACA Code of Ethics and Standards of Practice, the ASGW Professional Standards for the Training of Group Workers, these ASGW Best Practice Guidelines, the ASGW diversity competencies, the ACA Multicultural Guidelines, relevant state laws, accreditation requirements, relevant National Board for Certified Counselors Codes and

Standards, their organization's standards, and insurance requirements impacting the practice of group work.

A.2. Scope of Practice and Conceptual Framework
Group Workers define the scope of practice related to the core and specialization competencies defined in the ASGW Training Standards. Group Workers are aware of personal strengths and weaknesses in leading groups. Group Workers develop and are able to articulate a general conceptual framework to guide practice and a rationale for use of techniques that are to be used. Group Workers limit their practice to those areas for which they meet the training criteria established by the ASGW Training Standards.

A.3. Assessment

(a)   Assessment of self: Group Workers actively assess their knowledge and skills related to the specific group(s) offered. Group Workers assess their values, beliefs and theoretical orientation and how these impact upon the group, particularly when working with a diverse and multicultural population.
(b)   Ecological assessment: Group Workers assess community needs, agency or organization resources, sponsoring organization mission, staff competency, attitudes regarding group work, professional training levels of potential group leaders regarding group work; client attitudes regarding group work, and multicultural and diversity considerations. Group Workers use this information as the basis for making decisions related to their group practice, or to the implementation of groups for which they have supervisory, evaluation, or oversight responsibilities.

A.4. Program Development and Evaluation

(a)   Group Workers identify the type(s) of group(s) to be offered and how they relate to community needs.
(b)   Group Workers concisely state in writing the purpose and goals of the group. Group Workers also identify the role of the group members in influencing or determining the group goals.
(c)   Group Workers set fees consistent with the organization's fee schedule, taking into consideration the financial status and locality of prospective group members.
(d)   Group Workers choose techniques and a leadership style appropriate to the type(s) of group(s) being offered.
(e)   Group Workers have an evaluation plan consistent with regulatory, organization and insurance requirements, where appropriate.
(f)   Group Workers take into consideration current professional guidelines when using technology, including but not limited to Internet communication.

A.5. Resources
Group Workers coordinate resources related to the kind of group(s) and group activities to be provided, such as: adequate funding; the appropriateness and availability of a trained co-leader; space and privacy requirements for the type(s) of group(s) being offered; marketing and recruiting; and appropriate collaboration with other community agencies and organizations.

A.6. Professional Disclosure Statement

Group Workers have a professional disclosure statement which includes information on confidentiality and exceptions to confidentiality, theoretical orientation, information on the nature, purpose(s) and goals of the group, the group services that can be provided, the role and responsibility of group members and leaders, Group Workers' qualifications to conduct the specific group(s), specific licenses, certifications and professional affiliations, and address of licensing/credentialing body.

A.7. Group and Member Preparation

(a) Group Workers screen prospective group members if appropriate to the type of group being offered. When selection of group members is appropriate, Group Workers identify group members whose needs and goals are compatible with the goals of the group.

(b) Group Workers facilitate informed consent. Group Workers provide in oral and written form to prospective members (when appropriate to group type): the professional disclosure statement; group purpose and goals; group participation expectations including voluntary and involuntary membership; role expectations of members and leader(s); policies related to entering and exiting the group; policies governing substance use; policies and procedures governing mandated groups (where relevant); documentation requirements; disclosure of information to others; implications of out-of-group contact or involvement among members; procedures for consultation between group leader(s) and group member(s); fees and time parameters; and potential impacts of group participation.

(c) Group Workers obtain the appropriate consent forms for work with minors and other dependent group members.

(d) Group Workers define confidentiality and its limits (for example, legal and ethical exceptions and expectations; waivers implicit with treatment plans, documentation and insurance usage). Group Workers have the responsibility to inform all group participants of the need for confidentiality, potential consequences of breaching confidentiality and that legal privilege does not apply to group discussions (unless provided by state statute).

A.8. Professional Development

Group Workers recognize that professional growth is a continuous, ongoing, developmental process throughout their career.

(a) Group Workers remain current and increase knowledge and skill competencies through activities such as continuing education, professional supervision, and participation in personal and professional development activities.

(b) Group Workers seek consultation and/or supervision regarding ethical concerns that interfere with effective functioning as a group leader. Supervisors have the responsibility to keep abreast of consultation, group theory, process, and adhere to related ethical guidelines.

(c) Group Workers seek appropriate professional assistance for their own personal problems or conflicts that are likely to impair their professional judgement or work performance.

(d)   Group Workers seek consultation and supervision to ensure appropriate practice whenever working with a group for which all knowledge and skill competencies have not been achieved.

(e)   Group Workers keep abreast of group research and development.

A.9. Trends and Technological Changes

Group Workers are aware of and responsive to technological changes as they affect society and the profession. These include but are not limited to changes in mental health delivery systems; legislative and insurance industry reforms; shifting population demographics and client needs; and technological advances in Internet and other communication and delivery systems. Group Workers adhere to ethical guidelines related to the use of developing technologies.

Section B: Best Practice in Performing

B.1. Self Knowledge

Group Workers are aware of and monitor their strengths and weaknesses and the effects these have on group members.

B.2. Group Competencies

Group Workers have a basic knowledge of groups and the principles of group dynamics, and are able to perform the core group competencies, as described in the ASGW Professional Standards for theTraining of Group Workers. Additionally, Group Workers have adequate understanding and skill in any group specialty area chosen for practice (psychotherapy, counseling, task, psychoeducation, as described in the ASGW Training Standards).

B.3. Group Plan Adaptation

(a)   Group Workers apply and modify knowledge, skills and techniques appropriate to group type and stage, and to the unique needs of various cultural and ethnic groups.

(b)   Group Workers monitor the group and progress toward the group goals and plan.

(c)   Group Workers clearly define and maintain ethical, professional, and social relationship boundaries with group members as appropriate to their role in the organization and the type of group being offered.

B.4. Therapeutic Conditions and Dynamics

Group Workers understand and are able to implement appropriate models of group development, process observation and therapeutic conditions.

B.5. Meaning

Group Workers assist members in generating meaning from the group experience.

B.6. Collaboration

Group Workers assist members in developing individual goals and respect group members as co-equal partners in the group experience.

B.7. Evaluation

Group Workers include evaluation (both formal and informal) between sessions and at the conclusion of the group.

B.8. Diversity

Group Workers practice with broad sensitivity to client differences including but not limited to ethnic, gender, religious, sexual, psychological maturity, economic class, family history, physical characteristics or limitations, and geographic location. Group Workers continuously seek information regarding the cultural issues of the diverse population with whom they are working both by interaction with participants and from using outside resources.

B.9. Ethical Surveillance

Group Workers employ an appropriate ethical decision making model in responding to ethical challenges and issues and in determining courses of action and behavior for self and group members. In addition, Group Workers employ applicable standards as promulgated by ACA, ASGW, or other appropriate professional organizations.

Section C: Best Practice in Group Processing

C.1. Processing Schedule

Group Workers process the workings of the group with themselves, group members, supervisors or other colleagues, as appropriate. This may include assessing progress on group and member goals, leader behaviors and techniques, group dynamics and interventions; developing understanding and acceptance of meaning. Processing may occur both within sessions and before and after each session, at time of termination, and later follow up, as appropriate.

C.2. Reflective Practice

Group Workers attend to opportunities to synthesize theory and practice and to incorporate learning outcomes into ongoing groups. Group Workers attend to session dynamics of members and their interactions and also attend to the relationship between session dynamics and leader values, cognition and affect.

C.3. Evaluation and Follow-Up

(a)   Group Workers evaluate process and outcomes. Results are used for ongoing program planning, improvement and revisions of current group and/or to contribute to professional research literature. Group Workers follow all applicable policies and standards in using group material for research and reports.
(b)   Group Workers conduct follow-up contact with group members, as appropriate, to assess outcomes or when requested by a group member(s).

C.4. Consultation and Training with Other Organizations

Group Workers provide consultation and training to organizations in and out of their setting, when appropriate. Group Workers seek out consultation as needed with competent professional persons knowledgeable about group work.

Appendix 2

Group Counselling: Q-sort research*

Information to clients

Aim of the exercise:
To sort 60 statements about group counselling/therapy into your own rank ordering.

Instructions:
Enclosed with this is a list of 60 statements about the therapeutic factors of groups and seven envelopes. Please sort the statements into the seven envelopes marked:

1. Most helpful to me in the group (2 statements)
2. Extremely helpful to me in the group (6 statements)
3. Very helpful to me in the group (12 statements)
4. Helpful to me in the group (20 statements)
5. Barely helpful to me in the group (12 statements)
6. Less helpful to me in the group (6 statements)
7. Least helpful to me in the group (2 statements).

Then, within each envelope rank each statement in the order of helpfulness by writing a number (1–60) on the statement. Thus in the 'Most helpful to me in the group' you will have statements ranked 1 and 2, in the 'Extremely helpful to me in the group' you will have statements ranked and marked 3, 4, 5, 6, 7 and 8 and so on through the envelopes until you have ranked all the statements. You will probably find it easiest to sort the statements into the seven groups, then make any necessary adjustments in terms of the numbers of statements in each group, and then rank-order and number them and put them in the envelopes.

I am also enclosing a sheet of paper asking you to write your comments on the pre- and post-group time as well as what, if anything, happens outside the group, and any other comments you have about your experience of group counselling/therapy.

With thanks for your consideration.

1. Helping others has given me more self-respect.
2. Putting others' needs ahead of mine.
3. Forgetting myself and thinking of helping others.
4. Giving part of myself to others.
5. Helping others and being important in their lives.
6. Belonging to and being accepted by a group.
7. Continued close contact with other people.
8. Revealing embarrassing things about myself and still being accepted by the group.

* Based on Yalom (1995).

9. Feeling alone no longer.
10. Belonging to a group of people who understand and accept me.
11. Learning I'm not the only one with my type of problem; 'We're all in the same boat.'
12. Seeing that I am just as well off as others.
13. Learning that others have some of the same 'bad' thoughts and feelings I do.
14. Learning that others had parents and backgrounds as unhappy or mixed up as mine.
15. Learning that I'm not very different from other people gives me a 'welcome to the human race' feeling.
16. The group's teaching me about the type of impression I make on others.
17. Learning how I come across to others.
18. Other members honestly telling me what they think of me.
19. Group members pointing out some of my habits or mannerisms that annoy other people.
20. Learning that I sometimes confuse people by not saying what I really think.
21. Improving my skills in getting along with people.
22. Feeling more trustful of groups and of other people.
23. Learning about the way I relate to other group members.
24. The group's giving me an opportunity to learn to approach others.
25. Working out my difficulties with one particular member in the group.
26. The therapist's suggesting or advising something for me to do.
27. Group members suggesting or advising something for me to do.
28. Group members telling me what to do.
29. Someone in the group giving definite suggestions about a life problem.
30. Group members advising me to behave differently with an important person in my life.
31. Getting things off my chest.
32. Expressing negative and/or positive feelings towards another member.
33. Expressing negative and/or positive feelings towards the therapist.
34. Learning how to express my feelings.
35. Being able to say what was bothering me instead of holding it in.
36. Trying to be like someone in the group who is better adjusted than I.
37. Seeing that others could reveal embarrassing things and take other risks and benefit from it helps me to do the same.
38. Adopting mannerisms or the style of another group member.
39. Admiring and behaving like my therapist.
40. Finding someone in the group I can pattern myself after.
41. Being in the group is, in a sense, like reliving and understanding my life in the family in which I grew up.
42. Being in the group somehow helps me to understand old hang-ups that I had in the past with my parents, brothers, sisters, or other important people.
43. Being in the group is, in a sense, like being in a family, only this time a more accepting family.
44. Being in the group somehow helps me to understand how I grew up in my family.
45. The group is something like my family – some members or the therapist being like my parents and others being like my relatives. Through the

group experience I understand my past relationships with my parents and relatives (brothers, sisters etc.).

46. Learning that I have likes or dislikes for a person for reasons which may have little to do with the person and more to do with my hang-ups or experiences with other people in my past.

47. Learning why I think and feel the way I do (that is, learning some of the causes and sources of my problems).

48. Discovering and accepting previously unknown or unacceptable parts of myself.

49. Learning that I react to some people or situations unrealistically (with feelings that somehow belong to earlier periods in my life).

50. Learning that how I feel and behave today is related to my childhood and development (there are reasons in my early life why I am as I am).

51. Seeing others getting better is inspiring to me.

52. Knowing others have solved problems similar to mine.

53. Seeing others have solved problems similar to mine.

54. Seeing that other group members improve/d encourages me.

55. Knowing that the group has helped others with problems like mine encourages me.

56. Recognising that life is at times unfair and unjust.

57. Recognising that ultimately there is no escape from some of life's pain and from death.

58. Recognising that no matter how close I get to other people, I must still face life alone.

59. Facing the basic issues of my life and death, and thus living my life more honestly and being less caught up in trivialities.

60. Learning that I must take responsibility for the way I live my life no matter how much guidance and support I get from others.

Group Counselling – Before, After and Outside the Group

1. I am interested in your thoughts and feelings about the time you spend with people before the group. Please write as much or as little as you want.
   Some questions you may consider – Do you come for this time or aim to come for the starting time of the group at 7.30pm? What is the purpose of this time for you? What, if any value does it have? Has this time changed over the time you've been in the group?

2. I am interested in your thoughts and feelings about the time you spend with the group after I have left. Again, please write as much or as little as you want.
   Some questions you may consider – Do you stay on after the group, if so how regularly and for how long? Does this depend on anything and if so what? What's different about this time compared to the time in the group (7.30–9.30pm)? Are there particular therapeutic factors (e.g. the 60 statements) which are more relevant or pertinent to this time? Has any of this changed over the time you've been in the group?

3. I am also interested in any contact you have with group members, or indeed as a group, outside the group.

Some questions – Do you have any contact with any group member/s outside the group? Is this one or two particular people or with anyone in the group and if so how often? What is the nature and purpose of this contact? Has it changed over the time you've been in the group?

4. Any other comments about your experience of group counselling/therapy.

With thanks
Keith Tudor

Appendix 3

A Simple Group Contract

Using the parallel with legal contracts, Steiner (1971) outlines four basic requirements for contracts:

- *Mutual consent* – which, in turn, involves a request for treatment, an offer of treatment and an acceptance of treatment.
- *Valid consideration* – that is, the benefit to both parties, for instance, a service for a fee.
- *Competency* – that both parties are competent to agree to the contract and to fulfil their side of it. This is especially important in the case of working with minors or people whose mental facilities are impaired for some reason and will almost certainly involve a third party (see Chapter 6) such as a parent or legal guardian (also see Vanwynsberghe, 1998).
- *Lawful object* – that the object or outcome of the contract is legal and not illegal.

Updating Steiner's requirements in terms of British contract law, four elements create a legal 'simple contract' (as distinct from a contract by deed or a contract under seal): agreement, clarity, legality and valid consideration and, bearing in mind that some counsellors draw up written agreements with their clients, dates and signatures. The content of a written, legal counselling contract may be considered thus:

1. An introduction, outlining the purpose of the contract.
2. The definitions of terms, including any ambiguous terms such as 'getting better'.
3. The responsibilities of parties to the contract, including other parties, for example parents when working with children and other group members when working with groups.
4. A description of what is to be delivered.
5. Any issues as regards copyright – this may be relevant to any writing and publication of material about clients.
6. The delivery of service specified.
7. Agreed terms of payment.

8. An agreed disputes procedure – or access to an identified complaints or disputes procedure.

In the light of their empirical findings from studying group confidentiality and the law, Roback et al. (1996) suggest a model for an 'informed consent' form which includes a clear outlining of 'risks':

- The legal and professional position on the counsellor's obligation or choice to report any disclosure of child abuse. All counsellors, including group counsellors, need to be clear where they stand on this in terms of the law, their professional associations and codes of ethics and practice, any requirements arising from the setting of their work, for example in primary care, and morally (see BAC, 1997, especially B.3.3 and B.3.4).
- The risk of disclosure of any 'secrets' by other members of the group.
- The implications of telling other people outside the group of group members' secrets, including the possibility of legal action.
- The risk of expulsion from the group.

This model also proposes a signed and witnessed declaration of acceptance of the terms, conditions and risks of group counselling (see Roback et al., 1996, pp. 134–5).

Appendix 4

Training Courses in Groupwork

These are listed in terms of specialist courses leading to UKCP registration and other training courses in groupwork.

This is not intended as a comprehensive list. It is based on entries in and a brief survey of courses – of a minimum duration of one year, part time – listed in the BAC's (1995) *Directory of Training Courses*. Details of other group-work training courses may be sent to the author at Sage Publications for inclusion in future editions/publications.

Specialist training courses in groupwork leading to UKCP registration

Organisation:	**The Institute of Group Analysis**
Qualification:	**Diploma in Group Analysis**
Entry requirements:	One of the general courses approved by the IGA, university degree or equivalent, adequate experience of work with psychiatric patients, personal group analysis (see personal therapy requirements)
Course requirements	
Practice:	Two groups under supervision, individual client work
Supervision:	Weekly supervision seminar throughout the training period for each group
Personal therapy:	Twice-weekly personal group analysis with a training group analyst, commencing six months prior to formal training
Duration:	Four years (minimum), part-time (6 hours per week)
Further details:	Co-ordinator of Training, The Institute of Group Analysis, 1 Daleham Gardens, London NW3 5BY; or for details of UK Diploma in Group Analysis Group Analysis North, 79 Fog Lane, Didsbury, Manchester M20 6SL
Organisation:	**Westminster Pastoral Foundation**
Qualification:	**Diploma in Group Psychotherapy**
Entry requirements:	Certificate in groupwork or equivalent introductory course including experience in running groups, university degree or equivalent
Course requirements	
Practice:	Trainees set up and run their own group, once weekly for a minimum of two years. The course

	also provides co-conducting experience and observation of groups through a one-way mirror. Some groups are run by trainees in the WPF counselling service. Trainees are also expected to gain experience of one-to-one psychodynamic client work
Supervision:	Weekly, for the duration of the practice group. Also supervision of individual client work
Personal therapy:	Group psychotherapy at a minimum of once a week by the beginning of the course with a group psychotherapist approved by the WPF
Duration:	Three years (minimum) part-time (5 hours per week)
Further details:	The Training Department, Westminster Pastoral Foundation, 23 Kensington Square, London W8 5HN

In addition to these there are organisations currently seeking membership of the UKCP with a view to having their groupwork training accepted as leading to UKCP registration, including Cambridge Group Work (Diploma in Group Analysis) and Goldsmiths' College, London University (Diploma in Group Psychotherapy).

Other courses in groupwork

Organisation:	**Cambridge Group Work**
Course:	**Introductory General Course**
Duration:	1 year, part-time
Qualification:	Advanced Diploma in Group Work/Advanced Diploma in Educational Studies (University of Cambridge Institute of Education)
Duration:	3 years, part-time
Contact:	CGW Administrator, 4 George Street, Cambridge CB4 1AJ

Organisation:	**Group Analysis North**
Course:	**Manchester Course in Group Psychotherapy** (recognised by the IGA as equivalent to its Introductory General Course in Group Work)
Duration:	1 year, part-time
Course:	**Advanced Learning in Group Psychotherapy**
Duration:	1 year, part-time
Course:	**Diploma in Dynamic Psychotherapy**
Duration	3.5 years, part-time
Contact:	Group Analysis North (address above)

Organisation:	**The Institute of Group Analysis**
Course:	**Introductory General Course in Group Work**
Duration:	1 year, part-time
Contact:	IGA (address above)

Organisation: **Minster Centre**
Qualification: **Diploma in Integrative Group Psychotherapy**
                   (post-qualification)
Duration: 2 years, part-time
Contact: Minster Centre, 1 Drakes Court Yard, 291 Kilburn High
                   Road, London NW6 7JR

Organisation: **Westminster Pastoral Foundation**
Qualification: **Diploma in Groupwork Skills**
Duration: 1 year, part-time
Contact: WPF (address above)

References

Adler, G. (1979) *Dynamics of the self*. London: Coventure. (Original work published 1951).

Alford, C.F. (1994) *Group psychology and political theory*. New Haven, CT: Yale University Press.

Alladin, W. (1988) Cognitive-behavioural group therapy. In: M. Aveline and W. Dryden (eds), *Group therapy in Britain*. Milton Keynes: Open University Press. pp. 115-139.

American Counseling Association. (1995) *Code of Ethics and Standards of Practice*. Alexandria, VA: ACA.

Applebaum, P. and Greer, A. (1993) Confidentiality in group therapy. *Hospital and Community Psychiatry*, 44: 311-312.

ASGW (Association for Specialists in Group Work) (1989) *Ethical guidelines for group counselors*. Alexandria, VA: ASGW.

ASGW (Association for Specialists in Group Work) (1992) *Professional standards for the training of group workers*. Alexandria, VA: ASGW.

ASGW (Association for Specialists in Group Work) (1998) *Best Practice Guidelines*. Alexandria, VA: ACA.

AHPP (Association of Humanistic Psychology Practitioners) (1997) *Criteria for AHPP full membership in the category of group counsellor*. Available from the AHPP, BCM AHPP, London WC1N 3XX.

Atkinson, D., Morton, G. and Sue, D.W. (1989) *Counseling American minorities: a cross cultural perspective*. Dubuque, IA: William C. Brown.

Autton, N. (1989) *Touch: an exploration*. London: Darton, Longman and Todd.

Aveline, M. (1988) Issues in the training of goup therapists. In: M. Aveline and W. Dryden (eds), *Group therapy in Britain*. Milton Keynes: Open University Press. pp. 317-336.

Aveline, M. (1996) The training and supervision of individual therapists. In: W. Dryden (ed.), *Handbook of individual therapy*. London: Sage. pp. 365-394.

Aveline, M. and Dryden, W. (1988) A comparative review of small group therapies. In: M. Aveline and W. Dryden (eds), *Group therapy in Britain*. Milton Keynes: Open University Press. pp. 140-150.

Bach, G.R. (1954) *Intensive group psychotherapy*. New York: Ronald Press.

Bach, G.R. (1966) The marathon group: intensive practice of intimate interaction. *Psychological Reports*, 18: 995-1002.

Barrett-Lennard, G. (1979) The client-centered system unfolding. In: F.J. Turner (ed.), *Social work treatment: interlocking theoretical approaches* (2nd edn). New York: Free Press. pp. 171–241.

Barrett-Lennard, G. (1984) The topography of family relationships: a person-centered systems view. In: A. Segrera (ed.), *Proceedings of the First International Forum on the Person-Centered Approach*. Oaxtepec, Morelos, Mexico: Universidad Iberoamericana.

Barrett-Lennard, G.T. (1990) The therapy pathway reformulated. In: G. Lietaer, J. Rombauts and R. Van Balen (eds), *Client-centered and experiential psychotherapy in the nineties*. Leuven: Leuven University Press. pp. 123–153.

Becvar, R.J., Canfield, B.S. and Becvar, D.S. (eds) (1997) *Group work: Cybernetic, constructivist and social constructionist perspectives*. Denver: Love Publishing.

Berke, J.H., Masoliver, C. and Ryan, T.J. (1995) *Sanctuary: the Arbours Experience of alternative community care*. London: Process Press.

Berke, J.H. (ed.) (1990) The Arbours: Twenty years on [Special Issue]. *Therapeutic Communities*, 11(4).

Bernard, H. (1989) Guidelines to minimize premature terminations. *International Journal of Group Psychotherapy*, 39(4): 523–529.

Berne, E. (1961/1975a) *Transactional analysis in psychotherapy*. London: Souvenir Press.

Berne, E. (1963) *The structure and dynamics of organizations and groups*. New York: Grove Press.

Berne, E. (1964/1968) *Games people play*. Harmondsworth: Penguin.

Berne, E. (1966) *Principles of group treatment*. New York: Grove Press.

Berne, E. (1970/1973) *Sex in human loving*. Harmondsworth: Penguin.

Berne, E. (1972/1975b) *What do you say after you say hello?* London: Corgi.

Bindrim, P. (1968) A report on a nude marathon. *Psychotherapy: Theory, Research and Practice*, 5: 180–188.

Bion, W. (1961) *Experience in groups and other papers*. London: Tavistock.

Bloch, S. (1988) Research in group psychotherapy. In: M. Aveline and W. Dryden (eds), *Group therapy in Britain*. Milton Keynes: Open University Press. pp. 283–316.

Bloch, S. and Crouch, E. (1985) *Therapeutic factors in group psychotherapy*. Oxford: Oxford University Press.

Bloom, B.S., Engelhart, M.D., Furst, E.J., Hill, W.D. and Krathwohl, D.R. (1956) *Taxonomy of educational objectives. Handbook I: Cognitive domain*. London: Longman.

Bond, T. (1993) *Standards and ethics for counselling in action*. London: Sage.

Bowlby, J. (1981) *Attachment and loss: Volume 3. Loss: sadness and depression*. Harmondsworth: Penguin.

Boyd, R.D. (1991) *Personal transformations in small groups: A Jungian perspective*. London: Routledge.

Bozarth, J.D. (1981) The person-centred approach in the large community group. In: G. Gazda (ed.), *Innovations to group psychotherapy* (2nd edn.). Springfield, IL: Thomas.

Bozarth, J.D. (1984) Beyond reflection: emergent modes of empathy. In: R.F. Levant and John M. Shlien (eds), *Client-centered therapy and the person-centered approach: new directions in theory, research and practice*. New York: Praeger.

BAC (British Association for Counselling) (1992) *Code of ethics and practice for counsellors*. Rugby: BAC. (Amended 1993 and 1996)

BAC (British Association for Counselling) (1994) *Accreditation criteria. Leaflet*. Rugby: BAC.

BAC (British Association for Counselling) (1995) *Training in Counselling and Psychotherapy: A Directory* (12th ed.). Rugby: BAC.

BAC (British Association for Counselling) (1997) *Code of ethics and practice for counsellors*. Rugby: BAC.

Brown, A. (1992) *Groupwork*, 3rd edn. Aldershot: Arena.

Brown, R. (1988) *Group processes: dysfunction within and between groups*. Oxford: Blackwell.

Burrow, T. (1927) *The social basis of consciousness*. London: Kegan Paul.

Butler, S. and Wintram, C. (1991) *Feminist groupwork*. London: Sage.

Castel , R., Castel, F. and Lovell, A. (1982) *The psychiatric society*. New York: Columbia University Press.

Central Council for Education and Training in Social Work (1995) *Diploma in Social Work: rules and regulations for the Diploma in Social Work. Paper 20*, rev. edn. London: CCETSW.

Christ, J. (1975) Contrasting the charismatic and reflective leader. In: Z.A. Liff (ed.), *The leader in the group*. New York: Jason Aronson. pp. 104–113.

Clarkson, P. (1990) A multiplicity of psychotherapeutic relationships. *British Journal of Psychotherapy*, 7: 148–163.

Clarkson, P. (1991) Group imago and the stages of group development. *Transactional Analysis Journal*, 21: 36–50.

Clarkson, P. (1992) *Transactional analysis psychotherapy: an integrated approach*. London: Routledge.

Clarkson, P. (1995a) *Change in organisations*. London: Whurr.

Clarkson, P. (1995b) *The therapeutic relationship*. London: Whurr.

Clarkson, P. and Fish, S. (1988) Systemic assessment and treatment considerations in TA child psychotherapy. *Transactional Analysis Journal*, 18: 123–132.

Coche, J. and Coche, E. (1990) *Couples group psychotherapy: a clinical practice model*. New York: Brunner/Mazel.

Coghlan, D. and McIlduff, E. (1990) Structuring and nondirectiveness in group facilitation. *Person-Centered Review*, 5: 13–29.

Cohn, R. (1972) Style and spirit of the theme-based interactional method. In: C.J. Sager and H.S. Kaplan (eds), *Progress in group and family therapy*. New York: Brunner/Mazel.

Corey, G. (1995) *Theory and practice of group counseling*, 4th edn. Pacific Grove, CA: Brooks/Cole.

Cornell, W.F. (1997) Touch and boundaries in transactional analysis: ethical and transferential considerations. *Transactional Analysis Journal*, 27: 30–37.

Corsini, R. and Rosenberg, B. (1955) Mechanisms of group psychotherapy: Processes and dynamics. *Journal of Abnormal and Social Psychology*, 51: 406–411.

Cox, M. (1993) The group therapy interaction chronogram. *British Journal of Social Work*, 3(2): 243–256.

Craib, I. (1987) The psychodynamics of theory. *Free Associations*, 10: 32–56.

de Maré, P. (1972) *Perspectives in group psychotherapy*. London: Allen and Unwin.

de Maré, P. (1975) The politics of large groups. In: L. Kreeger (ed.), *The large group: dynamics and therapy*. London: Maresfield. pp. 145–158.

de Maré, P., Piper, R. and Thompson, S. (1991) *Koinonia: From hate, through dialogue, to culture in the large group*. New York: Brunner/Mazel.

de Marignac, D. (1984) Experimenting the person-centred approach in various groups of my close neighbourhood and aspects of my daily life. In: A. Segrera (ed.), *Proceedings of the First International Forum on the Person-Centered Approach*. Oaxtepec, Morelos, Mexico: Universidad Iberoamericana.

Dierick, P. and Lietaer, G. (1990) Member and therapist perceptions of therapeutic factors in therapy and growth groups: comments on a category system. In: G. Lietaer, J. Rombauts and R. Van Balen (eds), *Client-centered and experiential psychotherapy in the nineties*. Leuven: Leuven University Press. pp. 741–770.

Dies, R.R. (1985) Leadership in short-term group therapy: manipulation or facilitation? Short-term Group Treatment [Special Issue]. *International Journal of Group Psychotherapy*, 35: 435–455.

Douglas, T. (1979) *Group processes in social work: a theoretical synthesis*. Chichester: John Wiley.

Douglas, T. (1993) *A theory of groupwork practice*. London: Macmillan.

Dryden, W. and Feltham, C. (1994) *Developing counsellor training*. London: Sage.

Ebersole, G.O., Leiderman, P.H. and Yalom, I.D. (1969) Training the nonprofessional group therapist. *Journal of Nervous and Mental Disorders*, 149: 385.

Edelson, M. (1970) *Sociotherapy and psychotherapy*. Chicago, IL: University of Chicago Press.

Eissler, K. (1955) *The psychiatrist and the dying patient*. New York: International Universities Press.

Embleton Tudor, L. and Tudor, K. (1994) The personal and the political: power, authority and influence in psychotherapy. In: P. Clarkson and M. Pokorney (eds), *The handbook of psychotherapy*. London: Routledge. pp. 384–402.

Embleton Tudor, L. and Tudor, K. (1995) Acting up as acting out: containing anxiety in Social Services. *Changes*, 13: 241–253.

Embleton Tudor, L. and Tudor, K. (1997) *Sharing life therapy*. Presentation at 'Ten Years On' International Conference on the Person-Centred Approach, University of Sheffield, September 1997.

Embleton Tudor, L. and Tudor, K. (in preparation) *Temenos: the creation of psychotherapeutic space*.

English, F. (1975) The three-cornered contract. *Transactional Analysis Journal*, 5: 383–384.

Erikson, E. (1968) *Identity, youth and crisis*. New York: W.W. Norton.

Ernst, F.H. (1971) The OK corral: the grid for get-on-with. *Transactional Analysis Journal*, 1(4): 33-42.

Erwin, E. (1997) *Philosophy and psychotherapy*. London: Sage.

Feder, B. and Ronall, R. (1994) *Beyond the hot seat: Gestalt approaches to group*. Highland, NY: The Gestalt Journal Press.

Feltham, C. (1997a) Challenging the core theoretical model. *Counselling*, 8(2): 121-125.

Feltham, C. (1997b) *Time-limited counselling*. London: Sage.

Fiumara, R. (ed.) (1989) Jungian analysts and group analysis [Special Issue]. *Group Analysis*, 22(2).

Fleming, P. (1998). Seven levels of listening. In *Contribution training manual*. Available from Pellin Institute, 15 Killyon Road, London SW8 2XS.

Foulkes, S.H. (1964) *Therapeutic group analysis*. London: George Allen and Unwin.

Foulkes, S.H. (Speaker) (1972) *Group-analytic psychotherapy* [Cassette recording]. Fort Lee, NJ: Sigma Information.

Foulkes, S.H. (1975) Problems of the large group from a group-analytic point of view. In: L. Kreeger (ed.), *The large group: dynamics and therapy*. London: Maresfield. pp. 33-56.

Foulkes, S.H. (1983) *Introduction to group-analytic psychotherapy*. London: Marsefield. (Original work published 1948)

Freire, P. (1972) *Pedagogy of the oppressed*. Harmondsworth: Penguin.

Freire, P. (1974) *Education: the practice of freedom*. London: Readers and Writers.

Freud, S. (1913/1958) On beginning the treatment. In: J. Strachey (ed. and trans.), *The standard edition of the complete psychological works of Sigmund Freud; Volume 12*. London: Hogarth Press. pp. 123-144.

Freud, S. (1921/1985a) Group psychology and the analysis of the ego. In: A. Dickson (ed.), *Civilization, society and groups* (J.Strachey, trans.). Harmondsworth: Penguin. pp. 93-178.

Freud, S. (1930/1985b) Civilization and its discontents. In: A. Dickson (ed.), *Civilization, society and groups* (J. Strachey, trans.). Harmondsworth: Penguin. pp. 243-340.

Furedi, F. (1997) *Culture of fear: risk-taking and the morality of low expectation*. London: Cassell.

Gans, J.S. (1989) Hostility in group psychotherapy. *International Journal of Group Psychotherapy*, 39(4): 499-516.

Gelso, C.J. and Carter, J.A. (1985) The relationship in counseling and psychotherapy: components, consequences and theoretical antecedents. *The Counseling Psychologist*, 13(2): 155-243.

Gelso, C.J. and Carter, J.A. (1994) Components of the psychotherapy relationship: their interaction and unfolding during treatment. *Journal of Counseling Psychology*, 41(3): 296-306.

Gendlin, E.T. and Beebe, J. (1968) Experiential groups. In: G.M. Gazda (ed.), *Innovations to group psychotherapy*. Springfield, IL: Thomas. pp. 190-206.

Giesekus, U. and Mente, A. (1986) Client empathic understanding in client-centered therapy. *Person-Centered Review*, 1: 163-171.

Ginott, H.G. (1961) *Group psychotherapy with children*. Northvale, NJ: Jason Aronson.

Glassman, U. and Kates, L. (1990) *Group Work: a humanistic approach*. Newbury Park, CA: Sage.

Gordon, R. (1978) *Dying and creating: a search for meaning*. London: The Society of Analytic Psychology.

Gottlieb, S. (1989) The pregnant psychotherapist: a potent transference stimulus. *British Journal of Psychotherapy*, 5: 287-299.

Gottschalk, L.A. (1966) Psychoanalytic notes on T-groups at the Human Relations Laboratory, Bethel, Maine. *Comprehensive Psychiatry*, 7: 472-487.

Harris, J.B. (1996) The power of silence in groups. *British Gestalt Journal*, 5(1): 24-30.

Hawkins, P. and Shohet, R. (1989) *Supervision in the helping professions*. Milton Keynes: Open University Press.

Helms, J.E. (1984) Towards a theoretical model of the effects of race on counseling: a black and white model. *The Counseling Psychologist*, 12: 153-165.

Henry, M. (1988) Revisiting open groups. *Groupwork*, 3: 215-228.

Herman, J. and Schatzow, E. (1984) Time-limited group therapy for women with a history of incest. *International Journal of Group Psychotherapy*, 34(4): 605-616.

Hillery, G.A. (1955) Definitions of community: areas of agreement. *Rural Sociology*, 20: 111-123.

Hillman, J. (1993) Loving the community and work. In: R. Bly, J. Hillman and M. Meade (eds), *The rag and bone shop of the heart*. New York: HarperCollins. pp. 229-232.

Hillman, J. and Ventura, M. (1992) *We've had a hundred years of psychotherapy and the world's getting worse*. San Francisco, CA: Harper.

Hinshelwood, R.D. (1987) *What happens in groups: psychoanalysis, the individual and the community*. London: Free Association Books.

Hobbs, N. (1951) Group-centered leadership and administration. In: C.R. Rogers, *Client-centered therapy*. London: Constable.

Holland, S. (1990) Psychotherapy, oppression and social action: gender, race and class in black women's depression. In: R. Perelberg and A. Miller (eds), *Gender and power in families*. London: Routledge. pp. 256-269.

Holloway, E. (1995) *Clinical supervision: A systems approach*. London: Sage.

Holloway, W.H. (1974) Beyond permission. *Transactional Analysis Journal*, 4: 15-17.

Hopper, E. and Weyman, A. (1975) A sociological view of large groups. In: L. Kreeger (ed.), *The large group: dynamics and therapy*. London: Maresfield. pp. 159-189.

House, R. and Totton, N. (1997) *Implausible professions: arguments for pluralism and autonomy in psychotherapy and counselling*. Ross-on-Wye: PCCS.

Houston, G. (1982) *The red book of gestalt*. London: Rochester Foundation.

Houston, G. (1990) *The red book of groups*, 3rd edn. London: Rochester Foundation.

Hunter, M. and Struve, J. (1997) *The ethical use of touch in psychotherapy*. London: Sage.

Hyde, K. (1988) Analytic group psychotherapies. In: M. Aveline and W. Dryden (eds), *Group therapy in Britain*. Milton Keynes: Open University Press. pp. 14–42.

Igwe, A. (1997/8) An exploration of the impact of multi cultural issues on the supervision process. *RACE Journal*, No. 15, 30–32.

Ivey, A.E., Ivey, M.B. and Simek-Morgan, L. (1993) *Counseling and psychotherapy*, 3rd edn. London: Allyn and Bacon.

Jacobs, A. (1987) Autocratic power. *Transactional Analysis Journal*, 17: 59–71.

James, M. (1971) *Breaking Free*. Reading, MA: Addison-Wesley.

Jenkins, P. (1997) *Counselling, psychotherapy and the law*. London: Sage.

Jung, C.G. (1931/1968) Commentary on "The secret of the golden flower" In: H. Read, M. Fordham and G. Adler (eds) and R.F.C. Hull (trans.), *The collected works of C.G. Jung: Volume 13*. London: Routledge and Kegan Paul. pp. 1–56.

Kaplan, S.R. and Roman, M. (1961) Characteristic responses in adult therapy groups to the introduction of new members: a reflection on group process. *International Journal of Group Psychotherapy*, 11(4): 374–381.

Kennard, D. (1988) The therapeutic community. In: M. Aveline and W. Dryden (eds), *Group therapy in Britain*. Milton Keynes: Open University Press. pp.153–184.

Kingdom, R. (1992) *No such thing as society? Individualism and community*. Buckingham: Open University Press.

Klass, D., Silverman, P. and Nickman, S. (eds) (1996) *Continuing bonds: new understandings of grief*. Washington, DC: Taylor and Francis.

Klein, D.C. (1968) *Community dynamics and mental health*. New York: Wiley.

Klein, R.H. (1985) Some principles of short-term group therapy. *International Journal of Group Psychotherapy*, 35: 309–329.

Kopp, S. (1974) *If you meet the Buddha on the road, kill him!* London: Sheldon Press.

Knowles, J. (1995) How I assess for group psychotherapy. In: C. Mace (ed.), *The art and science of assessment in psychotherapy*. London: Routledge.

Kreeger, L. (ed.) (1975) *The large group: dynamics and therapy*. London: Maresfield.

Krueger, D. (1986) *The last taboo*. New York: Brunner/Mazel.

Kübler-Ross, E. (1973) *On death and dying*. London: Tavistock.

Lacoursiere, R. (1980) *Life cycle of groups*. New York: Human Sciences Press.

Lago, C. (1996) Computer therapeutics. *Counselling*, 7(4): 287–289.

Lago, C. and Macmillan, M. (1999) *Experience in relatedness: Group work and the person-centred approach*. Llangarron: PCCS Books.

Lambert, M.J. (1985) Implications of psychotherapy outcome research for eclectic psychotherapy. In: T.C. Norcross (ed.), *Handbook of eclectic psychotherapy*. New York: Brunner/Mazel. pp. 436–462.

Lazarus, A.A. (1968) Behavior therapy in groups. In G.H. Gazda (ed.), *Basic approaches to group psychotherapy and group counseling*. Springfield, IL: Charles C. Thomas.

Le Bon, G. (1896/1920) *The crowd: a study of the popular mind* (B. Niall, trans.) London: Fisher Unwin.

Leopold, H.S. (1961) The new member in the group: some specific aspects of the literature. *International Journal of Group Psychotherapy*, 11(4): 367-371.

LeVine, R.A. (1990) Infant environments in psychoanalysis: a cross-cultural view. In: J.W. Stigler, R.A. Shweder and G. Herdt (eds), *Cultural psychology*. Cambridge: Cambridge University Press. pp. 454-476.

Levitan, A. (1998) *Arabic-Jewish relationships in Israel: observed in the person-centered approach to counseling and supervision*. Paper presented at the Person Centred Approach Forum, Johannesburg, July 1998.

Lewin, K. (1952) *Field theory in social science*. London: Tavistock.

Liddell, H.G. and Scott, R. (1901) *A Greek-English lexicon*, 8th edn. Oxford: Oxford University Press.

Lieberman, M., Yalom, I. and Miles, M. (1973) *Encounter groups: first facts*. New York: Basic Books.

Lietaer, G. and Dierick, P. (1996) Client-centered group psychotherapy in dialogue with other orientations: commonality and specificity. In: R. Hutterer, G. Pawlowsky, P.F. Schmid and R. Stipsits (eds), *Client-centered and experiential psychotherapy*. Frankfurt am Main: Peter Lang. pp. 563-583.

Liff, Z.A. (ed.) (1975) *The leader in the group*. New York: Jason Aronson.

Lindemann, E. (1944) Symptomatology and management of acute grief. *American Journal of Psychiatry*, 101: 141-149.

Lukas, E. (1989) *From self-actualization to global responsibility*. Paper presented at the Seventh World Congress of Logotherapy, Kansas City, KS, June 1989.

Lynch, G. (1997) Words and silence: counselling after Wittgenstein. *Counselling*, 8(2): 126-128.

MacKenzie, K.R. (1996) Time-limited group psychotherapy. *International Journal of Group Psychotherapy*, 46(1): 41-60.

MacKenzie, K.R. and Livesley, W.J. (1983) A developmental model for brief group therapy. In: R.R. Dies and K.R. MacKenzie (eds), *Advances in group psychotherapy*. New York: International Universities Press. pp. 107-116.

Mackewn, J. (1997) *Developing gestalt counselling*. London: Sage.

Macmillan, M. and Lago, C. (1993) Large groups: critical reflections and some concerns. *The Person-Centred Approach and Cross-Cultural Communication: An International Review*, 2: 35-53.

Macmillan, M. and Lago, C. (1996) The facilitation of large groups: experiences of facilitative moments. In: R. Hutterer, G. Pawlowsky, P.F. Schmid and R. Stipsits (eds), *Client-centered and experiential psychotherapy*. Frankfurt am Main: Peter Lang. pp. 599-609.

Main, T. (1946) The hospital as a therapeutic institution. *Bulletin of the Menninger Clinic*, 10: 66-70.

Manor, O. (1994) Group psychotherapy. In: P. Clarkson and M. Pokorney (eds), *The handbook of psychotherapy*. London: Routledge. pp. 249-264.

Marcovitz, R.J. and Smith, J.E. (1983) Patients' perceptions of curative factors in short-term psychotherapy. *International Journal of Group Psychotherapy*, 33(1): 21-39.

Marrone, R.L., Merksamer, M.A. and Salzberg, P.M. (1970) A short duration group treatment of smoking behavior by stimulus saturation. *Behavior Research and Therapy*, 8: 347-352.

Marx, K. (1932/1975) Economic and philosophical manuscripts. In L. Colletti (ed.), *Karl Marx. Early writings* (G. Benton, trans.). Harmondsworth: Penguin. pp. 279–400.

Marx, K. and Engels, F. (1846/1970) *The German ideology* (C. Arthur, ed.). London: Lawrence and Wishart.

Maslow, A.H. (1962) *Towards a psychology of being*. New York: Van Nostrand.

Masson, J. (1989) *Against therapy*. London: Collins.

McDougall, W. (1920) *The group mind*. Cambridge: Cambridge University Press.

McGraw, W. (Producer and Director) (1973) *The steel shutter* [Film] La Jolla, CA: Center for the Studies of the Person.

Mearns, D. (1994) *Developing person-centred counselling*. London: Sage.

Mearns, D. (1997) *Person-centred counselling training*. London: Sage.

Mente, A. (1990) Improving Rogers' theory: toward a more completely *client*-centered psychotherapy. In: G. Lietaer, J. Rombauts and R. Van Balen (eds), *Client-centered and experiential psychotherapy in the nineties*. Leuven: Leuven University Press. pp. 771–778.

Menzies Lyth, I.E.P. (1959/1988) The functioning of social systems as a defence against anxiety: a report on the nursing service of a general hospital. In: *Containing anxiety in institutions*. London: Free Associations Books. pp. 43–85.

Merry, T. (1995) *Invitation to person centred psychology*. London: Whurr.

Merry, U. and Brown, G.I. (1987) *The neurotic behaviour of organizations*. New York: Gardner Press.

Midgley, D. (1994) *Character disorder: the flipside of neurosis. A practitioner's guide to diagnosis and treatment*. Middlesborough: New Directions.

Miller, A. (1988/1990) *Banished knowledge: facing childhood injuries* (L. Vennewitz, trans.). London: Virago.

Mindell, A. (1992) *The leader as martial artist*. New York: HarperCollins.

Mindell, A. (1995) *Sitting in the fire*. Portland, OR: Lao Tse Press.

Moreno, J.L. (1958) Fundamental rules and techniques of psychodrama. In: J.H. Masserman and J.L. Moreno (eds), *Techniques of psychotherapy*. New York: Grune and Stratton.

Moreno, J.L. (1946/1964) *Psychodrama: Volume 1*, rev. edn. Beacon, NY: Beacon House.

Mosse, J. (1994) Introduction: the institutional roots of consulting to institutions. In: A. Obholzer and V.Z. Roberts (eds), *The unconscious at work: individual and organizational stress in the human services*. London: Routledge. pp. 1–8.

Mowbray, R. (1995) *The case against psychotherapy registration: a conservation issue for the human potential movement*. London: Trans Marginal Press.

Murphy, M. and de Smith, J. (1997) On the death of a client. *Counselling*, 8(3): 176–177.

Nitsun, M. (1996) *The anti-group: destructive forces in the group and their creative potential*. London: Routledge.

Nobles, W.W. (1973) Psychological research and the black self-concept: a critical review. *Journal of Social Issues*, 29: 11–31.

Novellino, M. (1985) Antileadership in TA groups. *Transactional Analysis Journal*, 15(2): 64-167.

O'Hara, M. (1989) Person-centered approach as conscientizaçao: The works of Carl Rogers and Paulo Freire. *Journal Of Humanistic Psychology*, 29(1): 11-36.

Older, J. (1982) *Touching is healing*. New York: Stein and Day.

O'Sullivan, G. (1996) Behaviour therapy. In: W. Dryden (ed.), *Handbook of individual therapy*. London: Sage. pp. 282-303.

Parkes, C.M. (1972) *Bereavement: studies of grief in adult life*. New York: International Universities Press.

Patterson, J.E. (1973) Effects of touch on self-exploration and the therapeutic relationship. *Journal of Counselling and Clinical Psychology*, 40: 170-175.

Pavlov, I.P. (1941) *Conditioned reflexes and psychiatry* (W.H. Gantt, trans.). New York: International Universities Press.

Peck, S. (1987) *A different drum*. London: Rider and Co.

Perls, F.S., Hefferline, R.F. and Goodman, P. (1973) *Gestalt therapy*. Harmondsworth: Penguin. (Original work published 1951)

Perls, F. (1967) Group vs. individual therapy. *Etc. Review of General Semantics*, 24: 306-312.

Pines, M. (ed.) (1983) *The evolution of group analysis*. London: Routledge and Kegan Paul.

Piper, W.E. and Klein, R.H. (eds) (1996) Termination in Group Therapy [Special Issue]. *International Journal of Group Psychotherapy*, 46(1).

Price, J. (1988) Single-sex therapy groups. In: M. Aveline and W. Dryden (eds), *Group therapy in Britain*. Milton Keynes: Open University Press. pp. 254-280.

Rapoport, R.N. (1960) *Community as doctor*. London: Tavistock.

Rawson, D., Buddendiek, H. and Haigh, R. (1994) Trident Housing Association Therapeutic (THAT) Community. Community study: Basic principles and values. *Therapeutic Communities*, 15(3): 193-207.

Reich, W. (1933/1975) *The mass psychology of fascism* (V.R. Carfagno, trans.), 3rd edn. Harmondsworth: Penguin.

Rice, A.K. (1965) *Learning for leadership*. London: Tavistock.

Rice, C.A. (1996) Premature termination of group therapy: a clinical perspective. *International Journal of Group Psychotherapy*, 46(1): 5-23.

Rigby, A. (1974) *Communes in Britain*. London: Routledge and Kegan Paul.

Rigney, M. (1981) *A critique of Maslow's self-actualization theory: the 'highest good' for the aboriginal is relationship*. Videotape. Aboriginal Open College, Adelaide, Australia.

Roback, H.B., Moore, R.F., Bloch, F.S. and Shelton, M. (1996) Confidentiality in group psychotherapy: empirical findings and the law. *International Journal of Group Psychotherapy*, 46(1): 117-135.

Roberts J.P. (1982) Foulkes' concept of the matrix. *Group Analysis*, 15: 111-126.

Robinson, J. (1998) Reparenting in a therapeutic community. *Transactional Analysis Journal*, 28(1): 88-94.

Rogers, C.R. (1951) *Client-centered therapy*. London: Constable.

Rogers, C.R. (1957) The necessary and sufficient conditions of therapeutic personality change. *Journal of Consulting Psychology*, 21: 95-103.

Rogers, C.R. (1958/1990b) The characteristics of a helping relationship. In: H. Kirschenbaum and V.L. Henderson (eds), *The Carl Rogers reader*. London: Constable. pp. 108–126.

Rogers, C.R. (1959) A theory of therapy, personality, and interpersonal relationships, as developed in the client-centered framework. In: S. Koch (ed.), *Psychology: a Study of a Science: Volume 3. Formulations of the person and the social context*. New York: McGraw–Hill. pp. 184–256.

Rogers, C.R. (1961) *On becoming a person*. London: Constable.

Rogers, C.R. (1967) The process of the basic encounter group. In: J.F.T. Bugenthal (ed.), *Challenges of humanistic psychology*. New York: McGraw-Hill. pp. 261–278.

Rogers, C.R. (1970/1973) *Encounter groups*. Harmondsworth: Penguin.

Rogers, C.R. (1973/1990a) Some challenges to the helping professions. In H. Kirschenbaum and V.L. Henderson (eds), *The Carl Rogers reader*. London: Constable. pp. 357–375.

Rogers, C.R. (1975) In retrospect: Forty six years. In: R.I. Evans (ed.), Carl Rogers: The man and his ideas. New York: E.P. Dutton. pp. 121–146.

Rogers, C.R. (1978) *Carl Rogers on personal power: inner strength and its revolutionary impact*. London: Constable.

Rogers, C.R. (1983) *Freedom to learn for the 80's*. New York: Macmillan.

Rogers, C.R. and Sandford, R. (1980) Client-centred psychotherapy. In: H. Kaplan, B. Sadock and A. Freeman (eds), *Comprehensive textbook of psychiatry Vol. 3*. Baltimore, MD: Williams and Wilkins.

Rogers, C.R. (1986) Rogers, Kohut and Erickson: a personal perspective on some similarities and differences. *Person-Centered Review*, 1: 125–140.

Røine, E. (1997) *Group psychotherapy as experimental theatre*. London: Jessica Kingsley.

Roller, B. and Nelson, V. (1991) *The art of co-therapy: how therapists work together*. London: Guildford Press.

Rosenfield, M. and Smillie, E. (1998) Group counselling by telephone. *British Journal of Guidance and Counselling*, 26(1): 11–20.

Rowan, J. (1976) *The power of the group*. London: Davis-Poynter.

Russell, J. (1993) *Out of bounds: Sexual exploitation in counselling and therapy*. London: Sage.

Samuels, A. (1993) *The political psyche*. London: Routledge.

Satir, V. (1982) The therapist and family therapy: Process model. In: A. Horne and M. Ohlsen (eds), *Family counseling and therapy*. Itasca, IL: F.E. Peacock. pp. 12–42.

Schiff, A.W., Mellor, K., Schiff, E., Schiff, S., Richman, D., Fishman, J., Wolz, L., Fishman, C. and Momb, D. (1975) *Cathexis reader: transactional analysis treatment of psychosis*. New York: Harper and Row.

Schilder, P. (1936) The analysis of ideologies as a psychotherapeutic method, especially in group treatment. *American Journal of Psychiatry*, 93: 601–617.

Schilder, P. (1939) Results and problems of group psychotherapy in severe neurosis. *Mental Hygiene*, 23: 97.

Schmid, P.F. (1996) 'Probably the most potent *social* invention of the century': person-centered therapy is fundamentally group therapy. In R. Hutterer, G.

Pawlowsky, P.F. Schmid and R. Stipsits (eds), *Client-centered and experiential psychotherapy*. Frankfurt am Main: Peter Lang. pp. 611–625.

Schutz, W. (1973) *Elements of encounter*. Big Sur, CA: Joy Press.

Scott, M.J. and Stradling, S.G. (1998) *Brief group counselling*. Chichester: Wiley.

Shaffer, J.B.P. and Galinsky, M.D. (1974) *Models of group theory and sensitivity training*. Englewood Cliffs, NJ: Prentice-Hall.

Shellow, R.S., Ward, J.L. and Rubenfeld, S. (1958) Group therapy and the institutional delinquent. *International Journal of Group Psychotherapy*, 8: 256–275.

Shohet, R. (1997) Reflections on fear and love in accreditation. In R. House and N. Totton (eds), *Implausible professions: arguments for pluralism and autonomy in psychotherapy and counselling*. Ross-on-Wye: PCCS Books. pp. 45–50.

Shorter Oxford English dictionary, 3rd edn (1973) Oxford: Clarendon Press.

Shweder, R.A. (1990) Cultural psychology – what is it? In: J.W. Stigler, R.A. Shweder and G. Herdt (eds), *Cultural psychology*. Cambridge: Cambridge University Press. pp. 1–43.

Sills, C. (1997a) Contracts and contract making. In: C. Sills (ed.), *Contracts in counselling*. London: Sage. pp. 11–35.

Sills, C. (ed.) (1997b) *Contracts in counselling*. London: Sage.

Singh, J. and Tudor, K. (1997) Cultural conditions of therapy. *The Person-Centered Journal*, 4(3): 32–46.

Skinner, B.F. (1938) *The behavior of organisms*. New York: Appleton–Century–Crofts.

Southwell, C. (1990) *Touch and the psychotherapeutic relationship*. Paper presented at the Conference of the Institute of Chiron Psychotherapy Centre, London, July 1990.

Speierer, G.W. (1990) Toward a specific illness concept of client-centered therapy. In G. Lietaer, J. Rombauts and R. Van Balen (eds), *Client-centered and experiential psychotherapy in the nineties*. Leuven: Leuven University Press. pp. 337–360.

Spotnitz, H. (1961) *The couch and the circle*. New York: Knopf.

Stafford, W. (1977) *Stories that could be true*.

Stamatiadis, R. (1990) Sharing life therapy: a personal and extended way of being with clients. *Person-Centered Review*, 5(3): 287–307.

Stein, T.S. (1982) Men's groups. In: K.L. Solomon and N.B. Levy (eds), *Men in transition: Theory and therapy*. New York: Plenum. pp. 275–307.

Stein, M. and Hollwitz, J. (1992) *Psyche at work: workplace applications of Jungian analytic psychology*. Wilmette, IL: Chiron.

Steiner, C. (1971) *Games alcoholics play*. New York: Grove Press.

Steiner, C. (1987) The seven sources of power: An alternative to authority. *Transactional Analysis Journal*, 17: 102–104.

Stewart, I. (1996) *Developing transactional analysis counselling*. London: Sage.

Stockwell, D. (1984) An attempt at an on-going, person-centred community. In: A. Segrera (ed.), *Proceedings of the First International Forum on the Person-Centered Approach*. Oaxtepec, Morelos, Mexico: Universidad Iberoamericana.

Stoller, F.H. (1972) Marathon groups: toward a conceptual model. In: L.N. Soloman and B. Berzon (eds), *New perspectives on encounter groups*. San Francisco: Jossey-Bass.

Stoltenberg, C.D. and Delworth, U. (1987) *Supervising counselors and therapists*. San Francisco, CA: Jossey-Bass.

Sturdevant, K. (1995) Classical Greek 'koinonia', the psychoanalytic median group, and the large person-centred community group: Dialogue in three democratic contexts. *The Person-Centred Journal*, 2(2): 64-71.

Syme, G. (1994) *Counselling in independent practice*. Milton Keynes: Open University.

Thomas, L.K. (1997) Reworking stereotypes for self identity in a black men's psychotherapy group. *RACE Journal*, No. 13, 23-25.

Thorne, B. (1995) The accountable therapist: Standards, experts and poisoning the well. *Self & Society*, 23(4): 31-38.

Traynor, B. and Clarkson, P. (1992) What happens when a psychotherapist dies? *Counselling*, 3(1): 23-24.

Tuckman, B.W. (1965) Developmental sequence in small groups. *Psychological Bulletin*, 63: 384-399.

Tuckman, B.W. and Jenson, K. (1977) Stages of small-group development revisited. *Group and Organization Studies*, 2(4): 419-427.

Tudor, K. (1995) What do you say about saying goodbye? Ending psychotherapy. *Transactional Analysis Journal*, 25(3): 228-233.

Tudor, K. (1996a) Mental health promotion at work. In: D.R. Trent and C.A. Reed (eds), *Promotion of mental health: Volume 5*. Aldershot: Avebury. pp. 115-143.

Tudor, K. (1996b) *Mental health promotion: paradigms and practice*. London: Routledge.

Tudor, K. (1996c) Transactional analysis *intra*gration: a metatheoretical analysis for practice. *Transactional Analysis Journal*, 26: 329-340.

Tudor, K. (1997a) A complexity of contracts. In: C. Sills (ed.), *Contracts in counselling*. London: Sage. pp. 157-172.

Tudor, K. (1997b) Being at dis-ease with ourselves: alienation and psychotherapy. *Changes*, 22(2): 143-150.

Tudor, K. (1997c) Counselling and psychotherapy: an issue of orientation. *ITA News*, No. 47, 40-42.

Tudor, K. (1997d) Social contracts: contracting for social change. In: C. Sills (ed.), *Contracts in counselling*. London: Sage. pp. 207-215.

Tudor, K. (ed.) (1997e) The person-centred approach and the political sphere [Special Issue]. *Person-Centred Practice*, 5(2).

Tudor, K. (1998a) Men in therapy: opportunity and change. In: J. Wild (ed.), *Working with men for change*. London: UCL Press. pp. 73-97.

Tudor, K. (1999a) Change, time, place and community: an integral approach to counselling. In: P. Lapworth, C. Sills and S. Fish (eds), *Integrative counselling*.

Tudor, K. (1999b) 'I'm OK, You're OK - and They're OK': therapeutic relationships in transactional analysis. In: C. Feltham (ed.), *The counselling relationship*. London: Sage.

Tudor, K. (1998b) Value for money? Issues of fees in counselling and psychotherapy. *British Journal of Guidance and Counselling*, 26(4): 477-493.

United Kingdom Council for Psychotherapy (1996) Ethical guidelines. In: *National register of psychotherapists 1996-97*. London: Routledge.

Vanwynsberghe, J. (1998) Therapy with alcoholic clients: guidelines for good contracts. *Transactional Analysis Journal*, 28(2): 127-131.

Wasdell, D. (1997) T-groups: the Tavistock Leicester experience. *Self & Society*, 25(2), 17-22.

Watson, J.B. and Rayner, R. (1920) Conditioned emotional reactions. *Journal of Experimental Psychology*, 3: 1-14.

Wender, L. (1936) Dynamics of group psychotherapy and its application. *Journal of Nervous Mental Diseases*, 84: 54-60.

Whitaker, C.A. and Malone, T.P. (1953) *The roots of psychotherapy*. New York: Blakiston.

Whitaker, D.S. (1985) *Using groups to help people*. London: Routledge.

Whiteley, J.S. (1975) The large group as a medium for sociotherapy. In: L. Kreeger (ed.), *The large group: dynamics and therapy*. London: Maresfield. pp. 193-211.

Whitman, R.M. and Stock, D. (1958) The group focal conflict. *Psychiatry: Journal for the Study of Interpersonal Processes*, 21: 269-276.

Whitney, N.J. (1982) A critique of individual autonomy as the key to personhood. *Transactional Analysis Journal*, 12: 210-212.

Wibberley, M. (1988) Encounter. In: J. Rowan and W. Dryden (eds), *Innovative therapy in Britain*. Milton Keynes: Open University Press. pp. 61-84.

Wolf, A. (1949) The psychoanalysis of groups. *American Journal of Psychotherapy*, 3: 525-558.

Wolf, A. (1975) The loving leader. In: Z.A. Liff (ed.), *The leader in the group*. New York: Jason Aronson. pp. 72-78.

Wolf, A. and Swartz, E.K. (1975a) The responsible leader. In: Z.A. Liff (ed.), *The leader in the group*. New York: Jason Aronson. p. 66.

Wolf, A. and Swartz, E.K. (1962) *Psychoanalysis in groups*. New York: Grune and Stratton.

Wolf, A. and Swartz, E.K. (1975b) The role of the leader's values. In: Z.A. Liff (ed.), *The leader in the group*. New York: Jason Aronson. pp. 13-30.

Wolpe, J. and Lazarus, A.A. (1966) *Behavior therapy techniques*. New York: John Wiley.

Wood, J.K. (1982) Person-centered group therapy. In: G. Gazda (ed.), *Basic approaches to group psychotherapy and group counseling*. Springfield, IL: Charles Thomas.

Wood, J.K. (1984) Communities for learning: A person-centred approach. In: R.F. Levant and John M. Shlien (eds), *Client-centered therapy and the person-centered approach: new directions in theory, research and practice*. New York: Praeger.

Wood, J.K. (1995a) *Communities for learning: Observations on the person-centred approach to large group workshops*. Privately circulated manuscript.

Wood, J.K. (1995b) *The person-centered approach to small groups: More than psychotherapy*. Privately circulated manuscript.

Wood, J.K. (1999) Towards an understanding of large group dialogue and its implications. In: C. Lago and M. Macmillan (eds), *Experience in relatedness: Group work and the person-centred approach*. Llangarron: PCCS Books, pp. 137-166.

Woodmansey, A.C. (1988) Are psychotherapists out of touch? *British Journal of Psychotherapy*, 5(1): 57–65.

Woollams, S. and Brown, M. (1978) *Transactional analysis*. Dexter, MI: Huron Valley Institute Press.

Worden, J.W. (1982/1983) *Grief counselling and grief therapy: a handbook for the mental health practitioner*. London: Tavistock.

Wruck, K.H. and Eastley, M.F. (1997) Landmark Education Coorporation: selling a paradigm shift. *Harvard Business School*. (Ms. No. 9-898-081)

Yablonsky, L. (1965) *The tunnel back: synanon*. New York: Macmillan.

Yalom, I.D. (1970) *The theory and practice of group psychotherapy*. New York: Basic Books.

Yalom, I.D. (1985) *The theory and practice of group psychotherapy*, 3rd edn. New York: Basic Books.

Yalom, I.D. (1995) *The theory and practice of group psychotherapy*, 4th edn. New York: Basic Books.

Yalom, I.D., Tinklenberg, J. and Gilula, M. (1968) Curative factors in group therapy. Unpublished study.

Zimmerman, J.M. and Coyle, V. (1996) *The way of council*. Las Vegas, NV: Bramble Books.

Author Index

242 *Group counselling*

Subject Index